Réviser son bac avec Le Monde & Courrier international

TERMINALE, SÉRIES L ES S

ANGLAIS

Une réalisation de rue des écoles

CAHIER SPÉCIAL
16 pages pour se tester avant le bac

Avec la collaboration de :
Laurence Doë de Maindreville
Wendy Benoît
Laurence Bordas
Pascale Guillomet

En partenariat avec MAIF
assureur militant

Courrier international apporte chaque semaine depuis vingt-cinq ans les meilleurs articles de la presse étrangère à ses lecteurs. Parmi ceux-ci, beaucoup proviennent de la presse américaine ou anglaise. Qu'il s'agisse d'une tribune du *New York Times*, d'une enquête de *The Economist*, d'un reportage du *Washington Post* ou d'une analyse sur les nouvelles technologies publiée dans le *Guardian*, *Courrier International* sélectionne les analyses ou les points de vue les plus pertinents parmi des milliers de sources et les traduit.

Souvent très bien écrits, ces articles offrent, outre un regard décalé et neuf sur l'actualité, une plongée dans une langue vivante, riche de ses usages, de ses idiomes spécifiques et de leur vocabulaire en perpétuelle évolution. Qu'il s'agisse de l'anglais des affaires, concis et rigoureux, du *Financial Times*, des expressions recherchées et littéraires du *New Yorker* ou du jargon des geeks de la Silicon Valley qui fleurit dans les médias en ligne, la presse constitue un outil efficace pour se perfectionner dans les subtilités et les constantes inventions de la langue de Shakespeare et de Mark Twain. Parce qu'il est le reflet toujours changeant d'une société, d'une époque et de ses courants, culturels, sociétaux ou technologiques, le journal est également un terrain de jeu rêvé pour se frotter à la profusion et à la diversité humaine.

En reproduisant une série d'articles variés tirés des plus grands journaux, tantôt accompagnés de leur traduction commentée en regard, tantôt exploités dans leur version originale en tant que supports de révisions, nous espérons apporter aux candidats à l'épreuve d'anglais une connaissance plus familière et spontanée de l'anglais et de l'américain d'aujourd'hui... mais nous voudrions aussi leur donner envie, munis de ce passeport, de visiter les formidables sites des journaux anglo-saxons.

Courrier international est ainsi heureux de s'associer au *Monde* dans ce volume Anglais de la collection *Réviser son Bac*, pour donner accès à tous les kiosques de la planète.

Eric CHOL, Directeur de la rédaction de *Courrier International*

MYTHES ET HÉROS

Madiba: South Africa's loss is the world's loss too

It didn't take long for the tributes to start pouring in, from all corners of the globe and from every conceivable source. As South Africans, we sometimes think that Madiba belongs only to us, but this sells his legacy short: Nelson Mandela's was a life that touched the whole world, as we can tell by its reaction.

Nelson Mandela once rescued me from a very dangerous situation. I was in Egypt, covering the Egyptian Revolution in 2011. My taxi had taken a wrong turn, and I found myself at a checkpoint manned by pro-Mubarak thugs, who were making something of a habit from arresting and assaulting foreign journalists. They forced me out of the vehicle at knifepoint, and started shouting at me. "Where you from? You England? America?" I gave them my passport. "South Africa? What is South Africa?"

I tried to explain–World Cup, Bafana Bafana, Nelson Mandela. Only Mandela struck a chord. "Nelson Mandela! He good man. In Egypt, we love Nelson Mandela." With that, they returned the passport, apologized for being rude and let me on my way.

Even here, in the heart of a brutal dictator's regime, Mandela's name meant something and carried real weight; his legacy was potent enough to earn this South African citizen a get-out-of-jail-free card.

I am reminded of this story in the midst of the outpouring of obituaries and tributes dedicated to Mandela coming from all over the world in the wake of his passing. Mandela was not just a South African hero, as much as South Africans like to lay claim to him; he was a global icon, a truly world-straddling figure that changed lives everywhere–invariably for the better, and sometimes in the most unlikely places. Losing him is not just South Africa's loss; it is the world's loss.

World leaders have been quick to offer their condolences, as they always do at the passing of a former colleague. Of these, it is extraordinary how many have strayed from the pro-forma diplomat-speak templates to offer what feels like expressions of genuine grief.

US President Barack Obama, for instance, credits Mandela with kick-starting his political career (imagine, for a moment, if someone had told a young Madiba that his actions would inspire a US President, and that that president would be black). "I cannot imagine my own life without the example that Nelson Mandela set," said Obama.

"Nelson Mandela lived for that ideal, and he made it real. He achieved more than could be expected of any man. And today he's gone home. He no longer belongs to us, he belongs to the ages."

And Ghanaian President John Dramani Mahama, in *The New York Times*, describes how he felt when he saw Mandela for the first time:

DICTIONARY

- **to pour in**: to flow, to flood
- **to belong to**: to be the property of
- **to sell the legacy short** : to value the legacy too low
- **thugs**: delinquents
- **to assault**: to attack
- **to strike a chord**: to resonate
- **to apologize**: to express regret, remorse
- **legacy**: heritage
- **in the midst of**: in the middle of
- **outpouring**: effusion
- **in the wake of**: following
- **passing**: death
- **to stray**: to deviate
- **a template**: a pattern
- **genuine**: real
- **grief**: suffering
- **to kick-start**: to encourage
- **a lift**: an elevator
- **to glance**: to look at briefly
- **to nod**: to gesture with head
- **awe**: amazement, state of surprise
- **to weep (wept/wept)**: to cry
- **a flood**: overwhelming quantity
- **Oprah Winfrey**: very famous American TV host, producer and actress
- **gravitas**: seriousness
- **De Klerk**: President of South Africa from 1989 to 1994
- **to crush**: to destroy completely
- **savvy**: shrewd

MOTS CLÉS en lien avec la thématique

NOUNS

- a role model: *un modèle de référence, un exemple à suivre*

Ex.: Steve Jobs is a **role model** for aspiring young entrepreneurs.
- a father figure: *une figure paternelle*
- an icon: *une icône*

Ex.: Rosa Parks was one of the key **icons** in the civil rights movement.
- a symbol: *un symbole*
- a leader: *un dirigeant, un chef*
- a pioneer: *un pionnier*

Ex.: Martin Luther King is considered as a civil rights **pioneer**.
- a modern-day hero: *un héros des temps modernes*

Ex.: Oscar Pistorius is the perfect example of a **modern day hero's fall from grace**.
- a defender: *un défenseur*
- a war hero: *un héros de guerre*
- a fireman: *un pompier*
- a rescue worker: *un sauveteur*

ADJECTIVES

- impressive: *impressionnant*
- inspiring: *stimulant, exaltant*
- influential: *influent*
- outstanding: *exceptionnel*

VERBS

- to devote one's life to: *consacrer sa vie à*

Ex.: Mother Teresa **devoted her life to** others.
- to overcome: *surmonter*

Ex.: Oscar Pistorius **has overcome** personal hardships in his life.
- to embody: *incarner*

Ex.: Nelson Mandela **embodied courage** and humility.
- to be portrayed as: *être dépeint comme*
- to be regarded as: *être considéré comme*
- to be visionary: *être visionnaire*
- to impress: *impressionner*
- to achieve: *réussir*
- to dare: *oser*
- to change the face of the nation: *changer le visage de la nation*
- to change the course of history: *changer le cours de l'histoire*
- to make history: *marquer l'histoire, entrer dans l'histoire*
- to pave the way for: *ouvrir la voie*

FOCUS ON...

Nelson Mandela's political struggle started in 1942 when he joined the African National Congress, South Africa's major liberation movement and today the country's ruling party. In 1944, he formed the ANC Youth League to press the ANC towards effective protest. In 1948 the National Party took power in South Africa and set out to construct apartheid, a system of strict racial segregation and white domination.
Mandela was a lawyer and in 1952 he opened the first black law firm. He was first arrested for treason in 1956. In 1960 the government banned the ANC and Mandela became the leader of a secret army. He had to live underground as he was hunted by the police. He was arrested again in 1962 and was given a life sentence. Mandela spent 27 years in prison. When Mr de Klerk became president in 1989 he promised to phase out apartheid, unbanned the ANC and released some of the country's most prominent political prisoners. Nelson Mandela was freed in 1990 at the age of 71 and was determined to build a new South Africa based on dialogue and reconciliation. He and Mr de Klerk shared the Nobel Peace Prize in 1993.
When Mandela was elected President in April 1994 he was accepted by whites as well as blacks as the embodiment of South Africa's new democracy. *Long Walk to Freedom*, Mandela's autobiography based on the manuscript he wrote in prison, was published in 1995.
Mandela retired from the public eye in 2004 and died in 2013 at the age of 95.

"It was my first time in Cape Town. I had stayed out late with friends and was waiting to take the lift up to my hotel room. When the doors opened, there was Mandela. I took a step back, and froze. As he exited, Mandela glanced in my direction and nodded. I could not return the gesture. I couldn't move, not even to blink. I just stood there in awe, thinking: here was the man for whom we had marched, sung and wept; the man from the black-and-white photograph. Here was the man who had created a new moral compass for South Africa and, as a matter of course, the entire continent."
There has also been a flood of goodwill messages from various celebrities – some perhaps less meaningful than others. While we appreciate the sentiment, we're not sure that we'll be holding onto the messages from Nicole Sherzinger or R. Kelly. [...] But others knew him relatively well. Oprah Winfrey, for example, was a guest at his house for ten days, sharing meals during which she'd pick his brains about his experiences. "I feel that I don't know, nor have I ever met, read, or heard of another human being quite like Nelson Mandela," said Winfrey. "The courage and humility, it's the combination of the two, the courage and the humility that he embodied in order to change a nation and to impact a world. I haven't seen anything like that. And to try to even emulate a piece of that would make all of us ultimately better human beings."
Meanwhile, U2 frontman Bono tells a lovely story that shows, again, that for all his gravitas, Madiba had a sparkling sense of humour. "He could charm the birds off the trees—and cash right out of wallets. He told me once how Margaret Thatcher had personally donated £20,000 to his foundation. 'How did you do that?' I gasped. The Iron Lady, who was famously frugal, kept a tight grip on her purse. 'I asked,' he said with a laugh. 'You'll never get what you want if you don't ask.' Then he lowered his voice conspiratorially and said her donation had nauseated some of his cohorts. 'Didn't she try to squash our movement?' they complained. His response: 'Didn't De Klerk crush our people like flies? And I'm having tea with him next week ... He'll be getting the bill.'" [...]
The respect in which the rest of the world holds Mandela is obvious in the calibre of the editorials and obituaries published by the world's finest publications. *The New York Times*: "He was one of the most extraordinary liberation leaders Africa, or any other continent, ever produced." *The Guardian*: "A leader above all others." *The Economist*: "He was the world's most inspiring example of fortitude, magnanimity and dignity in the face of oppression." *Time*: "He was a repentant warrior and long-suffering martyr; a savvy saint and humble leader; he was both father of his nation and its conscience, the moral glue of its fragile polity."
Nelson Mandela is probably the greatest South African to ever live. There is little doubt on that score. And if there was any doubt of his importance beyond his country's borders, then let it be laid to rest by the overwhelming international response to his death.

Adapted from *Daily Maverick* (Simon Allison – December 6th, 2013)

TROIS ARTICLES DU *MONDE* À CONSULTER

- **L'assassinat de Martin Luther King** p. 18-19
(Marie-Claude Decamps, *Le Monde* daté du 11.04.1988)
- **Churchill, l'homme qui a écrit sa propre histoire** p. 19-20
(Jean-Pierre Langellier, *Le Monde* daté du 31.10.2014)
- **Mohamed Ali : une légende de la boxe** p. 21-22
(Mustapha Kessous, *Le Monde* daté du 06.06.2016)

S'EXPRIMER

EXPRESSING PURPOSE: IN ORDER TO

• "[...] the courage and the humility that he embodied **in order to** change a nation and to impact a world."
In formal language and writing, **in order to + infinitive** is used to express purpose (= *afin de*). Both verbs must have the same subject.
Ex.: The Prime Minister made a speech **in order to** defend his reforms.
• **So as to + infinitive** can also be used to express purpose.
Ex.: He took the course **so as to** get a better job.
• In spoken English it is much more common to use **to + infinitive** to express the same meaning.
Ex.: I went to the station **to** meet my parents.
• We can also use **so that** to talk about the purpose of an action (= *afin que*).
Ex.: She left school early **so that** she could go to her appointment.
Ex.: She'll give up her job **so that** she can take care of her daughter.
• **For** followed by a noun can be used to describe purpose.
Ex.: I went to the shops **for** some butter and eggs.

USING "ENOUGH"

"His legacy was potent enough to earn this South African citizen a get-out-of-jail-free card."
• **adjective + enough** (= *assez*)
Ex.: I'm old **enough** to know how to handle the situation.
Ex.: He is not tall **enough** to reach the top shelf of the cupboard.
• **adverb + enough**
Ex.: He doesn't speak loudly **enough**, no one can hear him..
Ex.: She doesn't work quickly **enough** to finish by noon.
• **enough + nom**
Ex.: I haven't got **enough** money to buy this expensive car.
Ex.: I've got **enough** time to finish my essay on Shakespeare.

Questions de compréhension

A. **True or False?**

1. The author of the article used to be a soldier in Egypt.
2. The author was rescued from a dangerous situation because the men who assaulted him admired Nelson Mandela.
3. Condolences offered from world leaders showed that they were really affected by Mandela's death.
4. Mandela helped Obama at the beginning of his political career.
5. Madiba was the name of Obama when he was young.
6. Mandela ignored the Ghanaian President when he first saw him.
7. The Ghanaian President admired Mandela but was afraid of him.
8. Oprah Winfrey was greatly impressed by Mandela when she spent time with him.
9. The donation made by Margaret Thatcher didn't please everybody in Mandela's entourage.
10. The author admires Nelson Mandela but points out his weaknesses in the article.

B. **Pick 5 nouns in the article used to describe Mandela.**

C. **Pick 5 nouns in the article used to describe Mandela's qualities.**

BOÎTE À OUTILS : LE SUPERLATIF

"He was **one of the most extraordinary** liberation leaders Africa (...) ever produced."
"Nelson Mandela is probably **the greatest** South African to ever live."

Le ***superlatif de supériorité*** *(= le plus...) est utilisé dans les phrases ci-dessus.*

• ***Formation du superlatif de supériorité***

- Pour les adjectifs d'une syllabe, pour les adjectifs de deux syllabes **en -y, -er, -ow** *et* **-e** *ainsi que pour l'adjectif* **late** : **the + -est**

Exemple : **the** low**est** mark I've had.

- Pour les adjectifs de deux syllabes et plus : **the most +** ***adjectif***

Exemple : **the most interesting** book I've ever read.

• ***Attention aux superlatifs irréguliers !***

- good: **the best**

- bad: **the worst**

- far: **the farthest** *ou* **the furthest**

- little: **the least**

• ***Most + adjectif*** *s'emploie au lieu de* very + *adjectif lorsqu'on veut insister.*

Exemple : She is a **most unpleasant** woman.

• *Pour le* ***superlatif d'infériorité****, on utilise toujours :*
the least + ***adjectif*** *(= le moins).*

Exemple : He is **the least hard-working** student in the class.

Exercices de grammaire

A. **Rewrite each sentence beginning as shown so that it has a similar meaning to the first sentence. Use a comparative or superlative form.**

1. Nobody in the class is taller than Mary.
Mary is the
2. My mobile phone is not as expensive as yours.
Your mobile phone is
3. Emma ate much less than David.
Emma didn't
4. Jane's hair isn't as long as Helen's.
Helen's hair is
5. No student in the school is noisier than I am!
I am the
6. We expected the play to be better.
The play wasn't

B. **Put one suitable word in each space.**

1. Today is .... cold .... yesterday so I'm wearing my shorts.
2. What a terrible novel. It's one of .... interesting I've ever read.
3. This is one of .... famous paintings in the world.
4. Nobody knows .... about computers .... Jane ....

C. **Complete each sentence with a comparative or superlative form of the adjective given. Include any other necessary words.**

1. This is .... TV programme I've ever watched. (**bad**)
2. Our house is .... the one next door. (**big**)
3. I think this book is much .... the other one. (**good**)
4. I was disappointed as the film was .... I expected. (**funny**)
5. Yesterday was one of the .... days of the year. (**hot**)
6. The Nile is .... river in the world. (**long**)
7. The first exercise was easy but this one is .... (**difficult**).
8. Today, I feel .... than I did yesterday. (**bad**)

Sujet national, septembre 2013, séries ES, L, S

Document A

21-Year-Old Poses as Fake Celebrity, Gets His 15 Minutes of Fame

Brett Cohen isn't your typical 21-year-old, at least not according to the tourists in New York City's Time Square on July 27. Cohen is now "famous" after pulling a huge prank on the city, posing as a celebrity and wandering the streets of Manhattan.
Accompanied by two bodyguards he hired on Craigslist, as well as three cameramen and four photographers acting as his own paparazzi, he attracted a huge fan following and caused quite a stir in response to what he calls his "social experiment."
"It was a social experiment. It confirms the theory of how our culture is so obsessed with celebrity and fame," Cohen told ABC News. [...] "I had photographers follow me around and act as paparazzi. There were 15 people in total that were actually in on it." [...] Cohen and his entourage began their walk toward Times Square. It didn't take long before crowds began to surround him on every block. [...] One little boy was particularly excited to meet the fake celebrity. Cohen said the boy went so far as to make an international call home on his cell phone, and was overheard screaming, "I just met Brett Cohen!" [...] From beginning to end, the whole thing took about three hours to shoot. Cohen said the hardest thing about the entire experience was stopping the frenzy, literally. "It was really hard to end the shoot. How the hell do you stop when there's so many people following you? We actually had to walk away from Times Square and into a small hotel," Cohen said. "One of my bouncers blocked off the door to the bar to keep the public from going in. It was the only way we were able to stop it."

Eliza Murphy, ABC *News Blogs*, Aug. 23, 2012.

EXPRESSION ÉCRITE : Do you agree with the fact that we live in a society "obsessed with celebrity and fame" (document A)?

Analyse du sujet

Le sujet s'appuie sur une citation tirée de l'article (document A), dans laquelle Brett Cohen affirme que nous vivons dans une société obsédée par la célébrité, la gloire, la notoriété... On vous demande votre avis personnel : êtes-vous d'accord avec cette affirmation ?

Repères essentiels

1. Préparez vos idées : des arguments pour et contre.
2. Rédigez votre réponse en respectant la structure d'un essai argumentatif :
– introduction (reformulation du sujet) ;
– 1er paragraphe : « thèse » (exemple : la société est obsédée par la célébrité, parce que...) ;
– 2e paragraphe : « antithèse » (exemple : cette obsession n'est que limitée, parce que...) ;
– conclusion (rappel du sujet et votre avis personnel circonstancié).
3. Contrôlez la qualité de votre anglais.

Proposition de corrigé

Reading Brett Cohen's story would lead anyone to conclude that we live in a society obsessed with celebrity and fame. But is it really the case? We will see first to what extent the star system rules our society and then, to what extent the contrary is true.

Cohen's successful prank underlines the role the media and means of communication play in the star system. These two dimensions have actually evolved in parallel with the leisure society of the twentieth century. In today's world, we have more free time, greater access to the media and a worldwide communications system. When you look at the media in the press, on the radio and TV or on the Internet, celebrities are often in the news and most people clearly enjoy hearing about stars'antics or accomplishments.
At the same time, it would be terribly wrong to infer that everyone is obsessed with fame.
It amuses us to know what stars get up to or how they live, but it is simply a form of entertainment. At the end of the day, we are all much more concerned about our family and our close friends, than about stars that we will probably never meet.
In conclusion, the obsession with celebrity and fame is simply a pastime for a society which is much more obsessed with its personal well-being and happiness than that of people we don't really know. ■

Ce qu'il ne faut pas faire

- livrer son opinion sans l'argumenter, confondre opinion subjective et réalité objective des faits ;
- ne développer qu'un seul point de vue, sans nuancer son propos ;
- se borner à commenter un sujet d'actualité, un fait divers récent, une polémique médiatique : il s'agit de dégager une problématique et de la mettre en perspective, en évitant de recourir à une approche trop superficielle et anecdotique du sujet.

NOTIONS CLÉS Pour un sujet de ce type, il vous faut mobiliser :

LES EXPRESSIONS D'OPINION
- to my mind/ in my opinion/ from my point of view/ as far as I'm concerned

LES MOTS DE LIAISON POUR ARTICULER VOTRE DISCOURS
- *en renforcement* : indeed/ moreover/ what's more
- *pour marquer une opposition* : however/ and yet/ on the one hand... on the other hand...

DES EXPRESSIONS POUR CONTEXTUALISER VOS ARGUMENTS
- *expressions de lieu* : on a world scale/ in the western world/ in the southern hemisphere...
- *expressions temporelles* : in the past/ before/ more recently/ in the present/ nowadays/ in the future...
- in theory/ in practice, in reality

LE LEXIQUE SPÉCIFIQUE EN LIEN AVEC LE SUJET
- a big name: *un grand nom, au sens de célèbre, reconnu*
- the buzz: *au sens littéral, le bourdonnement*
- fame: *la célébrité, la notoriété*
- a star/ fans/ success/ celebrity/ celebrities
- followers: *disciples, adeptes, amateurs... littéralement : suiveurs*
- glory: *la gloire*
- popular: *populaire au sens d'être à la mode, d'avoir du succès*
- the power of the media
- social networks: *les réseaux sociaux*
- the headlines: *les gros titres*
- a journalist/ a newsman: *un journaliste*
- the news: *les informations*
- the press: *la presse*
- the tabloids: *la presse à sensation*
- a weekly magazine: *un hebdomadaire*
- an advertisement: *une publicité*
- a reality show: *une émission de télé-réalité*
- an event: *un événement*
- to brainwash: *abrutir*

The meaning of Mandela

To fully grasp the meaning of Nelson Mandela's death, at the age of 95, imagine for a moment that his life had turned out differently. What if he'd perished as a child, like so many youngsters of his generation in the rural backwaters of the Transkei? Think of what might have happened, or not happened, if he'd died in the mines of the City of Gold, Johannesburg, where he arrived as a young man after running away from his village. Of course, he survived not only the privations of apartheid—that savage and extreme system of racial segregation—but also the long liberation struggle as well.

Should it go without saying that Mandela was not shot in the back, like demonstrators at Sharpeville in 1960, or gunned down in the streets like young protestors in Soweto during the June 16 uprising in 1976? Though he believed in armed struggle, and became a leader of an armed guerrilla insurrection, he escaped the fates of so many other comrades who were killed in the bush, blown to pieces by letter bombs sent by the authorities, poisoned by secret agents or hanged for treason or sabotage, which seemed the likely result when sentence was pronounced for him and other top leaders of the African National Congress after a long trial back in 1964.

Rolihlahla Dalibhunga Mandela was spared the death penalty a half-century ago. He wasn't forced into exile, like so many others, and did not lose his sanity or have his spirit broken from decades of imprisonment. He managed to survive tuberculosis and prostate cancer, outliving nearly all of the closest friends of his generation. Though it was once illegal to publish his photograph or quote him by name in South Africa, his image was picked as the rallying symbol of a global campaign against apartheid in a massive international organizing drive much like the effort to end slavery a century earlier. It was only natural then, and just, that when Mandela emerged from prison in 1990, he felt such a powerful sense of obligation to the fallen. It would be a shame if, in celebrating the remarkable arc of his life, we neglected to mention millions of others not lucky enough to become—like him—exceptions to old rules.

Time has exposed Mandela's own failings. In office, he failed to respond to the rise of HIV/AIDS. He protected cronies accused of corruption and failed to enforce distinctions between personal favors, party business and government decision-making. His dedication towards the governing party, the African National Congress, meant that he subjected himself to the policies of its "collective leadership" and, after stepping down as president in 1999, supported two flawed successors during election campaigns, tarnishing his own image in the process. In the last decade, quarrels with old comrades also spilled wince-worthy details of dodgy financial arrangements into public view. There were even lawsuits within the family over money.

Even here, though, there was a kind of backhanded tribute: these facts emerged eventually into public view. That, too, was part of Mandela's legacy, because in spite of a deep reservoir of popular affection for Utata, or Madiba, as he's known, he and the party never allowed the trappings of the kind of cult of personality upon which so many other liberation struggles in Africa and elsewhere have foundered. Mandela's personal troubles, like the failures of his party, were part of the public record revealed by a free press. Nineteen years into the South African democratic experiment, there's a vibrant civic culture that exploded to great effect in protests over the government's former AIDS policies, an independent if quite pressurized judiciary and an impressive if embattled media.

The last time I saw Mandela at his home after the World Cup three years ago, he greeted my son and me with a well-worn line: "It's nice that young people still come around to see an old man even though he has nothing new to say." He loved little jokes, but here the pat phrase revealed a deeper intention, I think, to signal that it was time for young South Africans to step up and take the revolution he'd begun much further. More than half of the South Africa's population is under 25, which means that young people grew up entirely in the new dispensation. For them, Nelson Mandela was always a grandfatherly figure; after all, he was 72 years old by the time he was released from prison.

As it turned out, this was a subject often on the mind of Mandela's grandson, who'd taken us to see his grandfather. "Here was a man who came from nothing," Ndaba Mandela said. "He was a young boy running around on the farms of Xhosa-land, and he became something he himself never imagined!" Now, the grandson added, it was time for the next generation to stop relying so heavily on his grandfather's generation. He thought young South Africans needed to more forcefully tackle the demands of the poor, liberated in terms of political rights by the election of 1994 but still denied economic and social justice in a still savagely unequal society.

The elder Mandela had done his best over the years to prepare South Africans for the next stage in the struggle to create a new nation. Now it was part of his legacy that so many of his countrymen had grown tired, even angry, at being asked whether the dream of establishing a new kind of society would outlive him. Of course, the vision of creating a new kind of nation was always bigger than a single leader. It was perhaps his most enduring gift that this question, asked ritualistically by outsiders, should sound so silly, so wide of the mark, on the day he died. In the end, there was a period but no question mark. Would the dream survive? The answer: it already had. ■

Adapted from Douglas Foster – *The Nation*, December 5th, 2013

KEY POINT

Nelson Mandela's legacy

This article from *The Nation* deals with Nelson Mandela's legacy. Mandela was elected South Africa's president in 1994 and served as president until 1999 when he was succeeded by his deputy Thabo Mbeki. The African National Congress has enjoyed unbroken political power since 1994 even though the movement is now lacking effective leadership and is rapidly losing legitimacy.

South Africa faces major problems but having held four successful national elections as well as local polls since the end of the white rule, a democratic culture appears to be taking hold. South Africa is along with China, Brazil, Russia and India a member of the BRICS club of emerging world economic powers. South Africa also plays a leading role in diplomatic initiatives in Africa.

However, poverty is widespread and there is a high level of inequality as well as a high crime rate associated with high unemployment. Officially youth unemployment has gradually risen to 36% but many believe that real unemployment among that population is closer to 50%.

South Africa has also the second highest number of HIV patients in the world as around one in seven of its citizens is infected with HIV.

Mandela, passeur d'un rêve

Pour bien comprendre ce que signifie la disparition de Nelson Mandela, à quatre-vingt-quinze ans, imaginez un instant que sa vie ait pris un cours différent. Que se serait-il passé s'il avait péri enfant, comme tant de jeunes de sa génération, au fin fond des campagnes du Transkei ? Pensez à ce qui serait arrivé — ou à ce qui ne serait pas arrivé — s'il avait trouvé la mort dans les mines de Johannesbourg où il est arrivé après s'être enfui de son village. Bien sûr, il a survécu non seulement aux privations engendrées par l'apartheid — ce système brutal, extrême, de ségrégation raciale —, mais également à la longue lutte pour la libération de son peuple.

Faut-il passer sous silence le fait que Mandela n'a pas reçu une balle dans le dos, contrairement aux manifestants à Sharpeville en 1960 ? Ni été abattu comme ces jeunes descendus dans les rues de Soweto, lors du soulèvement du 16 juin 1976 ? Bien qu'il ait cru dans la lutte armée et soit devenu l'un des meneurs de l'insurrection, il a échappé au sort de tant de ses camarades tués dans la brousse, réduits en pièces par l'explosion de colis piégés envoyés par les autorités, empoisonnés par les services de renseignement ou pendus pour trahison ou sabotage — fin qui semblait promise à Mandela et à d'autres hauts dirigeants du Congrès national africain (ANC) à l'issue d'un long procès en 1964. Rolihlahla Dalibhunga Mandela n'a pas écopé de la peine de mort il y a un demi-siècle. Il n'a pas dû prendre le chemin de l'exil comme tant d'autres. Il n'a pas perdu sa santé mentale et n'a pas été psychologiquement brisé par des décennies d'emprisonnement. Il a survécu à la tuberculose et au cancer de la prostate. Il a vu mourir presque tous ses plus proches amis de la même génération. Il est donc parfaitement naturel et juste qu'à sa sortie de prison, en 1990, Mandela se soit senti si profondément obligé envers ceux qui étaient tombés. Il serait dommage, à l'heure où nous célébrons son itinéraire hors du commun, de ne pas mentionner les millions d'individus qui n'eurent pas la chance de devenir, comme lui, des exceptions à de vieilles règles.

Au fil du temps, les échecs de Mandela sont apparus au grand jour. Lorsqu'il était au pouvoir, il n'a pas réussi à juguler la propagation du sida. Il a protégé des personnes proches du pouvoir accusées de corruption et n'a pas fait la distinction entre faveurs personnelles, affaires du parti et décisions gouvernementales. Par loyauté envers le parti au pouvoir, il s'est soumis à sa politique de « direction collective » et, après avoir quitté la présidence du pays en 1999, il a soutenu deux successeurs qui ne le méritaient pas, ternissant du même coup sa propre image. Ces dix dernières années, les querelles avec d'anciens compagnons de lutte ont également porté à la connaissance du public des détails embarrassants sur des arrangements financiers douteux. Des membres de sa famille ont même engagé des actions en justice pour des questions d'argent.

Là encore, pourtant, il y a une sorte d'hommage implicite à Mandela : ces faits ont fini par apparaître au grand jour. Cela aussi fait partie de l'héritage laissé par le grand homme, parce que, malgré la profonde affection populaire pour Madiba, comme on l'appelle, lui et son parti n'ont jamais toléré l'espèce de culte de la personnalité où se sont abîmés tant d'autres combats pour la libération en Afrique et ailleurs. Les ennuis personnels de Mandela, tout comme les erreurs de son parti, ont été révélés au public par une presse libre. Dix-neuf ans après l'introduction de la démocratie en Afrique du Sud, le pays jouit d'une culture civique dynamique, d'une justice indépendante (bien que soumise à des pressions) et de médias impressionnants malgré l'adversité auxquels ils font face.

La dernière fois que j'ai rencontré Mandela chez lui, après la Coupe du monde de football en 2010, il nous a accueillis, mon fils et moi, avec une formule éprouvée : « Ça fait plaisir de voir des jeunes continuer à rendre visite à un vieil homme qui n'a rien de nouveau à dire. » Il adorait plaisanter, mais, à mon avis, ces propos anodins révélaient une intention plus profonde : celle de signaler aux jeunes Sud-Africains qu'il était temps pour eux de se lever et de porter bien plus loin la révolution qu'il avait initiée.

C'était un sujet souvent présent à l'esprit du petit-fils de Mandela, qui nous avait conduits auprès de son grand-père. « Voici un homme sorti de nulle part, avait commenté Ndaba Mandela. C'était un garçon qui courait dans les fermes de Xhosa, et il est devenu ce que lui-même n'avait jamais imaginé ! » Maintenant, avait ajouté le petit-fils, il était temps pour la jeune génération de cesser de compter autant sur celle du vieil homme. Les jeunes Sud-Africains devaient agir énergiquement pour répondre aux revendications des pauvres, libérés sur le plan des droits politiques par l'élection de 1994, mais toujours privés de justice économique et sociale. [...]

Le patriarche a fait de son mieux pour préparer les Sud-Africains à l'étape suivante de la lutte. Maintenant, nombreux sont ses compatriotes à en avoir assez de s'entendre demander si le rêve d'établir une nouvelle société lui survivra. Cela aussi fait partie de son héritage. À l'évidence, le désir de créer une nouvelle nation va toujours au-delà de la personnalité d'un seul dirigeant. C'est peut-être son legs le plus durable que cette question, posée de manière rituelle par les étrangers, ait paru aussi incongrue, voire déplacée, le jour de sa mort. À la fin, il ne restait plus d'interrogation. À la question : « le rêve lui survivra-t-il ? », la réponse était : le rêve est déjà devenu réalité.

D'après Douglas Foster – *The Nation*, December 5th, 2013
Extrait de *Courrier International*

VOCABULARY AND STRUCTURES TO REMEMBER!

- **to fully grasp**: *pour bien comprendre*
- **think of what might have happened**: *pensez à ce qui serait arrivé*
- **to run away from**: *s'enfuir de*
- **though he believed in armed struggle**: *bien qu'il ait cru dans la lutte armée*
- **Mandela was spared the death penalty**: *Mandela n'a pas écopé de la peine de mort (= il a échappé à...)*
- **he managed to survive**: *il a survécu à (= il a réussi à survivre à)*
- **it would be a shame**: *il serait dommage*
- **he failed to respond to the rise of AIDS**: *il n'a pas réussi à juguler la propagation du sida*
- **after stepping down as president**: *après avoir quitté la présidence*
- **lawsuits**: *actions en justice*
- **failures**: *erreurs (= échecs)*
- **even though he has nothing new to say**: *même s'il n'a rien de nouveau à dire*
- **to tackle the demands of the poor**: *répondre aux revendications des pauvres*
- **his most enduring gift**: *son legs le plus durable*

A Chronicler of Syria's Conflict Returns to the Spotlight, Minus a Disguise

Mary Atwan, a trained nurse, has been a journalist in Syria since 2012, but only when she traveled to Italy this week to receive a prestigious award did the world learn her real name: Maisa Saleh. It was also a first chance for the world outside a narrow circle in Syria to see a sample of her work, which in addition to meriting this year's Anna Politkovskaya Award for investigative journalism has earned her an arrest, imprisonment and exile in just a few short years. Her home now is in the Turkish city of Gaziantep, 30 miles from the border with Syria. Although she got her start as a reporter for the Syrian opposition channel Orient TV, it was her work as the host of a weekly talk show beginning in January of last year that vaulted her into prominence. A natural brunette, on air Mrs Saleh wore a short blond wig with bangs, sunglasses with large round frames and a scarf that covered her mouth and nose. Her voice was altered. Even her family was unaware that the woman they watched on television every week was their beloved Maisa. "I absolutely couldn't show my face because they would kill me," said Mrs Saleh, who was arrested in April of last year by the Syrian government on suspicion of being Mrs Atwan. She was released months later when the authorities could not prove their case. "They know I am a reporter, but they don't know I am the same one who makes this show," she said. "Still, many, many friends and activists don't know." The relative anonymity has been a comfort to Mrs Saleh, 31, who has feared—with good reason—that her political affiliations could compromise her family's safety, either with the government or the extreme militants fighting for control of Syria. When she was released from prison last October, she learned that her youngest sister had been taken by militants with the Islamic State. "There is nothing, no information," Mrs. Saleh said. "Is she alive? Has she died? We don't know." Born in Aleppo, Syria, into a family of freethinkers, Mrs Saleh has long lived in fear of the government, first Hafez al-Assad's and then that of his son, the current president, Bashar al-Assad. Her father, an elementary school teacher, was a Marxist who liked to read philosophy in his spare time. "My family was very open-minded," said Mrs Saleh, who was taught at an early age about human rights and social freedoms—far from a normal upbringing in a police state. "We knew something needed to change."

A trained intensive care nurse, she was first arrested in 2004 after meeting covertly with a politically minded group of friends. "The regime had control of all things in Syria," Mrs Saleh said. "We were looking for freedom." When the Arab Spring unrest erupted, in March 2011, she was targeted by Mr Assad's secret police. "The police came to the hospital and warned me," she said. Mrs Saleh soon left her job as the head nurse in a Damascus hospital and went into hiding. She began to set up field hospitals in Damascus, the capital, to treat wounded demonstrators, who could not receive medical care at government hospitals. "I was going without cover, but the Free Army helped me to get to these areas," she said, referring to the Free Syrian Army, the pro-Western rebel faction.

Her life in perpetual danger, she became frustrated by the portrayal of revolutionaries in the Syrian state-run news media as sectarian terrorists. "All TV channels, they were talking about the war in Syria between armies," said Mrs Saleh, who said she and many activists expressed their dissent through peaceful means. "We are not all of us Free Army." Her transition from medical work to journalism was for ideological reasons, as well as practical ones. She needed the money. So she took a job with Orient TV, a Syrian satellite channel that had been based in Damascus but relocated to Dubai, in the United Arab Emirates, after the conflict began, and started reporting from the field via Skype. In January 2013, in an audacious move, Mrs Saleh began producing her own program, "From the Capital," right under the noses of the secret police in Damascus, as the program's title suggested. The show brought together civilian activists for discussions on issues such as sectarian violence and the role of the arts in the uprising. She shot segments from secret locations in Damascus, brazenly going through checkpoints and hiding her wig, scarf and other incriminating items in her handbag, which the police at that time were too polite to search. Eventually, she said, a friend cracked under torture and told the police where to find her. She was captured at a local cafe in cinematic fashion. She was beaten, but not badly, she said. For many others, prison has meant torture, even death. "I am not a story," she said. The local news media do not agree, and she has been pressed for interviews since her release in October 2013 in a prisoner exchange involving Lebanon, Turkey, Qatar and the Palestinian Authority. She repeatedly denied the news media requests. Things, however, are changing, as both she and most of her immediate family are now out of Syria. She is about to re-enter the spotlight, this time as herself, on a television show on Orient TV about Syrian female activists. "There are many stories I want people to know," she said.

Adaptated from Rebecca White – *The New York Times*, October 3rd, 2014

KEY POINT

The annual toll of journalists killed in connection with their work is very high as 71 were killed in 2013 according to Reporters Without Borders. Syria has become the world's deadliest country for the media. There has also been a big increase in abductions of journalists. In Syria, news providers are increasingly being targeted by Islamist armed groups and the murder of US citizen James Foley in August 2014 by Islamic State militants shocked the whole world.

There are no statistics kept on male vs. female reporters in the Middle East but the bureau chiefs of the main American and British publications in Beirut, where many of the journalists covering Syria live, are all women.

Besides, a report released by Human Rights Watch in July 2014 showed that the conflict in Syria impacts women in particular. Women profiled in the report experienced violations by government and pro-government forces as well as by armed groups opposed to the government. Some female activists and humanitarian aid providers said that they had been threatened, arbitrarily arrested and detained, and tortured by government or armed opposition forces.

Maisa Saleh : une journaliste face au régime Assad

Mary Atwan, infirmière de formation, est journaliste en Syrie depuis 2012, mais ce n'est que lorsqu'elle s'est rendue début octobre en Italie, pour y recevoir un prix de journalisme d'investigation [le prix Anna Politkovskaïa du festival organisé par la revue *Internazionale*], que le monde a découvert son identité : Maisa Saleh. C'est la première fois que le public, jusque-là limité à un cercle restreint en Syrie, a pu avoir un aperçu de son travail, qui lui a valu en deux ans une arrestation, la prison, puis l'exil. Elle vit aujourd'hui en Turquie, à une cinquantaine de kilomètres de la frontière syrienne.

D'abord reporter pour Orient TV (une chaîne de l'opposition en Syrie), c'est comme animatrice d'un talk-show hebdomadaire lancé en janvier 2013 qu'elle s'est fait connaître. Brune dans la vie, elle arborait à l'écran une courte perruque blonde avec une frange, d'imposantes lunettes de soleil à monture ronde et un foulard couvrant sa bouche et son nez. Sa voix était modifiée. Même ses proches ignoraient que la femme qu'ils voyaient tous les jours à la télé était en fait leur chère Maisa.

« Hors de question que je montre mon visage, ils m'auraient assassinée », assure Maisa Saleh. En avril 2013, elle est arrêtée par le gouvernement, qui la soupçonne d'être Mary Atwan ; elle sera libérée plusieurs mois plus tard, faute de preuves. « Ils savent que je suis journaliste, mais pas que je suis précisément cette journaliste. Il y a encore beaucoup de militants et même d'amis à moi qui l'ignorent. »

Cet anonymat relatif est rassurant pour Maisa Saleh, qui craint – à juste titre – que ses opinions politiques n'attirent sur sa famille la vindicte des forces gouvernementales ou des extrémistes en lutte pour le contrôle de la Syrie. À sa sortie de prison, en octobre 2013, elle découvre que sa plus jeune sœur a été enlevée par des proches de l'État islamique. « On n'a pas la moindre information. Est-ce qu'elle est vivante, morte ? On n'en sait rien. »

Née à Alep, en Syrie, dans une famille de libres penseurs, Maisa Saleh, trente et un ans, vit depuis longtemps dans la peur des autorités, que ce soit de Hafez El-Assad ou de son fils Bachar, l'actuel président. Son père, instituteur, était marxiste et philosophe à ses heures. « J'ai grandi dans une famille très ouverte d'esprit », dit la jeune femme, qui a entendu parler dès son plus jeune âge de droits de l'homme et de libertés sociales – sujets qu'il était bien rare d'aborder avec des enfants dans un État policier. « Nous avions conscience que les choses devaient changer. »

Infirmière diplômée en soins intensifs, elle est arrêtée pour la première fois en 2004, après une rencontre clandestine avec des amis militants. « Le régime contrôlait tout. Nous étions dans une quête permanente de liberté. » Au moment des Printemps arabes, en mars 2011, Maisa Saleh reçoit un avertissement direct de la police secrète d'Assad, qui vient la voir à l'hôpital de Damas où elle est infirmière en chef. Elle quitte son poste, passe dans la clandestinité et crée des postes de secours à Damas pour les manifestants blessés, qui ne peuvent se rendre dans les hôpitaux. « Je n'avais aucune protection, mais l'Armée libre m'aidait à rejoindre le lieu des affrontements », précise-t-elle, en référence à l'Armée syrienne libre, le groupe insurgé pro-occidental.

Vivant dans un danger permanent, elle s'agace que le portrait des révolutionnaires dressé par les médias d'État syriens soit celui de terroristes fanatiques. « Toutes les chaînes de télévision parlaient de la guerre en Syrie entre des armées », explique Maisa Saleh, qui précise qu'elle et bien d'autres militants exprimaient leur opposition par des voies pacifiques. « Nous ne sommes pas tous ralliés à l'Armée syrienne libre. » Quand elle passe des soins médicaux au journalisme, c'est autant pour des raisons idéologiques que pour des raisons pratiques : elle a besoin d'argent. Elle accepte un poste à Orient TV, une chaîne syrienne diffusée par satellite, basée d'abord à Damas puis à Dubaï, aux Émirats arabes unis, après le début du conflit, et qui propose des reportages depuis le théâtre des affrontements via Skype.

En janvier 2013, elle prend la décision audacieuse de produire sa propre émission, baptisée *Depuis la capitale* – à Damas donc, au nez et à la barbe de la police secrète. Des militants de la société civile débattent sur des sujets comme les violences religieuses ou le rôle des arts dans le soulèvement. Elle tourne dans des endroits secrets de Damas, passant effrontément les postes de contrôle avec sa perruque, son foulard et des accessoires compromettants cachés dans son sac à main, que la police est encore trop polie pour fouiller.

Mais un jour, raconte Maisa Saleh, un de ses amis a craqué sous la torture et donné à la police les informations pour la localiser : son arrestation dans un café a été spectaculaire. Elle a été battue – mais pas trop, minimise-t-elle : pour bien d'autres, la prison est synonyme de torture, voire de mort. « Mon histoire n'a rien de particulier », estime-t-elle. Les médias de la région ne sont pas de cet avis : depuis sa libération, en octobre 2013, à la faveur d'un échange de prisonniers avec le Liban, la Turquie, le Qatar et l'Autorité palestinienne, elle a reçu d'innombrables demandes d'interview – qu'elle a presque toutes refusées. Mais les choses changent, maintenant que Maisa Saleh et la majeure partie de ses proches ont quitté la Syrie. Elle va revenir sous les projecteurs, sous sa véritable identité, pour une émission sur les femmes militantes en Syrie, toujours pour Orient TV : « Il y a tellement d'histoires que j'ai envie de faire connaître... »

D'après Rebecca White – *The New York Times*, 3 octobre 2014
Extrait de *Courrier International*

VOCABULARY AND STRUCTURES TO REMEMBER!

- **an award**: *un prix*
- **a narrow circle**: *un cercle restreint*
- **a sample**: *un aperçu, un échantillon*
- **a border**: *une frontière*
- **a TV channel**: *une chaîne de télévision*
- **to be unaware**: *ignorer*
- **to be released**: *être libéré*
- **to fear**: *craindre*
- **to fight for (fought/ fought)**: *lutter pour*
- **in fear of**: *dans la peur de*
- **the current president**: *l'actuel président*
- **to go into hiding**: *passer dans la clandestinité*
- **dissent**: *opposition*
- **peaceful means**: *moyens pacifiques*
- **issues**: *des sujets*
- **to deny**: *refuser, nier*
- **to re-enter the spotlight**: *revenir sous les projecteurs*

Mary Shelley's, *Frankenstein (1831)*

I sat one evening in my laboratory; the sun had set, and the moon was just rising from the sea; I had not sufficient light for my employment, and I remained idle, in a pause of consideration of whether I should leave my labour for the night, or hasten its conclusion by an unremitting attention to it. As I sat, a train of reflection occurred to me, which led me to consider the effects of what I was now doing. Three years before, I was engaged in the same manner, and had created a fiend whose unparalleled barbarity had desolated my heart, and filled it forever with the bitterest remorse. I was now about to form another being, of whose dispositions I was alike ignorant; she might become ten thousand times more malignant than her mate, and delight, for its own sake, in murder and wretchedness. He had sworn to quit the neighbourhood of man and hide himself in deserts; but she had not; and she, who in all probability was to become a thinking and reasoning animal, might refuse to comply with a compact made before her operation. They might even hate each other; the creature who already lived loathed his own deformity, and might he not conceive a greater abhorrence for it when it came before his eyes in the female form? She also might turn with disgust from him to the superior beauty of man; she might quit him, and he be again alone, exasperated by the fresh provocation of being deserted by one of his own species.

> *"I shuddered to think that future ages might curse me as their pest, whose selfishness had not hesitated to buy its own peace at the price, perhaps, of the existence of the whole human race."*

Even if they were to leave Europe, and inhabit the deserts of the new world, yet one of the first results of those sympathies for which the demon thirsted would be children, and a race of devils would be propagated upon the earth who might make the very existence of the species of man a condition precarious and full of terror. Had I a right, for my own benefit, to inflict this curse upon everlasting generations? I had before been moved by the sophisms of the being I had created; I had been struck senseless by his fiendish threats: but now, for the first time, the wickedness of my promise burst upon me, I shuddered to think that future ages might curse me as their pest, whose selfishness had not hesitated to buy its own peace at the price, perhaps, of the existence of the whole human race.

I trembled and my heart failed within me, when, on looking up, I saw by the light of the moon, the demon at the casement. A ghastly grin wrinkled his lips as he gazed on me, where I sat fulfilling the task which he had allotted to me. Yes, he had followed me in my travels; he had loitered in forests, hid himself in caves, or taken refuge in wide and desert heaths; and he now came to mark my progress and claim the fulfilment of my promise.

As I looked on him, his countenance expressed the utmost extent of malice and treachery; I thought with a sensation of madness on my promise of creating another like to him, and trembling with passion, tore to pieces the thing on which I was engaged. The wretch saw me destroy the creature on whose future existence he depended for

MOTS CLÉS en lien avec la thématique

NOUNS
- a belief: *une croyance*
- a goal: *un objectif*
- a legacy: *un héritage*
- an achievement: *une réussite*
- fate: *le destin*
- fame: *la célébrité*
- a tribute: *un hommage*
- a hardship = an ordeal: *une épreuve*
- dedication: *le dévouement*
- bravery: *la bravoure*
- wisdom: *la sagesse*

ADJECTIVES
- brave, courageous: *courageux*
- bold: *audacieux*
- daring: *téméraire*
- outspoken: *franc*

Ex.: Malala has been **outspoken** about the importance of education.
- wise: *sage*
- legendary: *légendaire*
- heroic: *héroïque*

VERBS
- to look up to/ to admire/ to revere somebody: *admirer*

Ex.: Athletes are often **looked up to** as our **role models**.
- to worship: *vénérer*

Ex.: Nelson Mandela **is regarded as** a saint and **is worshipped by** a large number of people.
- to place somebody on a pedestal: *mettre quelqu'un sur un piédestal*
- to praise: *faire l'éloge de*

Ex.: Songs of **praise glorifying** Nelson Mandela are taught to school children in South Africa.
- to pay tribute to: *rendre hommage à*

Ex.: President Obama gave a speech **paying tribute to** 9/11's victims and heroes.
- to inspire: *inspirer*
- to speak out = to speak up: *parler franchement*

Ex.: Malala has continued **to speak out** as a fierce advocate for women's education since the assassination attempt.
- to stand up for a cause: *défendre une cause*
- to stand up against a government: *combattre un gouvernement*

Frankenstein and his creature – illustration from the title page of the 1831 edition.

happiness, and, with a howl of devilish despair and revenge, withdrew. I left the room, and locking the door, made a solemn vow in my own heart never to resume my labours; and then, with trembling steps, I sought my own apartment. I was alone; none were near me to dissipate the gloom and relieve me from the sickening oppression of the most terrible reveries.

Frankenstein by Mary Shelley (1831)

FOCUS ON...

The modern Prometheus

Mary Shelley

Mary Shelley was only 18 when she started writing her novel *Frankenstein*. As the subtitle *The modern Prometheus* indicates, she was strongly inspired by the myth of Prometheus – Prometheus both as defier of the divine will and as creator. Victor Frankenstein who is obsessed with occult scientific knowledge is a modern Prometheus of the scientific age. The central theme of the novel is therefore Man playing God, Frankenstein's pursuit of unlawful knowledge and his wish to penetrate Nature's secrets. Shelley's novel and the famous character of Frankenstein's monster have influenced popular culture for over a century and have inspired many films and television programs. The most famous adaptation of the story was the film directed by James Whale in 1931, which provided the definitive lasting visual image of the Frankenstein monster: to most people Boris Karloff as the Monster has become synonymous with Frankenstein. The following series of films contributed to a further change of the myth when people began to confuse the creator with the creation. In the end the Monster had become Frankenstein and the focus had been moved from the creator to the creation.

DICTIONARY

- **idle:** not working
- **to hasten:** to hurry
- **unremitting:** continuous
- **a fiend:** evil spirit
- **bitter**: causing pain or grief
- **to delight in:** to take great pleasure in
- **wretchedness:** evil
- **to swear (swore/sworn):** promised
- **to comply with a compact:** to act in accordance with an agreement
- **to loathe:** to hate
- **to thirst for:** to have a strong desire for
- **a curse:** a plague, a pest
- **sophisms:** false arguments
- **wickedness:** evil
- **to shudder:** to tremble
- **the casement:** the window
- **a ghastly grin:** a terrible smile
- **to gaze:** to look steadily
- **to loiter**: to wander, to move about without purpose
- **a wretch:** an unhappy person

S'EXPRIMER

CLAUSES OF TIME

• "**As I sat**, a train of reflection occurred to me."
"A ghastly grin wrinkled his lips **as he gazed on me**."
"**As I looked on him**, his countenance expressed the utmost extent of malice and treachery."
As means here "during the time that", to talk about something that happens when something else takes place (**as** = **when** = **while**).
Ex.: **As** I was working on my essay, the doorbell rang.
Ex.: **As** the meeting continued, it became clear that the two sides would not reach an agreement.

• "**On looking up**, I saw by the light of the moon, the demon at the casement."
The clause **on + V-ing** indicates **when**.
Ex.: **On returning** from China, I decided to start learning Chinese.
Ex.: **On returning** home, I found Jane waiting outside my front door.

• "**I was now about to form** another being."
To be about to + infinitive means that something will happen in the very near future (= *être sur le point de*).
To be on the point of + V-ing has the same meaning.
Ex.: I **was about to leave** when she phoned me.
Ex.: They're **on the point of getting** divorced.

• "She [...] **was to become** a thinking and reasoning animal."
Be to + infinitive is used to talk about events that are likely to happen in the near future (= *elle allait devenir*).
Note that **be to + infinitive** is commonly used in news reports and formal contexts, while **be about to + infinitive** is used in conversations.

Questions de compréhension

A. Compréhension générale

1. What is the narrator working on?

2. What had he done 3 years before?

3. What does the narrator fear for the future?

4. What does he decide to do at the end of the text?

B. Compréhension détaillée

1. True or false?

a. The narrator is the only character of this scene.

b. He is convinced that the creature and his new mate will get on well.

c. The creature and his new mate may have children.

d. He makes a new promise at the end of the text.

e. The narrator feels relieved at the end of the text.

2. What does the male creature look like? Justify your answer by quoting the text.

3. What does the narrator think of his male creature? Explain in your own words.

4. The narrator and the creature both made a promise. What were those promises?

BOÎTE À OUTILS : L'ÉVENTUALITÉ, LA POSSIBILITÉ ET LA PROBABILITÉ

"She **might** become ten thousand times more malignant than her mate."

"She [...] **might** refuse to comply with a compact made before her creation."

"They **might** even hate each other."

• **Might** exprime ici ***l'éventualité***, c'est-à-dire les chances qui existent pour que quelque chose se réalise.

• **May** et **could** peuvent également exprimer l'éventualité. **Might** et **could** expriment souvent ***un doute plus grand*** que **may**.

• ***L'éventualité négative*** peut être exprimée par **may not** et **might not**.

• ***La possibilité théorique*** que des actes ou situations soient réalisables peut s'exprimer avec **can** ou **could** (could exprimant une hésitation).

• ***L'impossibilité théorique*** peut s'exprimer avec **cannot** et **could not**.

• ***La forte probabilité ou quasi-certitude*** est exprimée par **must**. ***La forte improbabilité ou quasi-impossibilité*** est rendue par **cannot**.

• ***Observez les différences :***

He **must** be at work. (There is a strong probability that he is at work.)

He **can** be at work. (It is theoretically possible that he is at work.)

He **may** be at work. (There is a chance that he is at work.)

He **might/ could** be at work. (There is a small chance that he is at work.)

He **might not** be at work. (There is a small chance that he is not at work.)

He **may not** be at work. (There is a chance that he is not at work.)

He **could not** be at work. (It is theoretically possible that he is not at work.)

He **cannot be** at work. (It is almost impossible that he is at work.)

Exercices de grammaire

A. Choose the right modal auxiliary in each space (can, could, may, might, must).

1. ***Ils doivent être en train de travailler.***

They .... be working.

2. ***Il peut faire très chaud en Angleterre en été.***

England .... be very hot in the summer.

3. ***Elle doit avoir plus de quarante ans.***

She .... be over forty.

4. ***Il se peut qu'il parte à l'étranger demain.***

He .... go abroad tomorrow.

5. ***Son patron aurait pu la renvoyer.***

Her boss .... have fired her.

6. ***Il pourrait ne jamais revenir.***

He .... never come back.

B. Choose the correct word or phrase underlined in each sentence.

1. Look at those clouds. I think it can/might/must rain.

2. I've no idea where my sister is. She could be/must be anywhere!

3. Well done! You may be/might be/must be very pleased.

4. This is impossible. It mustn't be/can't be/may not be the answer.

5. Sue is not here yet. She can be/must be on her way.

6. I suppose it's possible. I might/can/must come to your birthday party.

7. Sorry, I can't come/may not come. I have to finish my homework.

8. That can't be/mustn't be Chris. He hasn't got a motorbike.

Sujet national, septembre 2013, séries ES, L, S

EXPRESSION ÉCRITE : Can one give too much importance to physical appearance? *(150 mots au moins)*

Analyse du sujet

Le sujet vous invite à disserter sur l'idée que l'on puisse attribuer trop d'importance à l'apparence physique. Quelle que soit la position que vous adoptiez, ce qui importe le plus c'est que vous démontriez votre capacité à argumenter. Vous pouvez fort bien présenter les deux faces du même argument et annoncer votre position personnelle dans la conclusion.

Proposition de corrigé :

How important is physical appearance? Can we give it too much importance? In this essay, we will see **first** why physical appearance is important **and then** when its importance should be relativized.

From a professional point of view, physical appearance can be very important, especially if you work in a commercial relationship in the presence of clients. Sales representatives and shop assistants are supposed to attract clients, even seduce them. If their appearance is unattractive, their company will lose clients to its rivals. **Even on a personal level**, physical appearance plays a major role in the game of seduction: people are generally initially attracted to their sexual partner by their looks.

However, too much importance is given to physical appearance when it leads to discrimination and prejudice. Thankfully, nothing is **more important than** one's personality.

As a result, all of us and not just "Beauty Queens" or "Mr Universes" can hope to find their soul mate. **Similarly**, on a professional level, I would say that skills and character are more important than physical appearance.

Liban, mai 2014, séries ES, L, S

EXPRESSION ÉCRITE : To what extent do you think it is important to make one's dreams come true?

Analyse du sujet

Vous devez dire dans quelle mesure vous pensez qu'il *est important de réaliser ses rêves.*

Pour répondre, il vous faudra mobiliser les expressions d'opinion ainsi que les mots de liaison qui vous permettront d'articuler votre discours. Vous pouvez également enrichir votre production à l'aide de références culturelles et lexicales en lien avec la thématique (voir la rubrique « Notions clés » ci-contre).

La question est posée de telle sorte (« ...dans quelle mesure... ») que la réponse attendue se doit d'être nuancée : quelle que soit votre opinion sur le sujet, tâchez de ne pas vous limiter à un avis tranché qui se résumerait exclusivement à l'expression de votre point de vue personnel.

Proposition de corrigé :

In this essay we will look at how important it is for people to make their dreams come true.

We can easily argue that it is essential for dreams to be fulfilled at least to some extent, **otherwise** people will no longer believe in them, and risk not even wanting to dream in the future. **In other words**, people need to dream in order to project themselves, to make plans and to aspire to self-fulfilment. It's rather like the National Lottery: if no one ever wins, people will eventually give up playing. Where there are dreams, there is hope, and where there is hope, people are willing to devote time and energy **so that** their dreams come true.

On the other hand, it is **quite possible** that what matters is not so much the realization of our dreams but the fact of dreaming. **Indeed**, it can be frequently noted that when someone's dream is fulfilled, **instead of** reaching a state of pure contentment, they generally transfer their desire to something else: they are never fully satisfied, as they actually gain pleasure from being in a constant state of waiting for a dream to come true. **If this is the case**, perhaps it does not really matter if the dream never comes true, **although** life will inevitably be less monotonous if our dreams are allowed to change and evolve as time goes by.

Personally, I don't believe that we can really make our dreams come true. **I think** we can try hard to make them happen, but there are often many external factors that we are unable to control that play an essential role as well as an element of chance. **I would say that** if we are able to control dreams, they are not really dreams, but simply stages in our lives.

NOTIONS CLÉS

RÉFÉRENCES CULTURELLES

- The cult of youth (*le culte de la jeunesse*) : James Dean, Marilyn Monroe, etc.
- The myth of eternal love (*le mythe de l'amour éternel*) : *Romeo and Juliet*, etc.
- The myth of Prometheus (*le mythe de Prométhée, la tentation humaine de se mesurer aux dieux*) : *Frankenstein*, etc.
- The quest for eternal youth (*la quête de la jeunesse éternelle*) : *Peter Pan, Dorian Gray*, etc.
- The American Dream: a dream of freedom and justice for all, equal opportunities and the pursuit of happiness; the belief that America offers everyone the chance to fulfil themselves and realise their dreams.
- The American way of life (Coca-Cola; Rock'n roll; Hollywood; the cult of the car... etc.).
- The myth of the self-made man (*le mythe de l'homme qui a réussi par ses propres moyens*).
- The Rags to Riches myth (*le mythe de l'ascension sociale, de l'extrême pauvreté à la grande richesse*).

LEXIQUE

- a challenge: *un défi*
- a model: *un modèle*
- adventurous: *aventureux*
- an inaccessible dream: *un rêve inatteignable*
- an obsession: *une obsession*
- aware: *conscient*
- beauty: *la beauté*
- freedom: *la liberté*
- grateful: *reconnaissant*
- to be in love: *être amoureux*
- to believe in: *croire en*
- to climb the social ladder: *monter dans l'échelle sociale*
- to die young: *mourir jeune*
- to dream of + V-ing: *rêver de*
- to encounter: *rencontrer*
- to go in search of: *partir à la quête de*
- to search for: *rechercher*
- to succeed in + V-ing: *réussir*
- to wish for: *souhaiter, désirer*
- to yearn for: *aspirer à*
- wisdom: *la sagesse*
- a wish: *un vœu, un souhait*

L'assassinat de Martin Luther King

Le printemps n'est pas toujours clément dans le Tennessee, mais en cette fin d'après-midi du jeudi 4 avril 1968, à Memphis, la fraîcheur de la brise était délicieuse. Fatigué, agacé même peut-être par les préparatifs si laborieux de cette marche qu'il tentait d'organiser pour soutenir la grève des éboueurs locaux, Martin Luther King avait décidé de s'accorder un moment de répit. Il était dix-huit heures. Dans moins d'une minute, il y aurait plusieurs détonations, et puis plus rien : le leader noir, l'apôtre de la non-violence, atteint en pleine tête et baignant dans son sang. Mais pour l'heure, dans ces derniers instants de grâce, accoudé à la balustrade de fer, au premier étage de ce Lorraine Motel, si banalement semblable à tous ces hôtels minables qu'il avait pratiqués dans les longues errances de sa vie militante, Martin Luther King se reposait. Peut-être même dressait-il en pensée son propre bilan.

Les menaces, si nombreuses, s'étaient faites pressantes ces jours-ci. Prenant la parole, la veille encore à Memphis, il avait prononcé un sermon prémonitoire : « *Je vois*, disait-il, *la Terre promise ! Ce qui va m'arriver maintenant n'importe guère. Car je suis allé au sommet de la montagne et je ne m'inquiète plus...* »

Pourtant, ces quatre mille gardes nationaux patrouillant dans une capitale du Tennessee encore fumante des émeutes qui venaient de faire, une semaine auparavant, un mort et soixante blessés, était-ce là la « *Terre promise* » ? Et que dire du couvre-feu instauré dans plusieurs villes de Caroline du Nord en novembre au terme d'une année 1967 désastreuse, qui avait vu la violence se répandre comme une traînée de poudre dans plus d'une centaine de grandes cités. Rien qu'à Détroit, dans le Michigan, la police devait relever quarante-trois morts et procéder à 7 000 arrestations. Dans ce pays, déjà malade d'un conflit vietnamien de plus en plus impopulaire – où bien des Noirs étaient en première ligne –, c'était maintenant l'Amérique des ghettos, exaspérée, qui réclamait sa part du mirage économique.

Quelle ironie, pour ce précurseur de la « non-violence active », nourri de la pensée de Gandhi, que ces explosions de haine raciale ! Quel échec aussi, pour ce jeune prix Nobel de la paix de trente-neuf ans, si respecté dans le monde entier, et incapable de se faire écouter dans son propre pays ! Pour les désespérés de Harlem ou de Watts, pour tous les laissés-pour-compte des mégapoles du Nord, ce petit pasteur du Sud, en dépit de son courage, n'est qu'un bourgeois. Un doux idéaliste, presque un « *oncle Tom* », faisant le jeu des Blancs.

Condamné à une lente mort politique

De fait, ses tentatives pour lancer une campagne de désobéissance civile à Chicago, en 1965, et l'année suivante une grève des loyers furent un fiasco. À quoi servait donc d'être allé « *en haut de la montagne* », pour en redescendre plus démuni encore ? Fallait-il renoncer pour autant ? Parce qu'après le grand élan de la fin des années 50, la longue croisade pour l'égalité des droits civiques piétinait ?

Rosa Parks, la petite couturière noire de Montgomery (Alabama), s'était-elle découragée, au soir du 1er décembre 1955, quand, lasse de céder systématiquement sa place aux Blancs dans l'autobus qui la ramenait chez elle, elle avait décidé de rester assise ? Cela devait déclencher le formidable boycottage des autobus de la ville.

Bien avant, il y avait eu aussi les neufs écoliers noirs de Little Rock, tremblant de peur sous les huées à l'entrée du collège « blanc », et les marcheurs de la liberté, impavides sous les aboiements des chiens policiers de « Bull » Connor à Birmingham, et les cris racistes de son patron le gouverneur Wallace : « *Ségrégation aujourd'hui, ségrégation demain, ségrégation toujours !* » Non, aucun n'avait renoncé. Pas même sur le pont de Selma, quand, sous les coups, plusieurs sont tombés.

Mais assurément le rêve, le beau rêve d'une Amérique fraternelle et égalitaire, que le pasteur avait fait partager à une foule vibrante à Washington, le 28 août 1963, au terme d'une marche « *historique* » sur la capitale, ce rêve était loin encore d'être réalisé. Un rêve qui tournait même au cauchemar. Edgar Hoover, le pugnace directeur du FBI, anxieux de discréditer King, en recherchant l'évidence que son mouvement, la Southern Christian Leadership Conference étant infiltrée par les communistes, n'avait cessé de le harceler. Enregistrant ses conversations téléphoniques, le traquant chez ses amis, et perçant dans le moindre motel jusqu'aux plus intimes secrets d'une vie privée agitée.

Personna non grata à la Maison Blanche depuis ses prises de position contre la guerre au Vietnam, il se savait condamné par le FBI et ses nombreux autres ennemis à une lente mort politique. L'évolution même du mouvement noir, toujours plus radical, poussait, elle aussi, Martin Luther King vers les coulisses de l'histoire immédiate. Depuis deux ans déjà, Stokely Carmichael et Willie Ricks avaient lancé le mot d'ordre d'un « *Black Power* » qui s'accommodait mal de l'illusion libérale d'un « *dialogue intégrationniste* ». Pourtant, jamais la phrase de l'ancien président Eisenhower n'avait, dans sa sécheresse lapidaire, été aussi désespérément vraie : « *Ce n'est pas avec des armes que l'on changera les mentalités.* »

Dix-huit heures une, un soir d'avril à Memphis : les coups de feu ont claqué, Martin Luther King s'est effondré. Son plus proche collaborateur, Ralph Abernaty, se précipite, le prend à bras-le-corps, le soutient : « *Mon Dieu, Martin est touché !* ». À l'étage du dessous, où il s'occupe de la voiture, le jeune Jesse Jackson, la « tête brûlée » de l'entourage de King, qui l'aimait pourtant bien, arrive lui aussi, mais il est trop tard. Le blessé a été transporté à l'hôpital Saint-Joseph en ville. Rapidement les médecins ne peuvent que constater le décès. Quelques heures plus

POURQUOI CET ARTICLE ?

Cet article, rédigé en 1988 à l'occasion de la commémoration du vingtième anniversaire de l'assassinat de Martin Luther King, présente un triple intérêt. D'abord, il retrace le parcours de la figure emblématique du Mouvement pour les droits civiques. Ensuite, il relate les circonstances tragiques de sa disparition, celles-ci ayant sans doute contribué à élever le leader charismatique au rang de héros pour tout le peuple afro-américain, et bien au-delà. Enfin, il fait écho à l'actualité récente, marquée par des émeutes et des tensions raciales aux États-Unis à la suite des décès d'Afro-Américains tués par des policiers blancs. La dernière phrase de l'article prend à ce titre un relief tout particulier : avec Obama, les afro-américains ont enfin réussi à atteindre la Maison Blanche, traduisant ainsi dans la réalité le fameux « I Have a Dream » de Martin Luther King – pour autant, le combat contre les discriminations raciales aux États-Unis ne semble toujours pas gagné.

tard, l'air buté et le pull-over ostensiblement maculé de sang, Jesse Jackson, sans se démonter, explique devant les caméras de télévision qu'il est le dernier a avoir parlé avec le pasteur assassiné et que celui-ci est « *mort dans ses bras* ». À peine versé, le sang du martyr de la cause noire était « *récupéré* ».

Dans les minutes qui suivent l'annonce de la mort de King, des bandes de jeunes noirs parcourent les rues de Memphis mais bientôt aussi celles de Washington, où pillages et incendies se multiplient en plein centre-ville, à moins d'un kilomètre de la Maison Blanche. La flambée de colère et de violence atteint bientôt Chicago, où des tireurs isolés s'en prennent aux pompiers. Deux jours après, c'est Baltimore, Kansas-City et même la Californie et la Floride qui sont touchées. Au total, plus d'une centaine de villes américaines sont à feu et à sang. On dénombrera plus tard quarante-six morts et deux mille six cents blessés. La capitale fédérale est une poudrière. Le maire a décrété le couvre-feu, et les points stratégiques sont gardés par des éléments de cette 82e division aéroportée qui sauta jadis sur la Normandie.

Le « rêve » récupéré

Inquiet, et comprenant qu'il lui faut faire très vite, le président Johnson décide de retarder, puis d'annuler son départ pour Honolulu où il doit assister à une conférence cruciale sur cette guerre vietnamienne, dont il tente déjà de se dégager un peu. Intervenant à la télévision quelques heures après le drame, il dit « *l'Amérique choquée* » par cet assassinat et « *demande à tous les citoyens de renoncer à la violence aveugle qui a frappé le pasteur King, qui vivait par la non-violence* ». Et tandis que, du monde entier, affluent les télégrammes de stupeur et d'indignation, une véritable veillée d'armes commence en Amérique. Que se passera-t-il aux obsèques, le 9 avril à Atlanta ?

Débordés devant cette Amérique qui brûle, les compagnons du pasteur assassiné tentent de faire entendre raison à la communauté noire. Coretta King, la veuve, deux de ses enfants à la main, a conduit elle-même à Memphis la marche à laquelle aurait dû participer son mari. Toute la nuit, les cent-quarante églises de la ville resteront ouvertes à la foule en prières. À peine brisé, le « *rêve* » de Martin Luther King est lui aussi récupéré.

Nourri du courage et des convictions de cet homme si simple et généreux, un mythe écrasant, déjà, se construit. À qui profitera-t-il ? À la Maison Blanche, où un président, sincère lui aussi, mais anéanti sous la tâche, s'efforce de réveiller les consciences blanches ? Drapeaux en berne, journée de deuil national, minute de silence à la Bourse, tout est fait pour utiliser le climat émotionnel. Le gouvernement souligne avec une ostentation satisfaite, que jamais pareilles mesures n'ont été prises pour honorer un Noir. À moins que, cette nouvelle « aura » posthume de King ne soit plus utile, finalement, à cette communauté noire qui, hier encore, était prête à le remettre en cause, lui et ses idéaux dépassés ?

La réponse s'impose d'elle-même le 9 avril. Plus de cent mille personnes suivent le corbillard, tiré par deux mules dans les rues d'Atlanta, jusqu'à la petite église baptiste Ebenezer, dont il était le pasteur. Dans la foule, au coude-à-coude, outre le vice-président Humphrey et plusieurs membres du gouvernement, des acteurs : Marlon Brando, Sammy Davis ; l'archevêque de New York Terence Cooke, le magnat Henry Ford II. Et, bien sûr, le « clan » Kennedy ; Jackie, la veuve du président, et Robert, le frère, les « parrains » politiques de King, auquel John en pleine campagne électorale, en 1960, avait pris le risque d'envoyer une lettre de soutien. Dans cette séance d'exorcisme collectif que sont les obsèques du pasteur assassiné, il y a comme la bonne conscience d'une unité retrouvée : le martyre du militant noir profite à l'Amérique tout entière.

À peine si l'on pense à l'assassin, cet escroc de deuxième zone, James Earl Ray, qui sera arrêté par la police britannique le 8 juin, alors que les États-Unis sont à nouveau sous le choc d'un autre assassinat. Celui, trois jours plus tôt à Los Angeles, de Robert Kennedy. Le 10 mars 1969, devant le tribunal de Memphis, Earl Ray, extradé pour la circonstance, après avoir toujours protesté de son innocence, plaide coupable pour sauver sa tête. Au cours d'une audience unique, après un compromis passé entre l'accusation et la défense, il est condamné à quatre-vingt-dix-neuf ans de prison. Pour tout un pays traumatisé, l'affaire est classée, et ce, en dépit de nombreuses incohérences. Personne, là non plus, n'a vraiment envie de savoir sur quelles pénibles vérités le « *mythe King* » a été fondé.

Vingt ans après [article rédigé en 1988], le message d'espoir du pasteur King, préservé pour l'éternité dans son mausolée de marbre comme la conscience de l'Amérique, a retrouvé toute son acuité : « *Après chaque vendredi saint*, disait-il, *Pâques arrive...* ». La Pâque noire américaine est encore un peu précoce, mais quel chemin parcouru !

Même si le pouvoir économique est trop inégalement partagé, les Noirs ont à présent suffisamment de poids en politique pour le réclamer. Un obscur gouverneur de l'Arizona vient d'être destitué, pour avoir, entre autres « maladresses », voulu annuler le jour férié dédié à la mémoire du leader noir assassiné. Enfin, son turbulent protégé, Jesse Jackson, vient de montrer au cours d'une incroyable percée dans les primaires présidentielles, que sa croisade contre la « *violence économique* », inspirée à bien des égards de King, pouvait rallier aussi des suffrages blancs.

Les marcheurs de Selma ont eu raison de ne pas s'arrêter. Ils ne sont pas encore à la Maison Blanche, mais déjà aux marches du palais.

Marie-Claude Decamps, *Le Monde* daté du 11.04.1988

Churchill, l'homme qui a écrit sa propre histoire

Au cœur de Londres, l'œil de Churchill scrute un bout de ciel sur lequel se dessine la silhouette de Big Ben, l'horloge du Parlement. Dans son pardessus de bronze, légèrement appuyé sur sa canne légendaire, épaule et jambe en avant, le vieux lutteur semble encore défier un invisible ennemi. Trapu, puissant, énergique, avec cet air de bouledogue belliqueux qui fut le sien à l'heure du plus grand péril. « *Ma statue sera ici !* » avait-il lancé, péremptoire, dans les années 1950, à l'un de ses ministres. Comme s'il avait voulu, à l'avance, régler la mise en scène de cet hommage posthume à sa gloire impérissable. Lui, déjà statufié pourtant de son vivant, et en partie par ses soins. Dès l'adolescence,

Churchill se croit voué à un grand destin, au point de confier à un ami qu'il sera, un jour, premier ministre. Mais que valent les plus beaux exploits s'ils ne sont ensuite exaltés ? Churchill ne cessera de manier le verbe et la plume pour accompagner et magnifier ses actions. Il fait l'histoire et la raconte. A chaud : jeune soldat de l'Empire et correspondant de guerre, en Inde, au Soudan, en Afrique du Sud, il relate ses faits d'armes, peaufine déjà son image, forge son mythe. A froid : des décennies plus tard, lorsqu'il s'agit, après l'épreuve, de s'ériger un mausolée avec les six volumes de ses Mémoires de guerre. *« L'Histoire me traitera bien, avait-il prévenu, car je l'écrirai moi-même. »* Entre-temps, il a accompli son destin, trop longtemps inachevé.

On a posé mille fois cette question, mais il faut la répéter : que serait le monde aujourd'hui, sans le Churchill de 1940 ? Que seraient le Royaume-Uni, la France, l'Europe, sans cet homme qui attendait son grand rendez-vous avec l'Histoire et que l'Histoire, elle-même, semblait attendre pour lui permettre de donner sa pleine mesure ? Imaginer la réponse, un seul instant, suffit à justifier que le principal artisan de la victoire sur l'Allemagne nazie occupe le premier rang au Panthéon des hommes d'Etat du XXe siècle.

Dans notre mémoire collective, Churchill reste à jamais le personnage providentiel qui, pendant plusieurs mois, tint, seul, la liberté de l'Europe à bout de bras et sauva l'honneur des démocraties. Un homme d'exception, et d'excès. Un chef de guerre implacable incarnant, aux heures les plus sombres, la résistance et l'espérance. Une figure déraisonnable au diapason d'une époque qui ne l'était pas moins. Sans Churchill, le nazisme aurait dominé l'Europe. Sans cet amoureux de « la France éternelle », il n'y aurait pas eu de gouvernement et de soldats français aux côtés des Alliés le jour de la victoire, et notre pays n'aurait obtenu ni zone d'occupation en Allemagne, ni siège permanent au Conseil de sécurité de l'ONU. La France, plus que d'autres, a une dette historique envers Churchill.

Meneur d'hommes et grand capitaine au milieu des tempêtes, Churchill incarne, pendant cinq ans, son peuple « au cœur de lion ». Il le rassemble, l'unifie, le galvanise. Il fait corps avec la nation britannique et lui dit la vérité, si dure soit-elle. Mais il lui insuffle aussi sa foi et lui transmet l'espoir. Il prédit le salut, le succès, la délivrance. *« Rira bien qui rira le dernier »*, promet-il, dès le 21 octobre 1940, sur les ondes de la BBC, dans son « discours aux Français », où il exhorte ces derniers à *« armer leur cœur à neuf »* face aux *« gangsters nazis »*. Chez cet homme, dont les talents et les faiblesses tissent une même trame, les défauts des temps ordinaires deviennent, face à l'adversité, autant de qualités qui s'ajoutent à ses vertus de toujours : le courage physique, l'énergie mentale, la confiance en soi, la force de travail, l'humour. L'obstination jusqu'à l'arrogance, la certitude d'avoir raison, l'ambition démesurée, l'intrépidité jusqu'à l'inconscience, le désir de préserver intact l'Empire britannique, l'autoritarisme, la volonté de se mêler de tout : ces traits de caractère l'ont aidé pendant les années de guerre à atteindre l'objectif qui le hantait à chaque instant. *« Il y avait en lui une extraordinaire concentration, qui allait jusqu'à l'obsession, sur un seul but, la victoire à tout prix »*, note son médecin personnel, Lord Moran.

Pendant la guerre, Churchill, fasciné, harcelé, tourmenté par l'action, dispose sur son bureau de petits pense-bêtes qui lui rappellent tout ce qu'il doit faire dans la journée. Le général de Gaulle écrira de lui : *« Par-dessus tout, il était de par son caractère, fait pour agir, risquer, jouer le rôle, très carrément et sans scrupule. »* « Agir » et *« jouer »* : voilà bien le double sens du verbe anglais « to act », tel que l'entend Churchill, ce personnage shakespearien pour qui le monde est un théâtre, et la guerre un drame exaltant où il déverse sa générosité, sa passion, ses colères et ses entêtements, où il répand son éloquence.

De Gaulle, lui-même grand tribun, admire la verve de Churchill et sa force de conviction : *« Quel que fût son auditoire : foule, assemblée, conseil, voire interlocuteur unique, qu'il se trouvât devant un micro, à la tribune, à table ou derrière son bureau, le flot original, poétique, émouvant, de ses idées, arguments, sentiments lui procurait un ascendant presque infaillible dans l'ambiance dramatique où haletait le pauvre monde. En politique éprouvé, il jouait de ce don angélique et diabolique.* [...] » Et le général conclut : *« Winston Churchill m'apparut, d'un bout à l'autre du drame, comme le champion d'une grande entreprise et le grand artiste d'une grande histoire. »*

Churchill n'est pourtant pas un orateur né. Bien au contraire. Souffrant d'un léger zézaiement, il peine à prononcer les « s ». Il surmontera ce handicap à force de discipline. Sa voix légèrement nasillarde et sa courte taille le préparent mal aux grandes envolées. N'ayant pas fréquenté l'université, il n'a jamais appris l'art du débat qu'on pratique à Oxford ou Cambridge. Mais, souligne l'un de ses biographes, l'historien François Bédarida, Churchill a deux atouts : une belle maîtrise de la langue et une excellente mémoire. Ayant, jeune député, perdu, un jour aux Communes, le fil de sa pensée, il prendra garde de ne plus jamais improviser. Et puis, il a un sens de la repartie qui deviendra légendaire, cinglant à souhait.

Dès ses années de collège, le jeune Winston découvre ses talents de conteur. Le reportage de guerre lui permet de travailler son style, de parfaire son art du récit, de polir ses métaphores. Entré en politique, le futur Prix Nobel de littérature privilégie le style oral, son langage naturel. Il dicte tout, ses discours et ses livres. A ses yeux, la rhétorique et la dialectique sont des armes majeures pour qui aspire à gouverner les hommes. Son exubérance verbale vogue sur tous les registres : *« Il tire parti de tout, note le général Eisenhower, depuis les classiques grecs jusqu'au canard Donald. »* ■

Jean-Pierre Langellier, *Le Monde* daté du 31.10.2014

POURQUOI CET ARTICLE ?

Dans cet article, Winston Churchill est salué comme le « personnage providentiel qui, pendant plusieurs mois, tint, seul, la liberté de l'Europe à bout de bras et sauva l'honneur des démocraties » lors de la Seconde Guerre mondiale. Avec son intarissable envie de briller et son exceptionnel talent d'orateur, il compte parmi les figures héroïques du XXe siècle. Ses traits de caractère, mêlant à la fois qualités admirables et défauts agaçants, rendent ce héros plus proche du commun des mortels que des dieux, mais la place qu'assigne la mémoire collective à son rôle dans l'histoire a fait de son parcours un véritable mythe. Rares sont les personnalités qui ont autant contribué à la naissance de leur dimension mythique et dont on pourrait également dire : « il fait l'histoire et la raconte ».

Mohamed Ali : une légende de la boxe

Ses ailes avaient séché depuis une éternité ; ses poings acérés avaient dû céder la place à des mains lourdes et tremblantes. Sa devise, *« vole comme un papillon et pique comme une abeille »* (« Float like a butterfly and sting like a bee »), s'était imposée à travers les continents comme un redoutable slogan publicitaire. « Le plus grand », comme Mohamed Ali aimait se décrire lui-même, est mort, vendredi 3 juin à Phoenix (Arizona), d'une insuffisance respiratoire, à l'âge de 74 ans. Après trente-deux années, la maladie de Parkinson a fini par terrasser l'une des dernières icônes planétaires du sport.

Ses sorties se faisaient rares ces dernières années. Son visage rond et son éternel air de chenapan appartenaient à l'histoire : il ne restait plus que l'image d'un vieil homme fatigué mais fier d'exposer son corps affaibli comme pour montrer – et démontrer – que la maladie ne pouvait atteindre l'ancienne gloire mondiale de la boxe. Orgueilleux, arrogant jusqu'au plus profond de sa peau. Mohamed Ali était un être à part, un duelliste hors catégorie à la beauté insolente.

Ali, c'est d'abord un style. Avec lui, la boxe était une chorégraphie : il était le chef d'orchestre de son propre combat, son adversaire devant se contenter de tenir la partition. Sa respiration était une musique que le public ne se lassait pas d'écouter dans les arènes les plus mythiques. Ali était un garçon qui dansait comme en apesanteur sur un ring, un cogneur de plus de 90 kg qui a marqué à coup de « jab » l'histoire du noble art.

La vie de cet athlète hors norme a tout d'un scénario hollywoodien : celui d'un « mauvais Noir » qui allait corriger une Amérique blanche et raciste. Mohamed Ali était ce genre de type, complexe et fascinant, qui aurait pu être croqué dans l'un des romans noirs du grand écrivain afro-américain Iceberg Slim. Dans ses livres, la destinée des personnages épouse l'histoire des Etats-Unis, celle qui opposa pendant tant de décennies les Noirs et les Blancs. Ali est le témoin de cet affrontement et en sera l'un des symboles les plus frappants.

Ali, c'est aussi une belle et grande gueule qui n'hésite pas à martyriser – avec sa verve ou ses poings – les adversaires qui lui avaient manqué de respect. Ali est né Cassius Clay à Louisville, dans le Kentucky, le 17 janvier 1942 dans un milieu, jure-t-il, pauvre même si sa famille a toujours préféré le terme « modeste ». Son père, Cassius Marcellus Clay senior, peint des affiches publicitaires et Jésus, qu'il aime dessiner *« blanc aux yeux bleus »*. Sa mère Odessa, femme de ménage chez de riches Blancs, élève ses deux garçons. Pour Cassius, l'école n'a rien d'épanouissant. La rencontre avec la boxe viendra en octobre 1954 lorsque à la fête du sport de son école, on lui vole son vélo, un Schwinn rouge et blanc. En pleurs, le jeune Cassius s'empresse de trouver un policier qui pourrait enregistrer sa plainte. Le voilà guidé vers le Columbia Gym, un club de boxe tenu par Joe Martin, qui est… policier. Joe Martin écoute le garçon. Le frêle Clay rêve d'attraper le voleur : il veut se venger, le punir d'avoir osé voler sa bécane.

Machine à distribuer les droites

« Tu devrais apprendre à te battre avant de commencer à te battre », lui répond Joe Martin. Quelques semaines plus tard, le voilà sur un ring pour affronter Ronnie O'Keefe dans un… show télévisé. « Tomorrow's Champions » est une émission de la chaîne locale où les combattants de Joe Martin sont souvent invités. Cassius gagne sur décision de l'arbitre mais quelque chose en lui a changé. *« Tout d'un coup, j'ai eu une nouvelle vie »*, déclarera plus tard le boxeur.

Le policier va s'occuper de Clay, l'emmener sur les plus hautes marches des podiums jusqu'à sa médaille d'or olympique, catégorie mi-lourds (75-81 kg), aux Jeux de Rome en 1960. Son palmarès chez les amateurs est vertigineux : 108 combats, 100 victoires, deux Golden Gloves… Cassius Clay, du haut de son 1,91 mètre, est une machine à distribuer les droites et les vannes provocatrices. Quand un journaliste russe lui demande aux Jeux de Rome ce qu'il pense de la ségrégation dans son pays, il répond : *« Dites à vos lecteurs que nous avons des gens qualifiés qui travaillent à cela et je ne suis pas inquiet sur l'issue. Pour moi, les Etats-Unis sont toujours le plus grand des pays y compris le vôtre. Il peut être difficile de trouver quelque chose à manger parfois, mais de toute façon, je ne combats pas les alligators et je ne vis pas dans une hutte de terre. »*

Le garçon va affûter ses répliques, s'affirmer en devenant professionnel. Le voilà entre les mains savantes d'Angelo Dundee, son nouvel – et dernier – entraîneur qui, tout au long de sa longue carrière, coachera une dizaine de champions du monde. Cassius enchaîne les victoires (19) avant son premier championnat du monde, prévu à Miami, le 25 février 1964, face au « vilain ours » Sonny Liston. Liston, 32 ans, est donné favori à huit contre un. Cassius est déjà surnommé le « boxeur poète », il se dit déjà *« le plus beau, le plus grand »*.

Et à la surprise générale, c'est le jeune apollon de 22 ans qui pousse son aîné, blessé à l'épaule gauche, à l'abandon avant la reprise du 7e round. Durant le combat, Sonny avait tenté d'aveugler le rejeton pour éviter de finir humilié dans les cordes. Liston touchera 1,15 million de dollars et Clay 650 000 dollars pour son premier sacre.

Mais pour la presse, ce combat est une *« combine »*. Le Sénat américain demande une enquête. La World Boxing Association réclame qu'on retire à Clay son titre pour avoir signé une revanche avant même d'avoir rencontré Sonny Liston et pour son comportement hors du ring qualifié de contre-exemple pour la jeunesse. *« Je suis jeune, je suis beau, je suis rapide, je suis joli, et je ne peux absolument pas être battu »*, lance-t-il comme pour narguer la vieille garde de la boxe.

Cette année-là, Cassius Clay n'existe plus. Il exige qu'on l'appelle Cassius X, renonçant ainsi à son nom d'esclave légué par d'anciens propriétaires blancs. Il fréquente un certain Malcolm X, et la secte politico-religieuse Nation of Islam, dirigée par Elijah Muhammad. Cassius X devient Mohamed Ali et exige qu'on l'interpelle uniquement par son nom musulman. Il se rend à La Mecque. Et il est reçu plusieurs fois par le président égyptien Nasser.

La revanche Liston-Ali se profile. Et le 25 mai 1965, à Lewiston, dès le premier round, Liston tombe. *« Debout et bats-toi, enfoiré »*, lance Ali. C'est la victoire la plus rapide de l'histoire des championnats du monde des poids lourds. Le coup de poing fatal – surnommé « le coup de poing fantôme » – est si furtif que personne ne semble l'avoir vu dans le public. Encore une fois, le combat est controversé au point que le *New York Times* demande *« l'interdiction »* de la boxe. Et on rappelle les liens qui rapprochent Liston à la pègre…

« Combat du siècle »

Ali défendra neuf fois son titre. Avec succès. Mais la guerre du Vietnam le rattrape en 1966. Il refuse d'aller au front car sa religion le lui interdit. Pour lui, *« les Vietcongs sont des Asiatiques noirs »*, et il n'a pas à *« combattre des Noirs »*. Il est condamné le 21 juin 1967 à cinq ans de prison et 10 000 dollars d'amende. On lui retire son titre et sa licence de boxe. Il ne sera pas incarcéré, mais ses détracteurs – à commencer par le gouvernement américain – veulent mettre son palmarès au cimetière des champions déchus.

D'une éloquence insolente, Ali parle, fait le tour des universités, devient un opposant farouche à la guerre au Vietnam et, aux côtés de Malcolm X (assassiné en 1965) ou de Martin Luther King (assassiné en 1968), une figure du mouvement pour les droits civiques. *« Ici, dans ma ville natale, de Louisville, nous sommes privés de liberté. Mais aujourd'hui, on nous demande d'aller dans un autre pays afin d'y offrir nos vies pour la liberté des autres »*, dénonce-t-il.

Ali ne baisse pas la garde. En 1970, on lui réattribue sa licence, un tribunal ayant reconnu qu'une condamnation pour insoumission ne justifiait pas qu'on lui retire son moyen d'existence. Le ring retrouve son maître et Ali enchaîne de nouveau les combats et les victoires. Une seule chose l'obsède : la reconquête du titre. Le 8 mars 1971, au Madison Square Garden de New York, deux boxeurs invaincus vont s'affronter dans le « combat du siècle ». Ali contre le champion du monde en titre, Joe Frazier.

Pour Ali, Frazier est un *« usurpateur »*. A lui de reprendre sa ceinture. Et pourtant, Ali va perdre ce duel aux points. Il lui faut alors repartir de zéro, affronter des seconds couteaux, des anonymes, des inconnus. Un long chemin pour devenir le challenger numéro un. L'ancien champion a vieilli et est moins agile. Mais l'homme vole encore comme un papillon et pique toujours comme une abeille. Cette année-là, la Cour suprême des Etats-Unis innocente définitivement Mohamed Ali : ses convictions – considérés comme politiques – ont fini par mettre KO le gouvernement américain.

Mais voilà, en 1973, face à Ken Norton, il perd une deuxième fois et quitte le ring avec une mâchoire fracturée. L'homme n'est pas abattu, et remonte sur le ring : il prend sa revanche sur Norton, puis sur Frazier et défie le champion du monde George Foreman. C'est probablement le combat le plus emblématique de sa carrière et le plus mythique de la boxe : c'est au Zaïre, à Kinshasa, grâce aux 10 millions de dollars du président Mobutu promis aux deux protagonistes, et grâce à l'entregent du promoteur de combats Don King, que les deux hommes vont s'affronter. L'Afrique, un retour aux sources. Dans les rues poussiéreuses de Kinshasa, Ali redécouvre brutalement sa notoriété et réalise qu'il a participé, d'une certaine manière, à changer le monde en refusant d'aller se battre au Vietnam. *« Ali boumayé »* (*« Ali, tue-le »*), hurle-t-on lorsque l'on croise sa grande silhouette.

Foreman, 25 ans, est surpuissant, invaincu. *« Foreman est lent comme un train de marchandises »*, ironise Ali. Mais en réalité, Ali n'est plus aussi rapide. Il va adopter une étonnante stratégie pour vaincre. Sous une chaleur étouffante, dans un brouhaha étourdissant, il va encaisser pendant sept rounds les coups rageurs de son adversaire jusqu'à ce que ce dernier s'épuise. Et au huitième round, Ali se lâche et envoie, le 30 octobre 1974, devant 100 000 personnes, Foreman au tapis. Dix ans après son premier titre, à 32 ans, Ali redevient *« le plus grand »* après un combat surnommé « The Rumble in the Jungle » (« Le grondement de la jungle »).

Quatre mariages et neuf enfants

Mohamed Ali défendra dix fois de suite son titre avant de le concéder aux points le 15 février 1978, à Las Vegas, face à Leon Spinks, 24 ans. Sept mois plus tard, il le reprendra, pour la troisième fois. Ali a 36 ans. Toujours aussi beau, mais moins flamboyant, il veut prendre sa retraite mais Don King sait comment lui parler. Ali n'est plus qu'une valeur marchande, il n'est plus ce boxeur lumineux. Il perd au 10e round contre son ancien partenaire d'entraînement Larry Holmes, en octobre 1980.

Pour son coach, Angelo Dundee, *« le petit jeu est terminé ! »* C'est la première fois qu'Ali perd avant la fin du match. Il combattra encore en 1981 avant de dire adieu aux cordes après vingt et un ans de professionnalisme. Son palmarès chez les pros : 61 combats, 56 victoires – dont 37 par KO – et 5 défaites.

Tout au long de sa carrière et surtout vers la fin des années 1970, Ali a encaissé des centaines de mauvais coups - parfois lors d'un seul combat – comme lors du violent « Thrilla in Manilla » (« Frisson à Manille ») aux Philippines face au « Gorille » Frazier, en 1975. En 1984, on lui diagnostique la maladie de Parkinson. L'homme consacre alors son existence à délivrer un message de paix, celui qu'il dit avoir trouvé dans l'islam. Il a une étoile sur Hollywood Boulevard, à Los Angeles. Mais elle est accrochée sur un mur à l'entrée du Kodak Theater, et non placée sur le trottoir comme pour les autres stars car il ne souhaite pas qu'on piétine le nom du prophète.

Sa vie personnelle ressemble étrangement à ses titres douloureusement conquis. Il s'est marié quatre fois et a eu neuf enfants. Une de ses filles se fera un prénom dans la boxe : Laila Ali sera au début des années 2000, championne du monde des poids super-moyens et mi-lourds (24 combats, 24 victoires dont 21 par KO).

Ali passa sa vie de boxeur à dénoncer le racisme et la ségrégation dans son pays. Paradoxalement, en vieillissant, l'anticonformiste finit par incarner « l'establishment » tant décrié : il est reçu à la Maison Blanche et par d'autres chefs d'Etat. Il voyage à travers le monde pour jouer, parfois, les médiateurs, comme en 1990, lorsqu'il obtient de Saddam Hussein la promesse de la libération de quatorze Américains pris en otage.

Il est aussi fait messager de la paix par les Nations unies, en 1998, pour avoir consacré sa vie à *« rapprocher les peuples de la planète en leur vantant les vertus de la réconciliation, quels que soient leurs race, religion ou âge. Au fil des ans, M. Ali s'est fait l'avocat des plus démunis et a accompli un travail humanitaire considérable dans le monde en développement. »* L'icône sportive devient aussi icône publicitaire et l'égérie de prestigieuses marques de luxe. Lucide sur les louanges qui lui étaient adressées, Mohamed Ali-Cassius Clay avait lancé : *« Dans cent ans, on dira que j'étais blanc, c'est ce qu'ils ont fait à Jésus. »*

Mustapha Kessous, *Le Monde* daté du 06.06.2016

POURQUOI CET ARTICLE ?

Cet article, écrit après le décès de Mohamed Ali le 3 juin 2016, retrace les grands moments de la vie de ce boxeur qui a non seulement marqué l'histoire du sport, mais dont la vie et le charisme ont également contribué à façonner une légende. Son parcours montre d'abord sa quête d'identité : né Cassius Clay, il rejettera son nom d'esclave – ironique, puisque c'était celui d'un célèbre abolitionniste – et s'appellera Cassius X avant de se convertir à l'islam et de devenir Mohamed Ali. Sa vie nous renvoie à l'histoire contemporaine des États-Unis et est marquée par des engagements, contre la guerre du Vietnam et pour le mouvement des droits civiques. Anticonformiste, rebelle et associé à Malcom X dans les années 1960, son message pour la paix, contre le racisme et la ségrégation fera ensuite de lui une personnalité plus consensuelle.

L'IDÉE DE PROGRÈS

The App That Lets You Spy on Yourself and Sell Your Own Data

Facebook and other social networking sites aren't free. They don't charge you money to connect with friends, upload photos, and "like" your favorite bands and businesses, but you still pay. You pay with your personal data, which these services use to target ads.

For *Citizenme*, the price you pay is much higher, and it's trying to shift Internet economics back in your direction. The long-term plan is to provide a way for you to sell your own online data directly to advertisers and others of *your* choosing. But it isn't there just yet. In the meantime, it's focused on helping you collect and analyze your social media data through a mobile app that connects to multiple social networks—giving you more insight into how things work today. "The very first step is raising awareness, helping people understand what's being done with their data," says *Citizenme* founder St John Deakins. Deakins, who has experience building mobile technologies for emerging markets, got the idea for *Citizenme* a few years ago, after selling mobile video company *Triple Media* to the private equity firm *NewNet* in 2010. "The biggest issue I could see for the Internet is our data and what happens to our data," he says. He acknowledges that personal data is essential to the health of the net because it drives the advertising that funds things. But today's invasive data collection policies have made people distrustful. *Citizenme* hopes to change that by making users more aware of this process and, ultimately, letting them decide how their data is used.

How It Works

You start by connecting your social profiles to the app, which stores your data locally on your phone. Nothing is stored on *Citizenme*'s servers. So far, the app handles *Facebook*, *LinkedIn* and *Twitter*, but other services, such as *Pinterest*, are planned for the future.

From there, you can see what data you share publicly on those networks, and get a better sense of the overall privacy settings and policies of those services. The app includes a guide to each network's terms of service. Particularly alarming policies—such as Facebook's broad license to your photos and other content—are highlighted in red to get your attention. And when a company updates its terms of service, *Citizenme* alerts you and lets you vote on whether you think it's a good or bad change. "It's like an anti-virus for terms of service," Deakins says, even though the outcome of such a vote is purely symbolic.

The company also worked with Cambridge University to create a series of personality tests that can be run against your data, letting you see how different networks might perceive you. For example, the app can predict whether you're politically liberal or conservative, and tell you whether you are more conservative on *LinkedIn* than you are on *Twitter*. It's fun, if not particularly useful, and it might help explain some of the ads *Facebook* sends your way.

DICTIONARY

- **to charge**: to ask in payment
- **data**: information
- **to target**: to aim at
- **an ad**: an advertisement
- **to shift**: to move
- **to provide**: to supply
- **to focus on**: to concentrate on
- **insight**: understanding
- **to raise awareness**: to make people more aware of
- **to acknowledge**: to recognize
- **distrustful**: doubtful
- **to store**: to stock
- **to handle**: to deal with
- **to highlight**: to underline
- **outcome**: end result
- **trust**: confidence
- **to release**: to deliver
- **accountable**: answerable
- **a cut**: a share
- **a subscription fee**: annual payment
- **fair**: honest
- **confident**: convinced
- **a lead**: a piece of information
- **pretty much**: almost
- **defunct**: no longer existing
- **ubiquity**: universality

MOTS CLÉS en lien avec la thématique

NOUNS

- virtual world/ reality: *monde virtuel/ réalité*
- the Internet/ the Web/ a website
- a network: *un réseau*
- a *Facebook* account: *un compte* Facebook
- technological improvements: *les progrès technologiques*
- software: *un logiciel*
- Internet users: *les utilisateurs d'Internet*
- a cellphone: *un portable*

Ex.: **Cellphones** reveal your location.

- surveillance cameras: *des caméras de surveillance*
- social networking: *le réseautage social*

Ex.: President Obama warned American teenagers of the dangers of putting too much personal information on **social networking sites**.

- social media tools: *les outils des medias sociaux*
- video games: *les jeux vidéo*
- a hacker: *un pirate informatique*

Ex.: **Hackers** often **steal data** from large companies.

- a threat: *une menace*
- privacy: *la vie privée*
- Web censorship: *la censure sur le Web*
- a police state: *un État policier*

VERBS

- to be connected to: *être connecté à*
- to be addicted to the Internet: *être « accro »à Internet*
- to block access to the Internet: *bloquer l'accès à Internet*
- to cut off Internet: *couper Internet*
- to hack into: *pirater*
- to launch cyber-attacks: *lancer des cyber-attaques*
- to steal data: *voler des données*
- to threaten: *menacer*

Ex.: New technologies can **threaten our privacy**.

- to monitor: *surveiller*

Ex.: The NSA **monitored** the calls of some world leaders.

- to spy on/ to snoop on: *espionner*

What the Future Holds

So far, the app is only available for *iOS*, but an *Android* version is planned for next month. Eventually, Deakins says, the team wants to offer the app for all operating systems and—with your permission—integrate far more information, including location data, statistics from health trackers, or even your genome, via services like *23andMe*. That would let you learn far more about your online self and how advertisers perceive you, while providing still more data you eventually could sell.

In order to build more trust, Deakins says the company will open source the client-side of the app "bit by bit," and it may release some server-side code as well. To keep itself accountable to users, the company also plans to establish an independent non-profit organization that will approve changes to *Citizenme*'s terms of service. Users will be able to vote on such changes.

The company plans to make money by taking a cut from any dollars that users earn by selling their data. If you choose not to sell your data, you'll have the option of paying a subscription fee. "The idea is that you sell your data for a fair price," Deakins says. "If you're selling your data so other people can get free access to the service, then you're not getting fair value. So some users need to pay. That's the fairest way that we can think of."

The Big Question

The big question is whether anyone will want to sell their data, but Deakins is confident they will. He says that so far users fall into two main groups. The first is older users who want greater control of their privacy and happily pay a subscription fee to have it. The second is younger users who, long since used to companies like *Facebook* profiting from their data, want to profit from it as well. He notes that selling the data could have other benefits as well.

"If I'm going to buy a new car in two weeks time, I want to share that, because I want advertising and discounts for my new car," he says. "For me, there's a big benefit because I get a discount on my new car. The advertiser wins because they get a verified, validated lead. For the publisher, the advertising is validated through the individual. Pretty much everyone wins in the ecosystem."

Citizenme isn't the first to try something like this. The defunct non-profit organization *Attention Trust* tried giving users tools to collect and sell their data as far back as 2005. But Deakins thinks the time is finally right, given the ubiquity of smartphones and social media. "We have an Internet ecosystem where all of our data is incredibly valuable," he says. "That means that market forces say that all our data needs to get sucked up into the cloud. But the natural next progression is giving people power over their own data."

Wired (Klint Finley–September 7th, 2014)

FOCUS ON...

Social networks

Today, *Facebook* and *Twitter* are the two most influential social networks. There are over 1.35 billion monthly active *Facebook* users worldwide and 284 million monthly active users of *Twitter*. 864 milion people log onto *Facebook* daily and they spend on average 21 minutes on *Facebook* per day. *LinkedIn* is another very influential social network and, with over 300 million users, it enables you to extend your professional network of contacts.

Facebook and *Twitter* have also played their part in political uprisings. In Arab countries many activists who played crucial roles in the Arab Spring used social networking as a key tool in expressing their thoughts concerning unjust acts committed by governments. Syrian rebel groups are now using *Twitter*, *Instagram* and *YouTube* to create new ways to recruit, train and raise money.

The question of privacy and the use of personal data is a key issue when we deal with social networks. More and more data is given to social networks, with very little understanding of where it actually ends up. Advertisers and retailers are using data from customers' online and social media activity to tailor their shopping experience. Privacy experts worry that *Facebook*'s business model runs contrary to people's interests as the more data you share, the more *Facebook* knows about you and the more powerful its ad-targeting machine becomes.

QUATRE ARTICLES DU *MONDE* À CONSULTER

- **San Francisco : smart d'entre les smart** p.36
(Corine Lesnes, *Le Monde* daté du 20.11.2015)
- **Les géants de la Silicon Valley, bâtisseurs du futur** p.37-38
(Corine Lesnes, *Le Monde Éco et entreprise* daté du 04.03.2015)
- **Les arts plastiques tentés par la réalité virtuelle** p. 38-39
(Laure Andrillon, *Le Monde* daté du 13.06.2017)
- **Google régale à l'œil** p.40-41
(Guillemette Faure, *Le Monde* daté du 14.09.2013)

S'EXPRIMER

PREPOSITIONS WITH A PRESENT PARTICIPLE

• "Deakins [...] got the idea for *Citizenme* a few years ago, **after selling** mobile video company *Triple Media* [...]."

"That would let you learn far more about your online self and how advertisers perceive you, **while providing** still more data."

After and **while** are used with a **present participle (V-ing)** clause.

• Other prepositions such as **before, without, through** and **since** can be used with a **present participle**.

Ex.: **Since** moving to London, I haven't had time to go the theatre.

Ex.: I need to learn a lot of vocabulary **before** taking the English exam.

• "*Citizenme* hopes to change that **by** making users more aware of this process."

"The company plans to make money **by** taking a cut from any dollars that users earn **by** selling their data."

By + V-ing indicates the **method or means used**.

• We can often use **by + V-ing** and **in + V-ing** with a similar meaning.

Ex.: **In/ by** writing my essay about Jane Austen, I came to understand English literature better.

STILL AND YET

• "[...] while providing **still** more data you eventually could sell."
(**still** = *encore*)

"But it **isn't** there just **yet**."
(**yet** = *déjà*/ **not yet** = *pas encore*)

Yet is used in questions and in negative sentences. **Yet** is usually at the end of the sentence.

Ex.: Has he arrived **yet**?/ He **hasn't** arrived **yet**.

LET + INFINITIVE

• "*Citizenme* alerts you and **lets** you **vote** on whether you think it's a good or bad change."

"That would **let** you **learn** far more about your online self."

The infinitive is used without "to" after the verb "to let" (= *laisser quelqu'un faire quelque chose*).

Questions de compréhension

True or false?

1. Social networks use your personal data for advertising purposes.
2. Social networks allow you to choose your advertisers.
3. For *Citizenme*, users should be able to make money with their data.
4. Thanks to *Citizenme* you can now sell your data to advertisers of your choosing.
5. Mr Deakins set up *Citizenme*.
6. Mr Deakins owns the mobile video company *Triple Media*.
7. Thanks to *Citizenme* users will be able to understand better how their data can be used.
8. The app enables you to understand the social networks' terms of service better.
9. You can vote whenever a company changes its terms of service.
10. If you do a personality test, the app can predict your political views.
11. *Citizenme* wants to become a non-profit organization.
12. *Citizenme* will take a percentage when you sell your data.
13. All *Citizenme* users will have to pay a subscription fee before using the service.
14. Younger users are more likely to be willing to sell their data than older users.
15. *Attention Trust* is going to be *Citizenme*'s main competitor.

Exercices de grammaire

A. Choose the correct word underlined in each sentence.

1. The girl whose/whom house I was staying at was an old friend.
2. Our house, which/that has been damaged by fire, hasn't been repaired yet.
3. The girl who/whom lives next door knows my brother.
4. The people who/where he works with are a bit strange.
5. The teacher who/whom taught us yesterday also teaches my sister.
6. The friend to who/whom I lent my book managed to lose it.
7. I'd like you to tell me what/who you were talking to.
8. The girl who/whose book I had borrowed wanted it back.

B. Rewrite each pair of sentences as one sentence, and include the word given. Begin as shown, and make any necessary changes.

1. We want to visit a museum. It opens at 10 am. (**that**)
The ....

2. A boy's bike was stolen. He went to the police station. (**whose**)
The ....

3. A friend met me at the station. He carried my bag. (**who**)
The ....

BOÎTE À OUTILS : LES PRONOMS RELATIFS

• "You pay with your personal data, **which** these services use to target ads."
Which *est ici un pronom relatif objet qui désigne une chose (*data*).*

• "The second is young users **who** [...] want to profit from it as well."
Who *est ici un pronom relatif sujet qui désigne des personnes (*young users*).*

• "The biggest issue I could see for the Internet is our data and **what** happens to our data."
On utilise* what *quand on veut dire ce qui, ce que.
Ex.: **What** I want now is a glass of water.

• "We have an Internet ecosystem **where** all of our data is incredibly valuable."
Where *signifie où.*

• Pour savoir quel pronom relatif utiliser il faut déterminer si l'information de la proposition relative est indispensable à la phrase ou non. Quand l'information n'est pas indispensable, les relatives sont séparées du reste de la phrase par une ou deux virgules.
Ex.: Have you read all the books **that** Jane Austen wrote?
Ici, l'information soulignée est indispensable : il s'agit donc d'une proposition déterminative.
Ex.: Jane, **who** lives in England, phoned me yesterday.
Ici, l'information soulignée n'est pas indispensable : il s'agit donc d'une proposition non déterminative.

		non détermina-tives	déterminatives
Pronom sujet	personnes	who	that ou who
	choses	which	that ou which
Pronom objet	personnes	whom	Ø
	choses	which	Ø

• On utilise* whose *quand on veut dire dont, de qui, duquel... ; c'est la forme possessive du pronom relatif.
Ex.: The woman **whose** wallet had been stolen went to the police station.

• On utilise* whom *après une préposition.
Ex.: No one knows **by whom** the victim was shot.

• Dans une proposition déterminative, le pronom objet peut être omis.
Ex.: The book **that** I'm reading at the moment is great! = The book I'm reading at the moment is great!

Sujet inédit, séries technologiques, LV1

EXPRESSION ÉCRITE : A parents' association writes an article about the dangers of computer games and offers advice.

Analyse du sujet

Il s'agit de rédiger un article sur les dangers des jeux vidéo, du point de vue de parents s'adressant à d'autres parents. Respectez bien la consigne : on vous demande de rédiger votre texte en adoptant le point de vue de parents hostiles aux jeux vidéo. Il s'agit donc de présenter les dangers (réels ou supposés) de ces jeux – ne vous lancez pas dans un argumentaire en leur faveur, même si vous estimez personnellement que les jeux vidéo ne représentent aucun danger !

Repères essentiels

1. Commencez par noter vos idées au brouillon en établissant la liste de tous les dangers potentiels liés à la pratique des jeux vidéo.
2. Réfléchissez au type de texte à produire et à ses principales caractéristiques.

Un article peut viser à :
- informer, expliquer, décrire ;
- alerter ou sensibiliser l'opinion publique à propos de tel ou tel sujet jugé préoccupant ;
- exprimer son propre point de vue sur un sujet qui fait débat, prendre position dans le cadre d'une controverse ou d'une polémique.

Dans l'article que vous devez rédiger, il s'agira principalement d'argumenter et de justifier votre point de vue (celui d'un parent hostile aux jeux vidéo en l'occurrence) de façon à convaincre d'autres parents et à les rallier à votre cause.

En règle générale, un article possède un titre : donnez donc un titre à votre production, en choisissant de préférence une formule simple et percutante.

3. Organisez vos idées en élaborant un plan structuré et cohérent.

Par exemple :

I. Les principaux risques liés à la pratique excessive des jeux vidéo
II. Les symptômes à surveiller chez l'enfant
III. Des conseils pratiques pour les parents

4. Rédigez l'article au brouillon.
5. Contrôlez sa précision linguistique.

Proposition de corrigé

Computer games are dangerous for your children

Many teenagers play video games, an activity that can be very dangerous for them. As parents, we have to be cautious and must keep an eye on the behaviour and reactions of our children. Quite often, playing video games becomes a major issue for teenagers and their family, as it may lead to a real addiction which can be compared to drug addiction. Furthermore, spending too much time on video games can lead to several problems including isolation, difficulties to concentrate, lack of sleep and appetite, irritability or even sudden outbursts of violence. These problems can severely affect the social life of our children, as well as their school results.

All families should be aware of these dangers, and there are some signs that parents must take into account in order to react as quickly as possible. If you notice the following signs in a teenager's behaviour, he is likely to become addicted. He stays in his room and plays video games hours on end. He loses his friends and doesn't speak a lot with his family, or even doesn't communicate with them any longer. He eats junk food so as to save time for his favourite activity. At school he gets lower grades than he used to, he misses some classes or even ends up dropping out of school.

Not only do many teenagers suffer from this kind of addiction, but young children may also become addicted. Eventually, they may even stop maturing. To avoid such a problem, the first thing to do is to put the computer in a common room, and not in the child's or teenager's room. This will allow parents to keep an eye on the time spent playing video games. Parents must insist on their children having meals with them, and grasp that opportunity to communicate as much as possible with their children. They must also talk with them about video games and warn them not to spend too much time playing those games. Ultimately, if the situation doesn't improve, parents may also seek advice from a psychiatrist specialized in the treatment of addiction related problems.

NOTIONS CLÉS

Pour un sujet de ce type, il vous faut mobiliser :

L'EXPRESSION DE LA CAUSE ET DE LA CONSÉQUENCE

- as/ since: *comme, puisque*

Ex.: As/ Since he was rather late, he decided to take a taxi. (*Comme il était assez en retard, il décida de prendre un taxi.*)

- because of: *à cause de*
- owing to/ on account of: *à cause de, en raison de*

Ex.: He was not allowed to enter the pub owing to his age. (*Il n'a pas été autorisé à entrer dans le pub en raison de son âge.*)

- out of: *par*

Ex.: He ruined all her plans out of sheer malice. (*Il a ruiné tous ses projets par pure malveillance.*)

- that's why/ that's the reason why: *c'est pourquoi, c'est la raison pour laquelle*
- for + V-ing: *pour + infinitif passé*

Ex.: He will be punished for telling lies. (*Il sera puni pour avoir raconté des mensonges.*)

- as a result/ as a consequence/ consequently: *en conséquence*
- if… then: *si… alors*

Ex.: If you have the required experience, then you might be given the job. (*Si vous avez l'expérience requise, alors il est possible que l'on vous confie le poste.*)

- therefore/ thus: *donc, ainsi*
- to/ in order to/ so as to: *pour, dans le but de*
- so that: *pour que, afin que*
- to lead to/ to result in: *conduire à, en résulter*

L'EXPRESSION DE LA PROBABILITÉ

- may/ might/ could + Verb
- be likely to/ will probably + Verb

L'EXPRESSION DE L'OBLIGATION

- have to + Verb
- must + Verb

LE LEXIQUE DE LA SURVEILLANCE

- to watch/ to keep an eye on: *surveiller*
- to warn: *prévenir, avertir*
- to inform: *informer*

Data Mining Reveals How Conspiracy Theories Emerge on Facebook

During the Italian elections last year, a post appeared on Facebook that rapidly became viral. The post's title was this: "Italian Senate voted and accepted (257 in favor and 165 abstentions) a law proposed by Senator Cirenga to provide policy makers with 134 billion euros to find jobs in the event of electoral defeat."

The post was created on Facebook page known for its satirical content and designed to parody Italian politics. It contains at least four false statements: the senator involved is fictitious, the total number of votes is higher than is possible in Italian politics, the amount of money involved is more than 10% of Italian GDP and the law itself is an invention. The parody struck a chord with disenchanted voters who shared it some 35,000 times in less than a month. Then things quickly became strange. The meme was re-posted with additional commentary on a Facebook page devoted to political commentary. The meme then spread all over again but this time with a new veneer of respectability. Today, this "law" is commonly cited as evidence of corruption in Italian politics by protesters in cities all over Italy.

Welcome to the murky world of conspiracy theories. The spread of misinformation over the Internet is a celebrated phenomenon. If you believe, for example, that the AIDS virus was created by the US government to control the African American population, then you're a victim. Episodes like this raise important questions about how people are exposed to false ideas and how they come to believe them. Today we get an important insight into this question thanks to the work of Walter Quattrociocchi at Northeastern University in Boston and a few pals who have studied the way that ordinary people interact with posts on Facebook that are known to be true or false.

These guys studied how over 1 million people treated political information posted on Facebook during the Italian elections in 2013. In particular, they looked at how these people 'liked' posts and commented on them from mainstream news organisations, from alternative news organisations and from pages devoted political commentary. They then studied how the same people reacted to false news injected into common circulation by "trolls" on pages known to produce satirical news content or otherwise false statements.

The results make for interesting reading. Quattrociocchi and co analysed how the long the debate about a post continued by measuring the date between the first and last comments about it. They say the length of debate is the same regardless of the type of content. In other words, people tend to discuss ideas on mainstream news pages, on alternative news pages and on political commentary pages for exactly the same length of time. That suggests the same kind of engagement, regardless of the type of content.

Quattrociocchi and co then found out that people who engage with debates on alternative news posts are much more likely to engage in the debate about false news posted by trolls. "We find that a dominant fraction of the users interacting with the troll memes is the one composed of users preeminently interacting with alternative information sources – and thus more exposed to unsubstantiated claims," they say. That's an interesting result. Quattrociocchi and co point out that many people are attracted to alternative news media because of a distrust of conventional news sources, which, in Italy, are strongly influenced by politicians of one persuasion or another.

But this search for other sources of news seems to be fraught with danger. "Surprisingly, consumers of alternative news, which are the users trying to avoid the mainstream media 'mass-manipulation', are the most responsive to the injection of false claims," they conclude.

This suggests an interesting mechanism for the emergence of conspiracy theories. Conspiracy theories seem to come about by a process in which ordinary satirical commentary or obviously false content somehow jumps the credulity barrier. And that seems to happen through groups of people who deliberately expose themselves to alternative sources of news.

Of course, there may be other ways that conspiracy theories emerge. Some theories may well be truths that have been deliberately suppressed by higher powers such as governments corporations and so on. But this work reveals that there is also a plausible mechanism through which false stories become thought of as true. The question now is how to exploit this new understanding to improve the flow and labeling of information, whatever its source.

Published on March 18th, 2014 in *Technology Review*,
Cambridge (Massachusetts)

KEY POINT

Information reliability on the Web

The Internet is generally assumed to be the main driving force behind the growth in conspiracy theories even though conspiracy theories have always followed in the shadows of major tragedies. For example, after Malaysia Airlines flight 370 vanished, theories of the plane's fate spread across websites and social media, ranging from the plausible to the absurd.

Conducting research on the Internet is convenient, but it can also be tricky. There are many thousands of Web pages that have little actual content and are mainly links to other pages. You can find distorted information on Web pages as many people get their information from other people's Web pages. The first person who posts information may make a few errors, the second repeats them and makes one or two more. In the end, it makes a difference in the information's reliability. Judging the reliability of sources found on the Internet is therefore crucial because there is no regulating body that monitors the reliability of what is on the Internet.

To make sure you have found a reliable source of information, you have to find out who is responsible for the website, who wrote the information, when the information was written and if sources are cited.

Elle court, elle court, la rumeur…

Dans le cadre des élections générales organisées en Italie l'an dernier, un message publié sur Facebook s'est propagé comme une traînée de poudre : « Le Sénat italien a adopté (à 257 voix pour et 165 abstentions) une loi proposée par le sénateur Cirenga, qui allouera 134 milliards d'euros à la recherche d'emploi des parlementaires s'ils perdent les élections. »
Ce titre est paru sur une page Facebook réputée pour son contenu satirique et conçue pour parodier la vie politique italienne. La phrase en question contient au moins quatre mensonges : le sénateur Cirenga n'existe pas, le nombre total de sénateurs est supérieur à la réalité, le montant représente plus de 10 % du PIB italien et la loi elle-même est une invention.
Cette parodie a trouvé un écho auprès des électeurs désenchantés, qui l'ont relayée 35 000 fois en moins d'un mois. La situation a toutefois pris un tour étrange par la suite. La fameuse phrase a été republiée sur une autre page Facebook consacrée à l'analyse politique, accompagnée d'un commentaire supplémentaire. Cette nouvelle version a été rediffusée partout mais, cette fois-ci, avec un semblant de respectabilité. Et désormais, dans toute l'Italie, des manifestants se servent de cette prétendue loi pour prouver que le monde politique est corrompu.
Bienvenue dans le monde obscur des théories du complot. La diffusion de fausses informations sur Internet est un phénomène bien connu. Si, par exemple, vous pensez que le virus du sida a été créé par le gouvernement américain pour maîtriser la population afro-américaine, alors vous êtes victime de l'une d'entre elles.
Les épisodes de ce type soulèvent de grandes questions : comment les personnes sont-elles exposées à de fausses idées et comment en viennent-elles à s'en persuader ? Nous pouvons en apprendre beaucoup sur le sujet grâce au travail de Walter Quattrociocchi, de la Northeastern University à Boston, qui a étudié avec quelques collègues la façon dont les gens ordinaires réagissent à des publications sur Facebook dont la véracité ou l'inexactitude sont attestées.
Ces chercheurs ont étudié comment plus de un million de personnes avaient interprété les informations politiques publiées sur Facebook au cours des élections italiennes de 2013. Ils ont notamment observé quels messages les internautes « aimaient » et commentaient selon leur source : de grands organes de presse, des médias non traditionnels ou des pages consacrées à l'analyse politique. Ensuite, ils ont étudié comment ces mêmes personnes réagissaient à de fausses actualités publiées par des « trolls », ou provocateurs, sur des pages réputées pour leur contenu satirique ou mensonger.
Les résultats sont fascinants. Walter Quattrociocchi et ses collègues ont analysé la durée des débats en comptant le temps passé entre le premier et le dernier commentaire. Cette durée est identique, quel que soit le type de contenu. En d'autres termes, les gens ont tendance à débattre sur les pages traditionnelles, non traditionnelles et satiriques pendant le même laps de temps : leur degré d'implication est le même quelle que soit la nature de l'information.
Les chercheurs ont ensuite remarqué que ceux qui s'expriment sur des pages n'appartenant pas à la presse traditionnelle étaient largement plus susceptibles de participer à un débat lancé par des agitateurs à partir de fausses informations. « Nous avons noté que la majorité des internautes qui interagissent à la provocation tirent essentiellement leurs informations de sources non traditionnelles, c'est pourquoi ils sont plus souvent exposés à des données sans fondement. »
C'est un résultat intéressant. M. Quattrociocchi et son équipe soulignent le fait que de nombreuses personnes sont attirées par les médias alternatifs, car les sources traditionnelles provoquent la méfiance – notamment en Italie, où les médias sont fortement influencés par tel ou tel camp politique.
Cette quête de sources indépendantes semble toutefois dangereuse. « Étonnamment, les consommateurs d'actualités qui sortent des sentiers battus, ceux qui veulent précisément éviter la manipulation de masse des médias traditionnels sont aussi ceux qui réagissent le plus aux fausses déclarations », précisent les chercheurs.
Cette conclusion suggère un mécanisme intéressant quant à l'émergence des théories du complot. Elles semblent naître d'un processus au cours duquel une analyse satirique ordinaire ou un contenu manifestement factice finissent par être jugés crédibles. Et ce processus semble issu de groupes qui s'exposent délibérément à des sources d'actualités alternatives au courant dominant.
Bien sûr, ce n'est pas nécessairement de cette seule façon que naissent les théories du complot. Certaines sont peut-être des vérités qui ont été étouffées délibérément par de grandes puissances, comme les gouvernements, les entreprises, etc. Toutefois, ces recherches révèlent qu'il existe un mécanisme plausible permettant d'expliquer comment de fausses théories finissent par être prises au sérieux. La question est maintenant de savoir comment exploiter ce résultat pour améliorer la diffusion et la classification des informations, quelles que soient leurs sources.

Publié le 18 mars 2014 dans *Technology Review*, Cambridge (Massachusetts). Extrait de *Courrier International*

VOCABULARY TO REMEMBER!

- **a law:** *une loi*
- **to provide somebody with something:** *allouer quelque chose à quelqu'un*
- **at least:** *au moins*
- **the amount of money:** *le montant, la somme d'argent*
- **GDP** *(Gross Domestic Product):* *le PIB (Produit intérieur brut)*
- **to strike (struck/ struck) a chord:** *trouver un écho*
- **devoted to:** *consacré à*
- **to spread (spread/ spread):** *se répandre, diffuser*
- **the spread of misinformation over the Internet:** *la diffusion de fausses informations sur Internet*
- **AIDS:** *le sida*
- **it raises important questions about…:** *cela soulève des questions importantes sur…*
- **thanks to:** *grâce à*
- **regardless of:** *quel que soit*
- **to tend to:** *avoir tendance à*
- **to be more likely to:** *être plus susceptible de*
- **thus:** *donc, c'est pourquoi*
- **to point out:** *souligner*
- **to be attracted to:** *être attiré par*
- **distrust:** *la méfiance*
- **to avoid:** *éviter*
- **to seem:** *sembler*
- **such as:** *tel que*
- **and so on:** *etc.*
- **to improve:** *améliorer*
- **whatever:** *quel que soit*

We can send humans back to space... if we fund Elon Musk instead of Nasa

"Elon Musk," the satellite industry insider told me over a beer, "has got to be the luckiest son of a bitch alive." Musk – the insanely dedicated, wealthy and polarizing founder of PayPal, Tesla and Space Exploration Technologies (SpaceX) – is on a hot streak when it comes to spaceflight. He's raiding revenue streams from Nasa and the US military to fund a private manned space program. His main weapon: low prices, with SpaceX offering satellite launches at about one-fifth the price of competitors at just over $60m a pop.

Sooner or later, the haters say, Musk's streak will end in a fiery accident. That kind of disaster, naturally, would undercut the current soaring confidence in SpaceX, from investors, private-space believers and even taxpayers.

Another group of doubters on Capitol Hill say the industries needed to keep private space exploration viable simply don't exist, necessitating a mini-Apollo push from Nasa, despite soaring progress from the Elon Musks of the world and soaring prices for government programs.

"There's a sense that America is falling behind," lamented Rep Lamar Smith of Texas on Wednesday, at yet another painful hearing of the House Committee on Science and Technology. "Today, America's finest spaceships and largest rockets are found in museums rather than on launch pads."

He's wrong: right now there are more space spacecraft and launch systems being designed and tested than any other moment in human history – but Washington doesn't know how to build a space program. Inconsistent planning and politics have so stultified Nasa, after all, that America today has no way to launch people into space.

Three years ago, Congress mandated $10bn in federal spending to develop a capsule-carry rocket, reversing President Obama's own reversal away from George W Bush's manned spaceflight program. Now the administration underfunds the effort, wasting billions with nothing to show for it.

Startups like SpaceX have already started launching private satellites to wean themselves off the government money that helped them get started. But the private-space industry will need customers, and that's where Congress could actually help. Politicians seem dead-set on handing out money – aerospace firm contracts, government programs, whatever creates jobs in Florida, Alabama or Texas – so why not help seed the space industries that will use startup-company rockets?

After all, it's more than thrill rides to the edge of the atmosphere. Asteroid mining operations, space-based power stations, orbital manufacturing centers and zero-G research labs are some fertile areas for private investment that could spur manned space travel. Government funding – even small demonstration programs of $25 to $50m – could absorb some risk and demonstrate new technologies.

Musk's satellite-launching business funds his effort to fly people to space, and not just for a few minutes like Richard Branson's Virgin Galactic. Musk wants to go farther – to Mars, and by 2026, a decade before Nasa's most optimistic plan.

He will use Nasa money to help develop the hardware to get there. SpaceX is one of three companies hired to fly cargo to the ISS, and now the company is one of three trying to compete to deliver astronauts to the station. That manned development program costs Uncle Sam $800m for three private development programs. That's a relatively cheap government investment for some private-sector ingenuity.

When space explorers can fund themselves, the ever-present "taxpayer money could be better spent" argument is irrelevant. Shareholders can defend themselves against idiotic waste better than taxpayers can.

I used to agree that Elon Musk was a lucky SOB. Then, year after year, his launch successes started adding up and his prices remained a bargain. I visited the SpaceX launch pad in Florida, the company headquarters in California, interviewed him one-on-one. Launching rockets is not a job for the lucky.

Musk may just be one of those industrial titans who come along in history to smash barriers. And the one he's busting really matters: cheap rockets are the key to opening up space, because that first step off the planet is the hardest. Once comfortable in our solar system, human beings can push even farther. Along the way, some people will make a buck. But at the end, even more people will get to go to space.

Adapted from Joe Pappalardo – *The Guardian*, June 26th, 2014

KEY POINT

The dawn of a new Space Age?

In 2017, NASA plans to test its Space Launch System, a rocket system designed for launches into deep space. More powerful than the Saturn V, which carried astronauts to the moon, the SLS would be larger than any other launch vehicles ever built. If on schedule, development to achieve this initial launch is estimated to cost $12 billion but NASA may be $ 400 million short to complete the project. A manned mission to Mars is the ultimate goal, but the SLS could open other doors for American space exploration. Currently, the only way for astronauts to reach even the International Space Station is through Russia; Americans have reportedly been paying Russia $70 million a seat to send astronauts to the ISS.

The private sector may hold solutions and private companies such as SpaceX and Orbital Sciences Corporation are beginning to gain momentum. Orbital and SpaceX already have billion-dollar contracts with NASA to transport cargo to the ISS. To help accomplish this, SpaceX began leasing a launch site from NASA in 2014. SpaceX ultimately aims to help people live on other planets.

Elon Musk, roi de l'espace

« Elon Musk est sûrement le salaud le plus chanceux du monde », m'avoue un spécialiste des satellites devant une bière. Elon Musk, le riche fondateur extrêmement zélé et charismatique du système de paiement PayPal, du constructeur d'automobiles électriques Tesla et de Space Exploration Technologies (SpaceX) est en passe de devenir le roi de l'espace. Il rafle les bénéfices obtenus grâce à ses contrats avec la Nasa et l'armée américaine pour financer un programme spatial privé et habité. Son arme principale ? Des coûts réduits qui permettent à SpaceX d'envoyer des satellites au cinquième du prix proposé par ses concurrents, soit environ 60 millions de dollars par lancement [45 millions d'euros].

Mais tôt ou tard, affirment ses détracteurs, Elon Musk ne sera plus en veine : il sera confronté à un accident explosif. Ce genre de catastrophe entamerait bien évidemment le crédit dont SpaceX jouit auprès des investisseurs, des partisans de la conquête spatiale privée et même des contribuables.

Selon un autre groupe de sceptiques au sein du Congrès américain, l'exploration spatiale privée – faute de s'être constitué en véritable secteur industriel autonome – ne pourrait pas se passer du soutien de la Nasa et de ses programmes. Et pourtant, malgré ces assertions, les progrès d'Elon Musk et de ses homologues sont aussi vertigineux que les coûts des programmes publics.

« Nous avons le sentiment que les États-Unis prennent du retard », se lamentait le 25 juin un représentant texan au Congrès, Lamar Smith, lors d'une pénible séance du Comité parlementaire des sciences et technologies. « Actuellement, les meilleurs vaisseaux et les plus grandes fusées des États-Unis sont dans les musées et non sur les pas de tir. »

Ce n'est pas vrai : il y a aujourd'hui plus de lanceurs en cours de conception et d'expérimentation qu'à n'importe quelle époque de l'Histoire. Ce qui est vrai, en revanche, c'est que Washington est incapable de mettre en œuvre un programme spatial. Les tergiversations politiques et les incohérences en termes de planification ont miné la Nasa au point qu'aujourd'hui les États-Unis n'ont plus aucun moyen d'envoyer des humains dans l'espace.

Il y a trois ans, le Congrès a alloué une enveloppe de 10 milliards de dollars au développement d'un lanceur permettant de réaliser des vols habités – une volte-face par rapport au choix initial de Barack Obama, qui avait lui-même pris ses distances vis-à-vis du programme spatial habité de George W. Bush. Actuellement, le gouvernement finance l'initiative, mais de façon insuffisante : des milliards de dollars sont ainsi gaspillés sans aboutir au moindre résultat.

Les start-up comme SpaceX ont déjà commencé à lancer des satellites privés pour se sevrer des fonds publics qui les ont aidés à prendre leur envol. Mais l'aérospatiale privée aura toujours besoin de clients et c'est dans ce domaine que le Congrès pourrait réellement être utile. La sphère politique semble déterminée à distribuer de l'argent – pour des contrats avec des sociétés aérospatiales, des programmes publics, tout ce qui peut créer des emplois en Floride, dans l'Alabama ou au Texas –, alors pourquoi ne pas contribuer au développement d'industries spatiales qui utiliseront les fusées conçues par des start-up ?

Après tout, il n'est pas seulement question de périples à sensations fortes. L'exploitation minière d'astéroïdes, les centrales installées dans l'espace ou les laboratoires de recherche en apesanteur sont des terrains fertiles pour les investissements privés. Ils pourraient être les fers de lance des vols spatiaux habités. Les financements publics – y compris pour de modestes programmes-pilotes à hauteur de 25 à 50 millions de dollars – pourraient absorber une partie des risques et mettre à l'épreuve de nouvelles technologies.

La mise en orbite de satellites permet à Elon Musk de financer son projet visant à envoyer des humains dans l'espace, et pas seulement pour quelques minutes, comme le propose Richard Branson avec Virgin Galactic. Elon Musk veut aller plus loin, en l'occurrence sur Mars, et avant 2026 – soit dix ans plus tôt que les projets les plus optimistes de la Nasa. Et, pour concevoir le matériel nécessaire, il prévoit d'utiliser l'argent de la Nasa. Car SpaceX est l'une des trois entreprises choisies pour envoyer des cargaisons vers la Station spatiale internationale (ISS). Et désormais, c'est aussi l'une des trois sociétés en compétition pour y envoyer des astronautes. Ce programme de développement de vols habités a coûté 800 millions de dollars aux États-Unis, répartis entre trois initiatives privées. C'est un investissement public relativement bon marché en échange de l'ingéniosité du secteur privé.

Lorsque les explorateurs de l'espace peuvent trouver leurs propres financements, l'argument récurrent selon lequel « l'argent des contribuables pourrait être mieux géré » devient hors de propos. Les actionnaires peuvent, mieux que les contribuables, se défendre contre un gaspillage inepte.

Avant, je pensais moi aussi qu'Elon Musk était un sacré veinard. Puis, année après année, les lancements réussis se sont accumulés et les prix sont restés bon marché. J'ai visité le pas de tir de SpaceX en Floride, le siège de l'entreprise en Californie et j'ai interviewé Elon Musk en tête-à-tête. Lancer des fusées n'est pas une question de chance.

Elon Musk pourrait bien être l'un de ces titans industriels qui marquent l'Histoire parce qu'ils ont fait tomber des obstacles. Et l'obstacle auquel il s'attaque est crucial : les fusées bon marché sont la clé de la conquête spatiale, car c'est le premier pas hors de notre planète qui est le plus difficile. Quand nous serons à l'aise dans notre système solaire, nous pourrons continuer de repousser les limites. Chemin faisant, quelques individus s'enrichiront. Mais au bout du compte, bien plus de personnes pourront aller dans l'espace.

D'après Joe Pappalardo – *The Guardian*, 26 juin 2014
Extrait de *Courrier International*

VOCABULARY TO REMEMBER!

- **wealthy**: *riche*
- **to fund**: *financer*
- **a weapon**: *une arme*
- **low prices**: *des coûts réduits, des prix bas*
- **sooner or later**: *tôt ou tard*
- **taxpayers**: *les contribuables*
- **to fall (fell/ fallen) behind**: *prendre du retard*
- **rather than**: *et non pas, plutôt que*
- **to waste billions on...**: *gaspiller des milliards sur...*
- **customers**: *des clients*
- **to be dead-set on**: *être déterminé à*
- **a rocket**: *une fusée*
- **to compete**: *être en compétition*
- **the argument is irrelevant**: *l'argument est hors de propos*
- **shareholders**: *les actionnaires*
- **a bargain**: *bon marché, une bonne affaire*

Jane Austen's *Pride and Prejudice* (1813)

Jane Austen

It is a truth universally acknowledged, that a single man in possession of a good fortune must be in want of a wife.
However little known the feelings or views of such a man may be on his first entering a neighbourhood, this truth is so well fixed in the winds of the surrounding families, that he is considered as the rightful property of some one or other of their daughters.
'My dear Mr. Bennet,' said his lady to him one day, 'have you heard that Netherfield Park is let at last?'
Mr. Bennet replied that he had not.
'But it is,' returned she; 'for Mrs Long has just been here, and she told me all about it.'
Mr. Bennet made no answer.
'Do not you want to know who has taken it?' cried his wife impatiently.
'*You* want to tell me, and I have no objection to hearing it.'
This was invitation enough.
'Why, my dear, you must know, Mrs Long says that Netherfield is taken by a young man of large fortune from the north of England; that he came down on Monday in a chaise and four to see the place, and was so much delighted with it that he agreed with Mr. Morris immediately; that he is to take possession before Michaelmas, and some of his servants are to be in the house by the end of next week.'
'What is his name?'
'Bingley.'
'Is he married or single?'
'Oh! Single, my dear, to be sure! A single man of large fortune; four or five thousand a year. What a fine thing for our girls!'
'How so? How can it affect them?'
'My dear Mr. Bennet,' replied his wife, 'how can you be so tiresome! You must know that I am thinking of his marrying one of them.'
'Is that his design in settling here?'
'Design! Nonsense, how can you talk so! But it is very likely that he *may* fall in love with one of them, and therefore you must visit him as soon as he comes.'

'Oh! Single, my dear, to be sure! A single man of large fortune; four or five thousand a year. What a fine thing for our girls!'

DICTIONARY

- **to acknowledge**: to recognize
- **to be in want of**: in need of
- **a neighbourhood**: district, region
- **surrounding**: neighboring
- **to let**: to rent
- **to reply**: to answer
- **a chaise and four**: a carriage pulled by four horses
- **to be delighted with**: to be very pleased with
- **Michaelmas**: a Christian holy day (Sept. 29th) in honour of Saint Michael
- **tiresome**: annoying
- **to settle**: to start to live in a place
- **it is very likely**: it is very probable
- **handsome**: beautiful
- **grown up**: adult
- **glad**: happy
- **hearty**: sincere
- **to get over something**: to find a way to deal with something
- **odd**: unusual
- **to fancy**: to imagine
- **solace**: comfort

MOTS CLÉS en lien avec la thématique

NOUNS

- right to vote: *le droit de vote*
- gender gap: *l'écart entre les sexes*

Ex.: **The gender gap is diminishing** in many developed countries.
- gender discrimination: *la discrimination fondée sur le genre*

Ex.: **Gender discrimination** affects girls and women throughout their lifetime.
- equal opportunities: *l'égalité des chances*
- glass ceiling: *le « plafond de verre »*

Ex.: Some women have managed **to break the glass ceiling**.
- earnings: *les revenus*

Ex.: Women's **earnings** are still lower than their male counterparts.
- wage discrimination: *la discrimination salariale*
- harassment: *le harcèlement*

Ex.: Many women have experienced **sexual harassment** at their workplace.
- second-class citizens: *les citoyens de seconde zone*

Ex.: In some parts of the world women are considered as **second-class citizens**.
- a milestone: *un événement marquant*

Ex.: Women gaining the **right to vote** was **a historical milestone**.
- motherhood: *la maternité*
- household tasks/ chores: *les tâches ménagères*

VERBS

- to progress / to go forward: *progresser, aller de l'avant*

Ex.: The condition of women **has progressed** over the last century.
- to be entitled to: *avoir le droit de*

Ex.: Many women in the world **are not entitled to** own property.
- to deny: *nier*

Ex.: Some women **are denied the right to** health and education.
- to achieve: *réussir*

Ex.: Women still have a long way to go **to achieve equality** in the workplace.
- to improve: *améliorer*

Ex.: Women have struggled **to improve** their condition.
- to make great strides: *faire de grands progrès*

'I see no occasion for that. You and the girls may go, or you may send them by themselves, which perhaps will be still better; for, as you are as handsome as any of them, Mr. Bingley might like you the best of the party.'
'My dear, you flatter me. I certainly *have* had my share of beauty, but I do not pretend to be any thing extraordinary now. When a woman has five grown up daughters, she ought to give over thinking of her own beauty.'
'In such cases, a woman has not often much beauty to think of.'
'But, my dear, you must indeed go and see Mr. Bingley when he comes into the neighbourhood.'
'It is more than I engage for, I assure you.'
'But consider your daughters. Only think what an establishment it would be for one of them. Sir William and Lady Lucas are determined to go, merely on that account, for in general you know they visit no new comers. Indeed you must go, for it will be impossible for *us* to visit him, if you do not.'
'You are over-scrupulous, surely. I dare say Mr. Bingley will be very glad to see you; and I will send a few lines by you to assure him of my hearty consent to his marrying whichever he chooses of the girls; though I must throw in a good word for my little Lizzy.'
'I desire you will do no such thing. Lizzy is not a bit better than the others; and I am sure she is not half so handsome as Jane, nor half so good-humoured as Lydia. But you are always giving *her* the preference.'
'They have none of them much to recommend them,' replied he; 'they are all silly and ignorant like other girls; but Lizzy has something more of quickness than her sisters.'
'Mr. Bennet, how can you abuse your own children in such a way? You take delight in vexing me. You have no compassion on my poor nerves.'
'You mistake me, my dear. I have a high respect for your nerves. They are my old friends. I have heard you mention them with consideration these twenty years at last.'
'Ah, you do not know what I suffer.'
'But I hope you will get over it, and live to see many young men of four thousand a year come into the neighbourhood.'
'It will be no use to us if twenty such should come, since you will not visit them.'
'Depend upon it, my dear, that when there are twenty I will visit them all.'
Mr. Bennet was so odd a mixture of quick parts, sarcastic humour, reserve, and caprice, that the experience of three-and-twenty years had been insufficient to make his wife understand his character. *Her* mind was less difficult to develope. She was a woman of mean understanding, little information, and uncertain temper. When she was discontented, she fancied herself nervous. The business of her life was to get her daughters married; its solace was visiting and news.

Pride and Prejudice, Jane Austen (1813)

UN ARTICLE DU *MONDE* À CONSULTER :

- **Aux Etats-Unis, les juges disent oui au mariage gay** p. 42
(Corine Lesnes, *Le Monde* daté du 29.06.2015)

FOCUS ON...

Jane Austen (1775-1817) is an English writer whose novels portray the lives of the gentry and clergy of rural England. The romantic world Jane Austen created offers insights into the lives of women at the turn of the 19th century in English Georgian society.
The female protagonists and the family's concern with marriage in all of Austen's novels mirror the condition of economic dependence suffered by women in those days. However, socio-economic changes brought about by the industrial revolution led to changes in the condition of women and in the traditional views of gender roles. Women began to gain equity in legal, educational, professional and personal aspects of their lives. In *Pride and Prejudice* some characters (such as Mr and Mrs Bennet) followed the traditional gender roles whereas others (Elisabeth, specifically) symbolized the changes in the role of women.

Jane Austen's house in Chawton, England.

S'EXPRIMER

GIVING REASONS: USING "FOR"

- "[...] or you may send them by themselves, which perhaps will be still better, **for**, as you are as handsome as any of them [...]"
"[...] **for** in general you know they visit no new comers."
"Indeed you must go, **for** it will be impossible for us to visit him."
In formal or literary written English, we can introduce reasons with "**for**". "**For**" is a formal alternative to "**because**".
Ex. He couldn't sleep **for** the pain in his leg (for = because of).

GIVING REASONS: USING "SINCE"

- "It will be no use to us if twenty such should come, **since** you will not visit them."
"**Since**" here means "**because**". When it means "because", "since" is rather formal. It is uncommon in conversation but frequently used in academic writing.
Ex.: **Since** the train was delayed more than an hour, passengers were given a full refund.

OTHER WAYS OF GIVING REASONS

- We can also begin a clause with "**as**", "**because**", "**seeing that**" and "**seeing as**" to give a reason for a particular situation.
Ex.: **Because** my mother has arrived, I won't be able to see you.
Ex.: **As** I had eaten five ice-creams, I didn't feel very well.
Ex.: **Seeing that** it's your birthday, I'll buy you lunch.
- "**Because of**", "**due to**" and "**owing to**" can also be used before a noun to give a reason for something.
Ex.: We were delayed **because of** an accident.
Ex.: I was unable to run **due to** a leg injury.
Ex.: Our company has less money to spend **owing to** budget cuts.

Questions de compréhension

A. **Choose the correct answer.**

1. Netherfield Park is ...... **a.** a garden/ **b.** an estate.

2. Netherfield Park has just been ...... **a.** sold/ **b.** rented.

3. a. Mr Morris/ **b.** Mr Bingley ...... will live in Netherfield Park.

4. Mrs Bennet is interested in Mr Bingley because he is ...... **a.** wealthy/ **b.** handsome.

5. Mrs Bennet ...... **a.** wants to visit Mr Bingley herself/ **b.** wants her husband to visit Mr Bingley.

6. Mrs Bennet has ...... **a.** three unmarried daughters and two married daughters/ **b.** five unmarried daughters.

7. According to Mrs Bennet ...... **a.** Lizzy/ **b.** Lydia ...... is her husband's favourite daughter.

8. Mr and Mrs Bennet have been married for .... **a.** 20 years/ **b.** 23 years.

9. Mr Bennett is ...... **a.** sarcastic/ **b.** pessimistic.

B. **Answer the questions using your own words.**

1. "Indeed you must go, for it will be impossible for us to visit him, if you do not." Explain in your own words what Mrs Bennet means.

2. How is Mr Bennet with his wife?

3. How is Mrs Bennet portrayed in this text?

Exercices de grammaire

A. **Employez les mots entre parenthèses pour exprimer une comparaison d'égalité et une comparaison d'égalité négative.**

1. She's friendly (**her sister**).

....

2. Your solution is good (**Sam's**).

....

3. The station is far (**the airport**).

....

4. The table is heavy (**the sofa**).

....

5. Her ring is expensive (**my car**).

....

B. **As** or **like?**

1. They closed the firm, ... it was no longer profitable.

2. I'd love to live in a house .... yours.

3. She was recruited .... a manager.

4. Our company is .... one big happy family!

5. Can I give you some advice .... a friend?

6. I, ... you, think that it's time to change.

BOÎTE À OUTILS : LES DIFFÉRENTS SENS DE "AS"

• "[...] as you are **as** handsome **as** any of them."

"She is not half **so** handsome **as** Jane, nor half **so** good-humoured **as** Lydia."

As est utilisé ici pour faire des comparaisons d'égalité.

***La comparaison d'égalité* s'exprime en effet ainsi : as... + as... (aussi... que...).**

Ex.: I came **as** quickly **as** I could.

• ***La comparaison d'égalité négative* s'exprime en utilisant not as... + as... ou en utilisant not so... + as... (pas aussi... que...).**

Ex.: This place is not **as** quiet **as** it used to be.

Ex.: This place is not **so** quiet **as** it used to be.

• "[...] **as** you are as handsome as any of them."

As signifie ici because.

Ex.: **As** I felt tired, I stayed at home and had a rest.

• "He is considered **as** the rightful property of some one or other of their daughters."

As est utilisé comme préposition après certains verbes comme consider as, describe as, regard as.

• **As s'utilise avec such pour introduire des *exemples*.**

Ex.: She has read a few English novels, **such as Emma** and **Sense and Sensibility**.

• **As s'utilise avec same.**

Ex. He works exactly the **same** hours **as** me.

• **Différences entre as et like:**

Like compare 2 personnes ou 2 choses tandis que as renvoie à l'identité ou à la qualité de la personne ou de la chose.

Ex.: She was **like** a daughter to him.

Ex.: He talks **like** a lawyer. **(Il parle comme un avocat, mais il n'est peut-être pas avocat.)**

Ex.: He works **as** a lawyer. **(C'est son métier.)**

• **Autres expressions utilisant as :**

– As long as (= tant que)

Ex.: You can go out **as long as** you promise to be back before midnight.

– As though (= comme si)

Ex.: I couldn't move my legs. It was **as though** they were stuck to the floor.

– As soon as (= dès que)

Ex.: I'll come and see you **as soon as** I arrive.

– As well as (= ainsi que)

Ex.: She was clever **as well as** kind.

Inde, avril 2013, séries ES, S, L, LV1

Document B

The scene is set in the late sixties.

But what I hadn't understood about my mother was that buried deep beneath this conventional exterior was the hardy little seed of a feminist. I'm sure that word never passed her lips, but it made no difference. Her certainty frightened me. She said it was my duty as a woman to go to Cambridge to study maths. As a woman? In those days, in our milieu, no one ever spoke like that. No woman did anything 'as a woman'. She told me she would not permit me to waste my talent. I was to excel and become extraordinary. I must have a proper career in science or engineering or economics. She allowed herself the world-oyster cliché. It was unfair on my sister that I was both clever and beautiful when she was neither. It would compound the injustice if I failed to aim high. I didn't follow the logic of this, but I said nothing. My mother told me she would never forgive me and she would never forgive herself if I went off to read English and became no more than a slightly better educated housewife than she was. I was in danger of wasting my life.

Those were her words, and they represented an admission. This was the only time she expressed or implied dissatisfaction with her lot.

Then she enlisted my father – 'the Bishop' was what my sister and I called him. When I came in from school one afternoon my mother told me he was waiting for me in his study. [...] He had made some enquiries. Cambridge was anxious to be seen to be 'opening its gates to the modern egalitarian world'. With my burden of triple misfortune – a grammar-school, a girl, an all-male subject – I was certain to get in.

Ian McEwan, *Sweet Tooth*, 2011.

EXPRESSION ÉCRITE : In document B, we are told that "Cambridge was anxious to be seen to be 'opening its gates to the modern egalitarian world.'" Generally speaking, do you think that our modern world has become egalitarian concerning equality between men and women?

Analyse du sujet

Il s'agit d'exprimer votre point de vue sur l'égalité des sexes au XXIe siècle dans un essai argumentatif. Cette égalité est-elle réellement acquise aujourd'hui ? Vous allez pouvoir démontrer d'un côté ce qui est acquis et de l'autre ce qui reste à acquérir. Dans la conclusion, vous pouvez exprimer un point de vue plus personnel : par exemple, expliquer pourquoi, pour vous, l'égalité des sexes n'est pas une question essentielle ou affirmer, au contraire, qu'il s'agit bien d'un objectif crucial à atteindre.

Proposition de corrigé

Sexual equality is **an issue** that regularly hits the news today, but which is relatively modern **with regards** to the history of the human race. **Indeed, over the course of history**, the physical superiority of males has always meant that they played the role of protector of women. The situation has evolved progressively in recent centuries with **first**, the active participation of women at work outside the home, **then**, the schooling of girls on an equal level with boys, **next**, the development of time-saving household equipment and more **recently**, the invention of the pill enabling women to choose when to have children.

In theory, men and women are considered equal in the twenty-first century. **However**, the reality is very different. **On a world scale**, there are still countries such as India or China, where parents are disappointed if their new-born baby is a girl. Sad to say, some go as far as infanticide to solve the "problem". **In the western world**, society encourages parents to treat their children the same way, **whether** they are boys or girls, and **yet** we often hear stories of parents continuing to produce children until they finally have their first son. Children of both sexes now receive an identical education, until the first choices have to be made **regarding** a future career. We still find more girls doing courses geared towards office work and more boys for technical, even scientific jobs.

Worse still, in jobs where men and women occupy the same post, the males very often are better paid than the women, and women with the same qualifications as men find themselves confronted by a "glass ceiling" that prevents them from progressing as far as their male counterparts. **On the other hand**, in the last century there has been considerable evolution in the way men and women handle their social and family life. **Indeed**, most men now play an active role in the home. They **no longer** come home, put on their slippers and watch TV while their wives cook a meal and look after the children. **As** most women also work outside the home, the husband shares the chores and taking care of the children. **More and more** men actually volunteer to take time off work when the baby is little to let their wife return to work.

In conclusion, I would say that **apart from** the discrimination that still exists in the professional world, men and women are more egalitarian today than ever before. **In modern society, it's not so much a matter of** one sex being able to do the same as the other, **but rather a matter of** sharing and accepting inevitable differences.

NOTIONS CLÉS L'idée de progrès

THE GREAT TECHNICAL AND SCIENTIFIC DISCOVERIES

- The evolution in means of communication: railway, canals, Morse, telephone, television, computers.
- The Industrial Revolution: Watt's steam machine, Fordism, Taylorization.
- The printing press: William Caxton.
- The Space Age.

MEDICAL AND SCIENTIFIC PROGRESS

- The invention of penicillin, treatment against scurvy, vaccination against smallpox (*l'invention de la pénicilline, le traitement contre le scorbut, le vaccin contre la variole*).
- The theory of evolution: Darwin.

PROGRESS AS WORK: A VECTOR OF SUCCESS

- Individual well-being and collective enrichment (*le bien-être individuel et l'enrichissement collectif*).
- The Protestant work ethic; individual fulfillment and the development of capitalism in the United States (*l'éthique protestante du travail ; l'accomplissement individuel et le développement du capitalisme aux États-Unis*).
- Working towards success – self-improvement, self-help books, personal coaching.

THE QUEST FOR SOCIAL PROGRESS

- The evolution in the perception of differences (gay rights).
- The evolution in racial perception – from a White society convinced of its own supremacy to a multicultural society looking to free itself from prejudice (*l'évolution de la perception raciale – d'une société blanche persuadée de sa suprématie à une société multiculturelle désireuse de se défaire de ses préjugés*).
- The status of women (*la condition de la femme*): the struggle for equal rights (right to vote, to work); contraception.

San Francisco : smart d'entre les smart

Entre solutions créatives et innovations écologiques, la ville du « zéro déchet » est à l'avant-garde.

San Francisco se vante d'être l'une des villes les plus intelligentes du monde. En janvier 2012, elle a été la première à nommer un *chief innovation officer*, un responsable de l'innovation, dont la mission est d'utiliser la technologie pour faire de la municipalité une entité *« réactive, flexible et efficace »*.

Dès 2009, le maire avait mis en place une politique de transparence dans les données municipales (DataSF). Plus de soixante applications ont été conçues à partir de celles-ci, qui listent les meilleurs parcours de santé ou identifient les espèces d'arbres que l'on rencontre dans les rues. Pour le maire, Edwin Lee, la technologie doit avant tout stimuler l'esprit de collaboration, les citoyens étant les mieux placés pour améliorer la cité.

Mais c'est surtout dans le domaine du développement durable que San Francisco est aux avant-postes. Depuis 2009, la ville a mis en place un système de recyclage obligatoire extrêmement contraignant. Les habitants – et les entreprises – sont tenus de séparer leurs déchets en trois catégories : les compostables, matières organiques qui seront transformées en engrais pour les fermes de la région ; les recyclables, cartons et autres papiers que la ville revend, notamment en Asie ; et les non-recyclables, destinés à la décharge. L'objectif est de réduire ces derniers à une quantité négligeable d'ici à 2020, d'où le nom de cette politique : « zéro déchet ».

En cinq ans, la ville a atteint un taux de récupération de 80 %, une performance sans précédent. On vient du monde entier pour étudier le programme, piloté par une coopérative de collecte des ordures, Recology, fondée en 1921, et photographier les trois poubelles (verte, bleue, noire) que chacun se doit d'avoir pour le tri des déchets. Non seulement la ville a réussi à réduire la pollution – la gestion des déchets représenterait 3 % des émissions de gaz à effet de serre –, mais elle a créé des emplois dans ce qui est devenu une nouvelle activité commerciale. En 2014, elle a aussi interdit les sacs plastique dans les magasins, les emballages en polystyrène et la vente des bouteilles d'eau en plastique dans les espaces publics.

« L'internet of things »

Dans un Etat qui compte la moitié du nombre de voitures électriques en circulation aux Etats-Unis (soit 160 000), San Francisco se doit de tenir son rang. La ville a déployé 110 stations de rechargement, soit 13,5 chargeurs pour 100 000 personnes : plus par habitant que toute autre agglomération américaine. Dans huit quartiers pilotes, des capteurs détectent les places de parking vides. Le système SFpark permet aussi d'augmenter le prix de stationnement dans les rues trop encombrées. Selon la municipalité, la recherche de place est source d'environ 30 % des embouteillages.

La sécheresse qui sévit depuis quatre ans en Californie a stimulé les idées : les citoyens ont accès à l'évolution de leur consommation d'eau et peuvent échanger leurs recettes pour la réduire. Sur la plate-forme SF Energy Map, ils peuvent entrer leur adresse et évaluer le potentiel de leur toit en termes de production d'énergie solaire et le coût d'une éventuelle installation, compte tenu des crédits alloués par les collectivités locales. La municipalité entretient un partenariat avec le portail Honest Buildings, qui évalue les entreprises de construction à l'aune de leur prise en compte des économies d'énergie.

San Francisco a enfin mis en place des « zones d'innovation vivante » où œuvrent des *fellows* (chercheurs) dont l'objectif est de développer des solutions créatives ou écologiques aux problèmes du quotidien. Certains s'attaquent au recyclage des déchets textiles, d'autres à la conception d'un outil simplifiant les règlements administratifs (San Francisco Decoded). Comme le dit le *chief innovation officer* Jay Nath, *« notre vision est de faire de San Francisco la capitale de l'Internet of Things, c'est-à-dire des objets connectés »*. Difficile de faire moins quand on se revendique la Mecque du high-tech.

Corine Lesnes (San Francisco, correspondante)
Le Monde daté du 20.11.2015

POURQUOI CET ARTICLE ?

La Californie est, depuis quelques décennies déjà, un État tourné vers les innovations technologiques et vers les utopies aussi bien sociétales qu'environnementales. Elle est en quelque sorte le laboratoire de l'Amérique de demain. Cet article évoque les solutions innovantes mises en place par San Francisco, la « Mecque du high-tech », devenue la championne mondiale de la gestion des déchets. De nombreuses mesures y ont en effet été prises pour lutter contre le gaspillage et parvenir au « zéro déchet » en 2020. Cet objectif de « zero waste », en anglais, repose sur un système incitant financièrement à recycler et à composter, mais qui ne peut fonctionner qu'avec l'investissement des citoyens et l'esprit de collaboration. San Francisco, pionnière dans le développement durable, fait figure d'exemple et a entraîné d'autres villes américaines dans son sillage, telles que Seattle et Minneapolis.

Les géants de la Silicon Valley, bâtisseurs du futur

Facebook, Google, Apple sont lancés dans des projets d'expansion monumentaux. Architectes de renom, espaces bucoliques, projets écologiques... Ils veulent révolutionner l'espace de travail.

Les géants de la Silicon Valley rivalisent dans les technologies mais aussi dans l'immobilier. Facebook, Google, Apple : ils se sont tous lancés dans des projets monumentaux à la mesure de leurs ambitions. Chacun avec des concepts audacieux, des architectes de renom et une prétention à révolutionner le concept d'espace de travail. *« Jusqu'ici, la technologie n'avait pas adopté un langage particulier pour la construction. On se contentait de s'installer dans des vieux bâtiments. Maintenant, nous avons l'occasion de donner au monde quelque chose qu'il n'avait pas »*, explique, en toute modestie, David Radcliffe, le directeur de l'immobilier de Google.

Signe du basculement de l'économie mondiale, les nouveaux empires se bâtissent sur les terrains délaissés par des sociétés établies comme HP ou Cisco. Ils sont uniformément « verts », bucoliques, comme si les ingénieurs, tout à leurs univers dématérialisés, avaient un besoin permanent de se ressourcer.

A part Apple, qui construit sa « navette spatiale » à l'écart du commun des mortels, la plupart des firmes affichent un souci de meilleure intégration dans les communautés locales. Sans doute ont-elles compris l'hostilité grandissante à San Francisco à l'égard de ces « techies » surpayés qui encombrent les autoroutes et font exploser les prix de l'immobilier.

Mark Zuckerberg, le fondateur de Facebook, a choisi la star des architectes, Frank Gehry, le concepteur du musée Guggenheim de Bilbao (Espagne), pour rénover son quartier général. Le réseau social, qui possède déjà onze bâtiments à Menlo Park (50 kilomètres au sud de San Francisco), achève un « West campus », qui pourra accueillir 2 800 employés. Le groupe a voulu conserver l'esprit start-up : l'édifice a la forme d'un énorme hangar de 40 000 mètres carrés, prétendument inachevé. Il s'inscrit dans un parc de 4 hectares, en bord de baie, et sera « enfoui » sous une forêt de 350 arbres plantés sur le toit. Les ingénieurs ne se trouveront *« jamais à moins de huit mètres d'un espace vert »*, assure la firme. Des télescopes leur permettront de se délasser en observant le survol des marécages par les espèces d'oiseaux protégées.

« Vaisseau spatial »

En juin 2014, Facebook avait déjà acheté le site voisin, un terrain de 24 hectares avec dix bâtiments appartenant à l'entreprise suisse TE Connectivity. Début février, il s'est aussi emparée de 22,6 hectares pour 400 millions de dollars (356 millions d'euros). Ces acquisitions ont alimenté les conjectures sur un projet de « ville Facebook », le long de la baie, avec des résidences pour les employés et des boutiques accessibles au public. Mais, selon le *Silicon Valley Business Journal*, aucun développement concret n'est prévu dans un futur proche. Il s'agit plutôt d'anticiper sur la croissance de la compagnie dans un contexte de pression immobilière forte dans la vallée.

De son côté, Apple a lancé, en novembre 2014 à Cupertino (75 kilomètres au sud de San Francisco), la construction d'un mégacomplexe appelé « Campus 2 », d'une superficie de 260 000 mètres carrés, soit plus de trois fois la surface du siège actuel. Les plans sont ultra-protégés, mais les images diffusées le 27 février par la municipalité montrent que le chantier en est au stade du creusement des fondations.

L'immeuble aura la forme d'un anneau géant de quatre étages d'un diamètre de 463 mètres. Un stade de football pourrait tenir en son centre. Imaginé par l'architecte britannique Norman Foster, il devrait être terminé fin 2016. Il pourra accueillir 12 000 employés – Apple emploie déjà 16 000 personnes à Cupertino et occupe 40 % de la superficie des bureaux disponibles dans la ville.

Le « vaisseau spatial », selon l'expression de Steve Jobs, qui avait présenté le projet en 2011 quatre mois avant sa mort, comportera aussi un auditorium souterrain de 1 000 places - pour les présentations à la presse des nouveaux produits –, un parking pouvant accueillir 5 870 véhicules et un parc de 6 000 arbres, avec des chênes, des abricotiers et des pruniers choisis par l'arboriste de la compagnie, dans une sorte de nostalgie pour l'époque où la Silicon Valley était encore un verger. Le complexe pourra supporter un déplacement de 1,20 mètre en cas de tremblement de terre. Selon Tim Cook, le PDG d'Apple, ce sera *« le bâtiment le plus écologique du monde »*.

Mais le projet le plus fou est celui de Google. Il a été présenté, vendredi 27 février, au conseil municipal de Mountain View (65 kilomètres au sud de San Francisco), la localité résidentielle qui abrite le moteur de recherche depuis 1999. A l'époque, l'entreprise y comptait une douzaine d'employés ; ils sont aujourd'hui plus de 19 000 (et 53 700 pour l'ensemble du groupe) répartis sur plusieurs immeubles logés dans un parc de 11 hectares. Le nouveau siège, composé de quatre édifices, pourra abriter 12 000 nouveaux employés sur 31 hectares de North Bay Shore, l'enclave de la firme située au nord de l'autoroute 101. Google a approché deux des jeunes architectes du moment, le Danois Bjarke Ingels, connu pour ses plans futuristes, et le Britannique Thomas Heatherwick, tout aussi anticonformiste. Comme ils n'arrivaient pas à les départager, ils ont embauché les deux.

L'objectif est de créer un endroit reconfigurable au gré des tâches. *« Les besoins des ingénieurs qui travaillent sur la voiture autonome ne sont pas les mêmes que ceux du moteur de recherche »*, décrit David Radcliffe. Et Google, qui continue à réaliser l'essentiel de son chiffre d'affaires sur la publicité, mais investit dans tout ce qui innove, des satellites aux robots, ne sait pas de quoi son avenir sera fait. Le design doit refléter ce besoin de flexibilité.

Les images sur la vidéo de présentation du projet ont stupéfié les observateurs. Le nouveau Googleplex est un ensemble utopique qui brouillera les distinctions entre intérieur et extérieur. Plus de béton, ni de murs, ni de toit rigide. Les éléments de base – planchers, plafonds – pourront être fixés à quelques structures permanentes métalliques ou détachés selon les besoins, comme des grilles dans un four. Les parois seront amovibles, assemblées comme des blocs sur un jeu de construction, à l'aide de petites grues robot (les « crabots »). *« Comme on déplace des meubles »*, dit David Radcliffe. Les

seules structures permanentes seront les toilettes et les escaliers. Google veut libérer la construction *« des limitations de l'architecture traditionnelle que sont les murs, les fenêtres et les toits »*...
Chaque site sera couvert d'un dôme translucide tendu comme une *« membrane super-transparente et ultralégère »*, selon l'expression de Bjarke Ingels, une sorte de toile de tente faite de verre souple. Le matériau, photovoltaïque, qui générera sa propre énergie, reste à inventer mais, comme dit David Radcliffe, *« les meilleurs ingénieurs et cerveaux du monde y travaillent »*, donc Google ne doute pas du succès. Le premier dôme devrait être prêt en 2020. De l'extérieur, les passants qui déambuleront dans les espaces verts et les potagers communautaires pourront voir les employés au travail, eux aussi parmi les arbres des jardins d'intérieur. Google ne veut plus être *« la forteresse qui exclut ses voisins »*, dit la présentation vidéo. On y entend aussi, dans une pique à peine voilée pour le « vaisseau » d'Apple, que, *« plutôt que se tourner vers l'intérieur comme nombre de* [leurs] *pairs, le campus privilégie la transparence et l'inclusion »*.

Une vallée déjà asphyxiée

Le projet sera examiné en avril par la municipalité, qui devra arbitrer entre les géants car LinkedIn convoite aussi une partie du terrain sur North Bay Shore. Mountain View, avec ses 80 000 habitants, entretient des relations tendues avec Google, qui est certes le premier employeur de la ville, mais qui détient déjà 65 000 hectares de bureaux, éparpillés entre 80 lots. Les élus sont ravis d'avoir vu les plans bucoliques de Google, mais plusieurs demandent déjà où tous ces nouveaux employés vont être logés et avec quel moyen de transport ils viendront travailler. Comme le déplore lui-même Bjarke Ingels, le campus actuel a été englouti dans *« une mer de parkings »*. L'architecte promet de *« renverser ce processus »* mais il n'explique pas comment.
D'autres font remarquer que, sur tous leurs plans, les architectes du high-tech montrent des personnages invariablement blancs, sveltes et cool, parcourant les allées arborées sur des vélos multicolores. Loin, autrement dit, de la réalité d'une vallée asphyxiée par l'insatiable croissance de ses géants.

Corine Lesnes (San Francisco, correspondante)
Le Monde Eco et entreprise daté du 04.03.2015

POURQUOI CET ARTICLE ?

Dans la Silicon Valley, la contribution des géants de la tech au progrès ne se limite pas à leur domaine de prédilection. Si les sociétés Google, Facebook et Apple développent des nouveautés en rapport avec l'informatique et Internet, elles cherchent aussi à expérimenter une réorganisation de l'espace du travail. Cette dernière passe bien souvent par la construction de nouveaux bâtiments dessinés par des architectes de renom et répondant à un cahier des charges qui insiste à la fois sur l'importance de la nature et sur la nécessité de créer des structures modulables, capables d'évoluer en fonction des besoins des ingénieurs. Chaque société envisage des solutions différentes, telle l'exploitation d'importantes zones souterraines prévue par Apple. Il est fort probable que le monde entier tirera par la suite profit des expérimentations les plus réussies.

Les arts plastiques tentés par la réalité virtuelle

Une génération d'artistes se saisit des outils numériques pour peindre sans toile ou sculpter dans l'air.

Drue Kataoka gesticule, bouche entrouverte, le visage tourné vers le plafond, pieds nus sur un grand écran vert qui recouvre le sol et les murs. Elle reçoit dans le pavillon de bois qui lui sert d'atelier, sur les hauteurs de Palo Alto, dans la Silicon Valley. Ce qu'elle a à montrer est bien là, flottant dans ces quelques mètres carrés, mais il faut, pour l'apercevoir, enfiler, comme elle, un casque de réalité virtuelle. On découvre alors, persuadé d'être seul, un univers fantastique qui s'étend dans toutes les directions, et dans lequel on peut se déplacer. Dans cette forêt orangée où la gravité n'existe pas, les arbres poussent racines au ciel, un lac de pierres se déverse dans un abîme, donnant autant le vertige que l'envie de s'y pencher.
Cette artiste d'origine japonaise a réalisé son œuvre à l'aide de Tilt Brush, une application de dessin en réalité virtuelle disponible pour les casques HTC Vive et Oculus. Vendu 20 dollars, l'outil aurait atteint, selon des chiffres non officiels, les 190 000 utilisateurs, un an après le début de sa commercialisation par Google, en avril 2016. Il permet de dessiner en 3D, sans support, à l'aide d'un casque et de deux commandes manuelles.
L'outil a pour vocation première, assumée par l'équipe de Google, de divertir un public d'amateurs. Une démonstration de quelques minutes suffit au novice pour balbutier une œuvre, mi-peinture mi-sculpture, qu'il peut archiver et partager. Mais, pour une nouvelle génération d'artistes, cette technologie annonce un tournant pour les arts plastiques.
« Nous sommes à l'aube d'une révolution, estime Drue Kataoka. *C'est une période fascinante pour être artiste. »* Peintures sans toile, graffitis sans mur, sculptures sans matérialité : les œuvres de réalité virtuelle sont paradoxales, et les galeries ne savent pas encore comment les exposer. Pour le spectateur également, la donne semble être changée. L'œuvre d'art n'est plus un objet matériel que l'on vient regarder ou que l'on peut vendre, mais une expérience dans laquelle il faut se plonger.

« La seule limite : l'imagination »

C'est le caractère immersif du dispositif qui a intrigué George Peaslee, un sculpteur de 29 ans originaire d'Hawaï, aujourd'hui installé à Los Angeles. Il a commencé à utiliser Tilt Brush il y a un an pour recréer en réalité virtuelle *La Nuit étoilée* de Van Gogh. *« Je rêvais de pouvoir envoyer un drone dans ce tableau,* se souvient-il, *ou de pouvoir plonger dedans, le voir depuis le ciel mais aussi depuis la ville. »*
Dans sa création, l'image a une réelle profondeur, et le spectateur

peut zoomer puis dézoomer à l'envi, la réduisant tantôt à une bulle, tantôt à un paysage de géant. *« Je ne suis jamais revenu à la sculpture traditionnelle depuis,* poursuit-il. *C'est trop de bazar, c'est trop contraignant. Avec la réalité virtuelle, la seule limite est l'imagination. On s'approche au plus près du rêve de l'artiste : mettre le spectateur dans son propre monde. »*

Parce que le spectateur n'est plus face à l'œuvre mais en elle, l'artiste doit modifier sa manière de travailler. *« Je pense souvent aux sculptures du fronton du Parthénon sur l'Acropole,* raconte Drue Kataoka. *Les artistes savaient que les dos des personnages ne seraient jamais visibles pour une personne qui se trouverait face au bâtiment. Mais ils les ont tout de même sculptés avec une finesse extraordinaire, pour que les sculptures soient dignes d'être vues par les dieux. En réalité virtuelle, il faut que chaque détail soit pensé avec minutie : le spectateur peut endosser ce point de vue divin, en allant autour, en regardant depuis en bas, depuis en haut, et même depuis l'intérieur de ce qui est peint ou sculpté. Il devient un agent dans l'œuvre, une sorte de cocréateur, en prenant un certain chemin et en faisant des choix. »*

C'est la différence majeure entre la réalité virtuelle préenregistrée, telle qu'elle est beaucoup diffusée au cinéma, et la réalité virtuelle volumétrique en temps réel, dans laquelle le spectateur peut se déplacer. Pour Rachel Rossin, artiste à New York, la réalité virtuelle investit davantage les salles de cinéma pour des raisons circonstancielles (de budget, d'audience, de popularité), et non parce qu'elle y serait plus légitime ou plus adaptée. *« Les réalisateurs ne tiennent pas encore suffisamment compte de la présence et de la conscience du spectateur,* explique-t-elle. *Dans beaucoup de films, l'expérience ressemble à une attraction Disney, on y est promené. La réalité virtuelle est un simple ajout à l'œuvre, alors qu'elle devrait la structurer. »*

La technologie Tilt Brush et ses applications concurrentes (Quill et Gravity Sketch pour le dessin, Medium pour la sculpture) peinent aussi à dépasser le stade du gadget. La plate-forme Tilt Brush Sketches, lancée par Google le 27 avril dans le but de centraliser les créations jusque-là dispersées sur les réseaux sociaux, ressemble davantage à un espace ludique qu'à un projet artistique. L'esthétique y est étonnamment répétitive, les couleurs souvent criardes, abusant des effets néon, fluo ou paillettes, très populaires auprès des utilisateurs. Elisabeth Morant, chef de produit chez Google, assure que cette patte Tilt Brush est due au goût du public, bien plus qu'aux limitations de l'outil : *« La palette de couleurs et de textures est immense,* insiste-t-elle. *Mais il est très tentant de peindre avec du feu quand on en a l'occasion pour la première fois. »*

« Un art encore non résolu »

Que cet art en friche n'ait pas encore atteint la maturité n'effraie pas Baldur Helgason, peintre islandais à Chicago. *« C'est un art encore non résolu,* commente-t-il. *Dans cette discipline, il n'y a ni maîtres, ni règles, ni canons. »* Quant au sculpteur George Peaslee, il attend avec impatience les améliorations de l'outil : pouvoir animer ses dessins ou réintroduire une forme de toucher dans la sculpture virtuelle en stimulant, avec les commandes, certaines parties de la main. Drue Kataoka, elle, rêve d'un mode *« multijoueur »* qui permettrait de travailler à plusieurs, depuis n'importe où, dans *« une sorte de version moderne des grands ateliers de la Renaissance ».*

Un problème plus pressant semble tout de même à résoudre pour cette génération d'artistes qui a fait de la réalité virtuelle sa spécialité. Comment exposer et monétiser ces œuvres-expériences ? Google a fait du mécénat un élément central de sa campagne de communication lors du lancement du produit, en organisant à San Francisco, New York et Paris des résidences artistiques. Une soixantaine de dessinateurs, sculpteurs, graphistes, peintres ou caricaturistes, rémunérés, y ont participé, mais une majorité d'entre eux semble être revenue à son médium d'origine, par passion ou par prudence. Pour les autres, il ne reste de cette résidence qu'une profonde fascination, et une précieuse visibilité.

Steve Teeple, artiste de 28 ans spécialisé dans le film d'animation, a été l'un des premiers à utiliser Tilt Brush depuis son studio d'Oakland, dans la baie de San Francisco. Il est aujourd'hui autant artiste que consultant VR (pour *virtual reality*), vendant ses services tour à tour pour collaborer avec une boîte de production, faire la publicité d'une marque de chaussures, plus rarement pour développer ses propres projets. Les artistes peuvent espérer être rémunérés lors de performances, en peignant par exemple pour des spectacles.

Le filon est d'autant plus prometteur que Google a mis au point des pinceaux sensibles aux sons, qui permettent aux traits de réagir à la musique en temps réel. Mais, pour l'instant, les plasticiens en réalité virtuelle doivent compter sur les produits dérivés. Steve Teeple vient d'exposer pour la première fois l'une de ses créations en réalité virtuelle dans une galerie d'Oakland. Il a pu vendre aux enthousiastes des *« sortes de cartes postales »,* à garder au plat pays des images en deux dimensions. Drue Kataoka envisage, elle aussi, de faire imprimer, en 3D cette fois, des détails de ses mondes fantastiques : *« Ce serait comme de petits talismans, entre le réel et le virtuel,* imagine-t-elle. *On les ramènerait d'un monde qu'on a vu, à la manière des héros qui rapportent une preuve de leurs exploits. »*

Pour l'heure, les musées et les institutions utilisent surtout la réalité virtuelle pour en revenir aux arts traditionnels, y voyant un moyen de séduire le jeune public ou de rendre leur collection visible à distance. *« C'est en partie pour des raisons de coût,* analyse l'artiste Rachel Rossin, *parce que les installations demandent du matériel et beaucoup de maintenance. Mais c'est aussi une question de connaissance, notamment en programmation. Toute une génération d'artistes est en train de cultiver des compétences qui transforment déjà cette situation. »* Dans son studio, l'artiste travaille d'ailleurs à l'élaboration de son propre casque de réalité virtuelle.

Laure Andrillon, *Le Monde* daté du 13.06.2017

POURQUOI CET ARTICLE ?

Cet article nous présente Tilt Brush, l'application de Google permettant de dessiner en trois dimensions dans l'espace, pratique inédite qui mélange peinture et sculpture. Laure Andrillon veut nous montrer que cette invention constitue peut-être un vrai tournant dans l'art : l'œuvre d'art n'est plus un objet mais devient une expérience, le spectateur devient agent et l'artiste peut plonger le spectateur dans son propre monde.

Mais s'agit-il d'une révolution ou d'un gadget ? Selon l'auteure de l'article, on ne peut pas encore à ce stade parler de projet artistique. De plus, des questions pratiques, telles que les modalités d'exposition des œuvres et la rémunération des artistes, restent en suspens. Ce qui est certain, c'est que cette application nous permet de nous demander si la réalité virtuelle est l'avenir de l'art.

Google régale à l'œil

Bar à sushis, cuisine indienne, tacos, pizzas, salades bio... Dans la Silicon Valley, les cantines du moteur de recherche ont des allures de banquets... gratuits. Capitalisme social ? L'objectif est plus pragmatique : s'assurer que, même à table, les salariés pensent Google.

«Vous avez peur des sept kilos de Google. Rejoignez les Weight Watchers. » L'affichette est installée à côté de l'ascenseur, près d'une des cafétérias du leader des moteurs de recherche. Sept kilos, c'est le poids que tout nouveau salarié est supposé gagner après son arrivée dans l'entreprise. Et, à naviguer entre les différents restaurants où les « googlers », comme ils s'appellent entre eux, mangent gratis, du comptoir à sushis aux machines à glaces, pas besoin d'explication supplémentaire. Il fut même un temps, se flatte Charlie Ayers, chef historique des cuisines de Google, où des employés qui avaient décidé de se remettre au sport portaient des tee-shirts imprimés de sa photo barrée.

Plus de 10 000 googlers mangent à l'œil dans la trentaine de restaurants du « campus » de Mountain View, au cœur de la Silicon Valley. Sans compter leurs invités et, vision assez rare dans des cafétérias d'entreprise, leurs enfants, pour lesquels des chaises hautes sont prévues. Certains sont présents en ce mois d'août, avec des ballons. Il y a aussi des chiens (mais qui doivent déjeuner dehors). Le modèle a essaimé dans toute la vallée où les entreprises high-tech ont fait des « *free lunches* » un atout pour leur recrutement.

Embauché en 1999, Charlie Ayers fut le 53e employé de Google. Cheveux mi-longs, tee-shirt noir, pantalon cargo et sabots blancs, il est bien plus souriant que la tête de mort de la grosse bague qu'il arbore au doigt. Sa silhouette indique qu'il a eu le temps, chez Google, d'amasser plusieurs fois les fameux sept kilos. « *Manger beaucoup, ça passe jusqu'à 25 ans, après, moins...*, s'excuse-t-il. *Quand j'ai rencontré Larry et Sergey* [Larry Page et Sergey Brin, les fondateurs de Google], *Google avait dix-huit ingénieurs. Ils étaient encore installés sur University Avenue, à Palo Alto*, se souvient-il. *Il y avait plein de restos pas chers dans le quartier, je ne voyais pas pourquoi ils avaient besoin de monter une cafétéria.* »

Les cofondateurs lui ont expliqué. Aller au resto, ça prend du temps. Ça commence une demi-heure avant le déjeuner par « tu veux aller déjeuner ? ». Ça traîne en discussions « *plutôt sushis ou plutôt tacos ?* ». Si vous sortez du quartier, il faut prendre la voiture... « *Et une fois que vous êtes à l'extérieur, vous vous sentez autorisés à passer plus de temps à table. Vous parlez plus volontiers de trucs qui n'ont rien à voir avec le travail alors qu'à la cafétéria, entre collègues, vous discuterez plus facilement des projets sur lesquels vous travaillez. À la cafétéria, les ingénieurs et commerciaux, deux populations qui se croisent peu, peuvent se retrouver. La productivité est bien meilleure. Financièrement, vous vous y retrouvez largement.* » Et, explique une responsable de la communication, manger sur son lieu de travail soulage de cette « *sorte d'anxiété adolescente : avec qui manger ?* ». Voilà comment Google en est arrivé à installer 30 restaurants (les « cafés ») et 150 cafés (les « *micro kitchens* ») sur ses terrains de la Silicon Valley. Tous sont gratuits.

Le modèle a fait des petits dans la Silicon Valley, de LinkedIn à Facebook en passant par Twitter. L'ex-adjoint de Charlie Ayers était parti diriger la restauration de Facebook. Ancienne de Google devenue patronne de Yahoo ! Marissa Mayers y avait tellement apprécié les déjeuners que revoir les cafétérias fut l'une de ses premières décisions à la tête du géant de l'Internet. Et « *dans tous les services de restauration de la Valley, vous retrouverez des anciens employés de Google* », assure Charlie Ayers, qui a quitté la compagnie en 2005 pour ouvrir son propre restaurant dans un centre commercial huppé de Palo Alto, mais est resté consultant dans le secteur. Pour lui, ces entreprises n'ont pas d'autre choix que d'épater leurs employés avec leur cuisine : « *Si vous ne pouvez pas payer très bien et que vous demandez beaucoup de travail, si vous voulez que les employés n'aient pas de raison de partir et qu'ils puissent rester tard...* » Malgré l'abondance de son offre de plats à emporter, New York a elle aussi commencé à copier cette formule. « *On essaie de les empêcher de quitter l'immeuble* », résume Jayson Brown, chef du Cafe 57, restaurant du groupe de médias Hearst, qui sert 1 200 repas (payants) par jour, avec chef pâtissier pour les goûters du mercredi. Pionnier des buffets de snacks et cafés à gogo dans les couloirs de son entreprise, le maire de New York, Michael Bloomberg, a expliqué que les clés du succès sont tout d'abord d'arriver tôt au bureau, de partir tard, et de quitter le moins possible son bureau pour manger ou aller aux toilettes – en réaction, le *New York Times* a interrogé un urologue, qui a déconseillé de se retenir de boire.

POURQUOI CET ARTICLE ?

Cet article nous permet de découvrir « les cuisines » – au sens propre comme au sens figuré – du géant américain Google, en éclairant sous un angle original certaines pratiques méconnues de cette entreprise phare de la Silicon Valley. La firme américaine, en offrant des repas gratuits à ses employés, met en avant sa bienveillante volonté de contribuer ainsi à leur bien-être – alors que l'objectif principal consiste à mieux contrôler les salariés, et accroître la productivité de l'entreprise. On retrouve ici cet étonnant mélange caractéristique de la Silicon Valley : des résidus d'esprit communautaire et de culture libertaire issus de la vague hippie des années 60 (très présente en Californie), une industrie à la pointe de l'innovation technologique, une culture *geek* omniprésente... et un sens aigu du *business*, au service d'un capitalisme aussi conquérant que décomplexé.

Hearst invite régulièrement des chefs new-yorkais à cuisiner dans sa cafétéria. Facebook a développé des partenariats avec des restaurants réputés qui ont décliné leur enseigne en interne. Plus la peine d'aller au restaurant, le restaurant vient à vous. « *C'est bien pour ceux qui aiment manger à l'extérieur*, approuve Charlie Ayers. *Il y a toujours des gens qui pensent qu'ils valent mieux que la cafétéria de l'entreprise.* »

Chez Facebook, on propose occasionnellement des stages de cuisine aux employés. Google s'interdit évidemment de faire moins. L'entreprise prépare un partenariat avec le Culinary Institute of America (l'autre CIA) pour ses employés qui souhaiteraient apprendre les fondamentaux de la cuisine. Sur le campus, Charlie's Cafe, avec ses avalanches de burgers, burritos, pizzas ou nouilles chinoises, est le Las Vegas de la cuisine. Le Baadal Cafe, un resto indien, est le seul à servir assis en salle et de préférence avec réservation. Le No Name Cafe a été remplacé par le Yoshka Cafe (du nom du premier chien à venir régulièrement sur le campus). Marque de l'époque, Google a introduit des *food trucks* sur son campus : ces camions qui historiquement servaient les ouvriers sur les chantiers viennent maintenant chez les *hipsters* du tertiaire, qui aiment y faire la queue debout. Google propose aussi un *mindful lunch* (« déjeuner de méditation »). *« Essayez de faire une seule chose à la fois pour le déjeuner,* propose une affichette à côté d'un coin zen au décor japonais. *13 h 15 : mangez en silence pendant trente minutes. 13 h 45 : présentez-vous à ceux qui sont assis avec vous »,* conseille encore l'affichette à proximité de la table basse prévue à cet effet.

« *Les entreprises de cette région se sont toujours battues pour attirer et retenir leurs employés* », résume Leslie Berlin, historienne de la Silicon Valley à Stanford. « *Dans les années 1950-1960, c'était tout ce qui touchait à la vie de la communauté, de l'équipe de sport au club de bowling. Dans les années 1970, c'était la façon de pouvoir s'habiller, la culture cool, la promesse d'un environnement professionnel moins formel. Maintenant, c'est la cuisine, d'autant que dans le nord de la Californie on y est plus sensible qu'ailleurs. Les mouvements bio et locavore* [consommateurs de production locale] *s'y sont développés très vite.* »

C'est à présent le côté naturel que Google met en avant. L'entreprise veut aider ses employés à « *faire des choix sains* », selon les mots de Scott Giambastiani, successeur de Charlie Ayers. Ainsi, on entre au Yoshka Cafe par le bar à salades plutôt que par une farandole des desserts, et la machine à faire des glaces est cachée derrière le dernier mur. Sur les étagères des armoires réfrigérées, l'eau est à hauteur des yeux, les sodas plus bas ou plus haut. Dans les MK (quand on passe plus d'une demi-heure sur le campus, on ne dit déjà plus *micro kitchen*), les bacs de fruits frais portent des étiquettes à rallonge sur lesquelles on apprend les origines de telle nectarine, le nom du producteur de ces framboises, l'intérêt nutritif de chaque fruit et comment il se consomme – juré, pour les bananes, il est inscrit que ça se mange épluché. À la différence des pommes, les sachets de chips ne sont plus à portée de main, les bonbons Haribo et les barres KitKat ont été rangés dans des bocaux fermés « *parce que ça demande plus d'énergie d'avoir à ouvrir la boîte* ». Sur les étiquettes des présentoirs, le code couleur indique ce que l'on peut manger à volonté (vert), ce sur quoi il vaut mieux ralentir (orange) ou s'arrêter (rouge). On propose des cuillers et des assiettes plus petites. Ce qui n'empêche pas, bien sûr, de croiser des gens avec une part de pizza juchée sur des frites.

Depuis quelques années, Google sous-traite la gestion de ses restaurants. Au siège, une petite pancarte indique les ressources humaines de Bon Appetit Management Company, une société spécialisée dans la gestion des cafétérias professionnelles de plusieurs grandes entreprises de la Silicon Valley, parmi lesquelles Oracle, Cisco, Yahoo ! et de grandes universités, dont Stanford. Pour Maisie Greenawalt, vice-présidente chargée de la stratégie, tout cela est cohérent : « *Les employés de Yahoo! d'aujourd'hui sont les étudiants de Stanford d'hier* » et c'est avec les jeunes que l'entreprise voit émerger les tendances. « *Manger végétalien ou sans gluten, on l'a d'abord vu sur les campus.* » Est-ce à dire que finalement on mange de la même façon chez Google ou chez Yahoo! ? Scott Giambastiani proteste : *« Google fait ça mieux. On crée un cadre pour ce qu'on autorise les chefs à mettre sur les assiettes Google. »*

À Mountain View, en dehors du campus Google, le Cucina Venti est un petit restaurant italien coincé entre un Starbucks et un fast-food. Une note derrière le comptoir rappelle aux serveurs que chaque client doit être servi de manière remarquable. Une affichette sur le parking indique qu'il y a d'autres places de parking disponibles pour les clients devant le cinéma. Au vu de la salle vide, ils n'en ont pas besoin. Bella Awdisho, la propriétaire, s'est récemment plainte dans un journal local, le *Mountain View Voice*, d'avoir perdu les deux tiers de son chiffre d'affaires à cause de l'offre gratuite de Google. Elle représente un groupe d'établissements en pourparlers avec l'entreprise. Dans un très long article publié en mai 2013 par le *New Yorker* et consacré à la Silicon Valley, le journaliste George Packer notait que ces bureaux, « *tournés vers eux-mêmes, empêchent les employés d'avoir ne serait-ce que des contacts accidentels avec la communauté qui les entoure* ». Pas de quoi émouvoir Charlie Ayers. Quand on évoque devant lui ces restos des environs, il fait la grimace : « *Ce sont des endroits qui de toute façon ne devraient plus être en activité.* » Dans une lettre de réponse, dont un extrait a été publié par le *Mountain View Voice*, Google suggérait aux restaurants de s'adapter en changeant de modèle pour se concentrer sur une offre complémentaire à la sienne, comme des dîners et repas à emporter pour le soir. Puisque Google ne le fait plus. Il y a quelques années, les googlers pouvaient, avant de quitter le travail, remplir des boîtes de « *take away* » pour leurs repas du soir. « *Mais il y a eu des abus* », se souvient Charlie Ayers. Les restos de Mountain View ont des bouches à nourrir en soirée pour quelque temps encore... Mais, prédit Scott Giambastiani, « *les repas à emporter du soir reviendront, sous une autre forme* ». Pourquoi pas payante.

Guillemette Faure, *Le Monde* daté du 14.09.2013

Aux Etats-Unis, les juges disent oui au mariage gay

Quand l'Histoire considérera les années Obama, elle y verra probablement une période de profonde transformation des Etats-Unis. Vendredi 26 juin a été *« une de ces journées »* où le progrès survient *« comme un coup de tonnerre »*, a déclaré le président américain après la décision de la Cour suprême de légaliser le mariage homosexuel sur tout le territoire.

Porté par les efforts de *« citoyens persévérants »*, le progrès survient par *« petites étapes »*, a-t-il souligné : *« Deux pas en avant, un pas en arrière. »* Le président lui-même est l'emblème de l'évolution du pays sur la question. Jusqu'en mai 2012, il refusait de se prononcer publiquement en faveur des unions homosexuelles. En 2015, la décision de la Cour a été fêtée sur le site de la Maison Blanche d'un logo White House aux couleurs de l'arc-en-ciel. *« Un grand pas dans notre marche vers l'égalité »*, s'est félicité M. Obama.

Les Etats-Unis sont devenus le 21e pays à approuver le mariage entre personnes du même sexe. Par 5 voix contre 4, la juridiction suprême a décidé que le 14e amendement à la Constitution, qui inscrit l'égalité de tous devant la loi, était applicable, et qu'il *« requiert d'un Etat qu'il célèbre un mariage entre deux personnes du même sexe »*.

C'est le juge-charnière de la cour, Anthony Kennedy, considéré comme centriste, qui a été chargé de rédiger l'opinion des *« sages »*. Le début de son texte, empreint d'émotion, a touché ceux qui militent depuis des années pour les droits des homosexuels. *« Ce serait ne pas comprendre ces hommes et ces femmes que de dire qu'ils manquent de respect à l'idée du mariage. Leur plaidoyer consiste à dire que justement, ils le respectent, le respectent si profondément qu'ils cherchent eux-mêmes à s'accomplir grâce à lui. Ils demandent une dignité égale aux yeux de la loi. »* Et, déclare le juge, *« la Constitution leur donne ce droit »*.

Le juge ajoute que *« toutes les parties »* reconnaissent que la plupart des couples homosexuels *« procurent des foyers aimants et soucieux de l'éducation de leurs enfants, qu'ils soient biologiques ou adoptés »*. Or, sans reconnaissance du statut de leurs parents, ces enfants subissent *« la stigmatisation de savoir que leur famille est moindre »*. Le droit au mariage ne saurait être *« conditionné à la capacité ou à l'engagement à procréer »*.

Les quatre juges conservateurs ont rédigé des opinions dissidentes, le président de la Cour, John Roberts, est même allé jusqu'à lire des extraits de son texte en séance, une première depuis dix ans qu'il appartient à la juridiction. Il a déploré que la Cour, par sa décision, ait pris *« l'extraordinaire initiative d'ordonner à chaque Etat d'émettre des licences* [de mariage] *et de reconnaître l'union entre personnes du même sexe »*. Alors que le mariage est du ressort des Etats, non du gouvernement fédéral, il a jugé dangereux que *« cinq juristes aient imposé leur vision personnelle du mariage comme une affaire de droit constitutionnel »*. Pour lui, l'argument de la conformité au principe d'égalité inscrit dans la Charte de 1787 n'est pas valide. Il a mis en garde contre le fait qu'un changement social aussi important, venant des juges et non du processus parlementaire, risque de le rendre *« beaucoup plus difficile à accepter »*.

Postérité

Le mariage homosexuel était reconnu dans 36 Etats sur 50. La saisine de la Cour avait été rendue possible par la plainte de Jim Obergefell, un agent immobilier de Cincinnati (Ohio) obligé d'aller épouser son compagnon, John Arthur, dans le Maryland, et plus précisément sur le tarmac de l'aéroport de Baltimore, en juillet 2013. Après la mort de celui-ci, d'une sclérose en plaques, trois mois et onze jours plus tard, Jim Obergefell avait souhaité que son nom figure sur le certificat de décès, ce qui lui avait été refusé dans l'Ohio.

Présent sur les marches de la Cour suprême avec la photo du défunt, M. Obergefell a reçu un appel de M. Obama. Celui-ci lui a dit à quel point les Etats-Unis pouvaient être *« fiers »* de lui. Devenu, l'espace d'une journée, une icône des droits civiques, M. Obergefell a indiqué qu'il était conscient que son nom allait passer à la postérité, dans la nomenclature de la Cour (*« Obergefell v. Hodges »*). Il a aussi indiqué que Cincinnati est maintenant acquise au mariage gay. *« C'était la seule ville qui avait adopté une mesure stipulant qu'aucune loi ne pouvait être passée pour protéger la communauté LGBT*, a-t-il relevé. *Les choses ont beaucoup changé. »*

Pour Barack Obama, la décision a clos une semaine exceptionnelle qui a vu le Congrès lui accorder le *« fast track »*, l'autorité de négocier en bloc l'accord de libre-échange avec la zone Asie-Pacifique, et la Cour suprême rejeter une nouvelle fois les arguments des républicains contre l'Affordable Care Act de 2010 (la réforme de l'assurance-santé, dite « Obamacare »). *« La décision d'aujourd'hui nous donne l'espoir que sur nombre de sujets auxquels nous sommes confrontés, parfois douloureusement, un vrai changement est possible »*, a-t-il encouragé.

La décision a aussi illustré le fonctionnement des institutions américaines. Le mariage entre personnes du même sexe a été une question de société traitée principalement au niveau des Etats, plutôt qu'au niveau du Parlement fédéral (le Congrès), lequel a jugé prudent de l'éviter. La Cour est venue harmoniser les différences de statut entre les Etats, mettant fin au *« patchwork »* législatif, selon l'expression de M. Obama. Pour les républicains opposés à la normalisation, la seule option est maintenant un amendement à la Constitution. Très hypothétique : il faudrait une majorité de deux tiers dans les deux Chambres et une ratification des trois quarts des Etats.

Corine Lesnes, *Le Monde* daté du 29.06.2015

POURQUOI CET ARTICLE ?

De nombreux peuples considèrent le mode de vie des États-Unis comme un modèle, mais cette nation, forgée par des croyances puritaines, est loin d'être en avance en matière d'évolution sociale. Comme pour l'abolition de l'esclavage, la déségrégation et le droit à l'avortement, des individus et de nombreux états fédéraux luttent contre le mariage gay, même s'il est entré dans la Constitution. L'histoire du peuple américain pèse lourd dans la balance et les opposants s'organisent pour faire de la résistance, comme par le passé avec la création d'écoles privées ou l'interdiction de construire des cliniques pratiquant l'IVG. Cet article souligne l'opposition des républicains à la décision historique de la Cour suprême de légaliser le mariage homosexuel sur tout le territoire et montre la transformation sociale qui a eu lieu sous la présidence d'Obama.

LIEUX ET FORMES DU POUVOIR

In Missouri, artists broadcasting pain through hip-hop

ST. LOUIS – It didn't take long for the lyrics to begin flowing from this city's hip-hop scene to the streets.

In the past 11 days, several tracks referencing the death of Michael Brown have surfaced, a spontaneous, organic and visceral reflection of what has been happening in Ferguson, Mo., since the 18-year-old African American was shot by a white police officer. The music – at least 10 songs, almost one a day – covers a range of emotions: anger and outrage, sadness and grief, and outright rebellion.

For the little-known but vibrant community of independent artists here, it's an expression of simmering frustrations that existed long before Brown was killed, they say.

If rap is the black community's CNN, as hip-hop pioneer Chuck D famously said, then the artists here have been working overtime to broadcast news from the small suburb of Ferguson, the nation's latest crisis point in the ongoing struggles around race and justice. [...]

Aside from the music, hip-hop producers, rap artists and DJs are organizing marches, buying food for protesters and planning political action, including drafting and raising money for a write-in candidate to challenge the county prosecutor in an upcoming election. Their actions are underscored by the soundtrack emerging from these days of unrest, music that documents the demonstrators' version of events. [...]

The artists encourage their fans, many of whom are listening to the tracks in Ferguson's streets, to protest peacefully even as they sympathize with the community's lingering anger. [...]

The raw aftermath of Brown's death was a moment for some artists to brandish their names, using the attention as an opportunity to promote themselves, but others have flexed new muscles as community organizers. Keem, whose biggest hit was the club record "Thick Wit It" [...] has found a more conscious streak.

He and local music producer Ronnie Notch, 30, have been picking up cases of water for a week to take to the site near Family Dollar on West Florissant Avenue, the staging area for the nightly protests. [...]

Rapper Tef Poe, one of the area's most popular independent artists, has been marching with demonstrators every night. For him, the situation is personal.

"When it happened, my younger brother called me," he said. "He was on the phone crying. He said, 'They killed Mike.' They had mutual friends."

Poe said he sees the potential for serious community action. He has been involved in failed attempts to bring local police forces and

DICTIONARY

- **lyrics**: the words of a song
- **tracks**: pieces of music
- **grief**: sorrow, feelings of suffering
- **outright**: complete
- **to work overtime**: to do extra hours
- **to broadcast**: to send out (radio or TV programme)
- **ongoing**: continuing
- **to raise money**: to collect money
- **upcoming**: about to happen
- **to underscore**: to underline
- **raw**: painful
- **aftermath**: the period following a bad event
- **to be involved in**: to be concerned with
- **attempts**: efforts made to do something
- **to back**: to support
- **to cloak**: to cover
- **to take a back seat**: a less important position
- **to drop**: to give up
- **tribute**: something done to show respect for someone
- **roots**: feeling of belonging to a place
- **grass-roots**: the ordinary members of a group
- **writ large**: on a larger scale

MOTS CLÉS en lien avec la thématique

NOUNS

- uprising (= unrest, upheaval, turmoil, revolt): *un soulèvement, une révolte*

Ex.: **The uprising** has led to economic trouble.

- a riot, rioting: *une émeute*
- looting: *le pillage*
- a curfew: *un couvre-feu*
- a demonstration: *une manifestation*
- demonstrators: *des manifestants*
- a union: *un syndicat*
- a unionist: *un syndicaliste*
- a crackdown on: *mesures de répression contre*
- terrorism: *le terrorisme*
- casualties: *victimes, pertes humaines*
- a slaughter: *un massacre*
- a bloodbath: *un bain de sang*
- gun control advocates: *les partisans d'un contrôle plus strict des armes à feu*
- mass shooting: *fusillade, tuerie*
- wounded (= injured): *blessé*

VERBS

- to take to the streets: *descendre dans la rue*
- to go on strike: *faire la grève*
- to demonstrate: *manifester*
- to stage a protest: *organiser une manifestation (pour protester contre...)*

Ex.: Hundreds of people **staged a public protest** against State censorship.

- to gather (= to rally): *se rassembler*

Ex.: Thousands of people **have rallied/gathered against** the regime.

- to protest: *protester, manifester*
- to call for: *appeler à, lancer un appel à*

Ex.: The **demonstrators have called for** reforms.

- to demand: *exiger*
- to erupt: *éclater, exploser, se déclencher*
- to blow up (= to explode): *exploser*
- to claim responsibility for: *revendiquer*

Ex.: An unknown terrorist group **has claimed responsibility for** the bomb attack.

- to carry a gun: *porter une arme*

QUATRE ARTICLES DU *MONDE* À CONSULTER :

- **Colin Gordon : « La ségrégation raciale contribue au déclin des villes américaines »** p. 56-57
(Gilles Paris, *Le Monde* daté du 30.08.2014)
- **Sadiq Khan, du HLM à la mairie de Londres** p. 57-58
(Philippe Bernard, *Le Monde* daté du 09.05.2016)
- **Le Royaume-Uni n'est plus le pays des libertés** p. 59
(Éric Albert, *Le Monde* daté du 28.08.2013)
- **Donald Trump, la volte-face permanente** p. 59-61
(Gilles Paris, *Le Monde* daté du 02.05.2017)

communities closer together and backed an effort to put the St. Louis police force under control of local elected officials. [...]
The activism is refreshing, said Tricia Rose, a professor of Africana studies at Brown University. [...] She called the crisis in Ferguson a potential turning point "for local artists to see themselves as having a mandate for developing a creative space where hip-hop is not a product, hip-hop is a nourishing community jewel."
The misogyny, macho bravado and consumerism that cloak much of the hip-hop industry has taken a back seat for the moment. Some big industry names have joined in. J. Cole, a well-known rapper from North Carolina, was among the first to release a record. [...] Cole emerged from a community meeting in street clothes, none of the routine bling or designer labels that mark the hip-hop culture. [...]
Even the local urban radio stations [...] have joined in. After Brown died, the programming director Boogie D stopped playing music for nearly 14 hours on both stations and allowed community members to call in. For more than a week, he dropped its typical playlist in favor of the tributes to Brown. "People want to hear the tributes, gospel and more socially conscious hip-hop," said Arthur "A Plus" Willis, a prime-time disc jockey.
The favored tributes have come from artists with roots in St. Louis. That's not surprising, Rose said.
"Localized grass-roots hip-hop still is a place for telling honest stories, and it's a brilliant context for young people to help each other with this crisis," she said.
The moment caused some introspection for Poe about the messages coming from the industry writ large.
"I've been thinking about the Mike Brown situation and the different types of music we all make and the messages we're putting out there," he said. In recent days, he has asked himself: "What are my intentions? What am I here for? What do I want from the music industry as an artist?"
He is aware that young Brown was an aspiring lyricist.
"I'm from here," Poe said. "I've walked the same streets that Mike Brown walked. We have a similar story. Like him, as a young kid, I wanted to be an entertainer."

Adapted from *The Washington Post* (Krissa Thompson – August 20th, 2014)

FOCUS ON...

The shooting of Michael Brown occurred in August 2014 in Ferguson, Missouri. Michael Brown, an 18-year-old black student was shot by Darren Wilson, a white police officer. The shooting sparked unrest in Ferguson as many people believed that Brown had his hands raised and was surrendering when he was killed; there have been longstanding tensions between the black community and the white government and police in Ferguson.
Peaceful protests and civil disorder lasted for several days. The shooting was also heavily debated throughout the nation. Following Michael Brown's death, police have begun wearing on-body cameras. The American Civil Liberties Union supports the use of cameras saying that "they have the potential to be a win-win, helping protect the police against misconduct and at the same time helping protect the police against false accusations of abuse."
A county grand jury as well as the FBI investigated the shooting and in November 2014, the grand jury decided not to indict police officer Darren Wilson. Protesters flooded the streets in more than 170 US cities to denounce the grand jury's decision and to demand greater equality.
Deep-seated racial tensions and inequalities have long plagued the St Louis region. There has been a dramatic demographic transformation of Ferguson from a largely white suburban enclave (it was 85% white in 1980) to a predominantly black community (it was 67% black by 2008). Ferguson has also been home to dramatic economic changes in recent years and poverty has skyrocketed. Ferguson is symbolic of growing suburban poverty in the US.

S'EXPRIMER

USING "FOR" AND "SINCE"

- "A spontaneous, organic and visceral reflection of what has been happening in Ferguson **since** the 18-year-old African American was shot by a white police officer."

Since is used here with **the present perfect continuous**.
Since describes when the period of time started (**since** = ***depuis***).
Ex.: I have worked here **since** September 10th.
Ex.: He has lived in London **since** 2010.

- "He and local music producer Ronnie Notch, 30, have been picking cases of water **for** a week to take to the site near Family Dollar [...]."

For is used here with **the present perfect continuous**.
For describes a period of time (**for** = ***depuis***).
Ex.: I have worked here **for** three months.
Ex.: He has lived in London **for** four years.

- "After Brown died, the programming director Boogie D stopped playing music **for** nearly 14 hours on both stations and allowed community members to call in."

For is used here with **the past simple** (**for** = ***pendant***).

- Note the difference:

They **were married for** five years. (*Ils ont été mariés* ***pendant*** *cinq ans*).
They **have been married for** five years. (*Ils sont mariés depuis cinq ans*).

USING "ASIDE FROM"

- "**Aside from** the music, hip-hop producers, rap artists and DJs are organizing marches, buying food for protesters and planning political action [...]."

Aside from means **as well as, in addition to**.
We can also use **apart from** and **besides** to express the same meaning.
Ex.: **Apart from** tennis (= aside from tennis, as well as tennis), I enjoy watching football on TV.

Questions de compréhension

Choose the right answer.

1. Michael Brown was ...... **a.** killed/ **b.** injured.

2. The police officer was ...... **a.** white/ **b.** an African American.

3. a. The police officer/ **b.** Michael Brown ...... was eighteen years old.

4. Ferguson is ...... **a.** a district/ **b.** a small suburb.

5. The songs ...... **a.** are all rebellious/ **b.** express different feelings.

6. Artists ...... **a.** refuse to be involved in political action/ **b.** are involved in political action.

7. Artists ...... **a.** want to prevent the reelection of the county prosecutor/ **b.** want the county prosecutor to be reelected.

8. Keem is concerned ...... **a.** about promoting his song "Thick Wit It"/ **b.** about helping the community.

9. Poe's brother ...... **a.** has friends who knew Michael Brown/ **b.** knew Michael Brown.

10. Tricia Rose thinks that as a result of the Ferguson shooting ...... **a.** hip-hop can become a commercial product/ **b.** hip-hop can be more than just a commercial product.

11. Cole is ...... **a.** a local rapper/ **b.** a rapper from another state.

12. Cole marched with demonstrators ...... **a.** wearing normal clothes/ **b.** wearing designer clothes.

13. After Brown's death, Boogie D ...... **a.** broadcast different music/ **b.** stopped broadcasting music for a week.

14. Michael Brown wanted ...... **a.** to write songs/ **b.** to be an actor.

Exercices de grammaire

Use the present perfect in one sentence and the present perfect continuous in the other one.

1. to disappear

a. An important document .... from my office.

b. Important documents .... from my office since the new assistant was taken on.

2. to stay

a. Steve .... in a flat since returning to London.

b. I .... at this hotel a couple of times before.

3. to run

a. I ran 20 miles today; I .... that far since I was a student.

b. I .... and I am exhausted.

4. to check

a. I .... those files since 9 am.

b. I .... already .... two files.

BOÎTE À OUTILS : PRESENT PERFECT AND PRESENT PERFECT CONTINUOUS

• "In the past 11 days, several tracks referencing the death of Michael Brown **have surfaced**."

"[...] others **have flexed** new muscles as community organisers."

***Dans ces deux phrases, c'est le* present perfect *qui est utilisé* (have + *participe passé*).**

• "The artists **have been working** overtime to broadcast news from the small suburb of Ferguson."

"**I've been thinking** about the Mike Brown situation and the different types of music we all make."

***Dans ces deux phrases, c'est le* present perfect continuous *qui est utilisé* (have been + verb-ing).**

• *Le* present perfect *et le* present perfect continuous *décrivent des événements qui ont un lien avec le présent. Il y a cependant certaines différences entre les deux.*

– Quand on se concentre sur le résultat d'une action on utilisera le* present perfect *plutôt que le present perfect continuous.

Ex.: Prices **have increased** by 3%.

– Quand on se concentre sur le procédé on peut utiliser le* present perfect continuous *(mais également le present perfect***)*.**

Ex.: Prices **have been increasing** in the last few months (***ou*** have increased).

• *On utilisera le* present perfect continuous *pour des actions qui sont répétées.*

Ex.: I **have been phoning** her for days but she's never at home.

***Le* present perfect *sera utilisé pour des activités qui ne se sont passées qu'une seule fois, ou un nombre de fois spécifique*.**

• *On utilisera le* present perfect continuous *pour souligner la durée de l'action.*

Ex.: I **have been waiting** here all afternoon.

On utilisera le* present perfect continuous *pour souligner que l'action est récente.

Ex.: You look exhausted! **Have you been working** all day?

• *On ne peut pas utiliser le* present perfect continuous ***avec des verbes tels que* belong, know, like, understand. *On utilisera alors le* present perfect.**

Ex.: I **have known** her for ages.

Ex.: I **haven't understood** the book.

Sujet national, juin 2013, séries ES, L, S

Document A

From the first day he could walk Simon had always wanted to outdistance his rivals. The Americans would have described him as 'an achiever', while many of his contemporaries thought of him as pushy, or even arrogant, according to their aptitude for jealousy. During his last term at Lancing Simon was passed over for head of school and he still found himself unable to forgive the headmaster his lack of foresight. Later that year, some weeks after he had completed his S-levels and been interviewed by Magdalen, a circular letter informed him that he would not be offered a place at Oxford; it was a decision Simon was unwilling to accept.
In the same mail Durham University offered him a scholarship, which he rejected by return of post.
"Future Prime Ministers aren't educated at Durham," he informed his mother.
"How about Cambridge?" she enquired continuing to wipe the dishes.
"No political tradition," replied Simon.
"But if there is no chance of being offered a place at Oxford, surely – ?"
"That's not what I said, Mother," replied the young man. "I shall be an undergraduate at Oxford by the first day of term." After eighteen years of forty-yard goals Mrs Kerslake had learned to stop asking her son.
"How will you manage that?"
Some fourteen days before the start of the Michaelmas Term at Oxford Simon booked himself into a small guest house just off the Iffley Road. On a trestle table in the corner of lodgings he intended to make permanent he wrote out a list of all the colleges, then divided them into five columns, planning to visit three each morning and three each afternoon until his question had been answered positively by a resident Tutor for Admissions: "Have you accepted any freshmen for this year who are now unable to take up their places?"
It was on the fourth afternoon, just as doubt was beginning to set in and Simon was wondering if after all he would have to travel to Cambridge the following week, that he received the first affirmative reply.
The Tutor for Admissions at Worcester College removed the glasses from the end of his nose and stared at the tall young man with a mop of dark hair falling over his forehead.
Alan Brown was the twenty-second don Kerslake had visited in four days.
"Yes", he replied. "It so happens that a young man from Nottingham High School, who had been offered a place here, was tragically killed in a motor cycle accident last month."
"What course – what subject was he going to read?" Simon's words were unusually faltering.
He prayed it wasn't Chemistry, Anthropology or Classics. Alan Brown flicked through a rotary index on his desk, obviously enjoying the little cross-examination. He peered at the card in front of him. "History," he announced. Simon's heartbeat reached 120. "I just missed a place at Magdalen to read Politics, Philosophy and Economics," he said. "Would you consider me for the vacancy?" The older man was unable to hide a smile. He had never in twenty-four years come across such a request. [...]
Mrs Kerslake was not surprised when her son went on to be President of the Oxford Union. After all, she teased, wasn't it just another stepping stone on the path to Prime Minister?

Jeffrey Archer, *First Among Equals*, 1984.

EXPRESSION ÉCRITE : Simon has decided to run for President of the University's Student Union. Write his first campaign speech. *(150 mots)*

Analyse du sujet

Simon se présente à l'élection du président du Syndicat des étudiants de l'université.

Vous devez rédiger son premier discours pour la campagne d'élection.

Repères essentiels

Pour un discours de campagne, vous cherchez à convaincre :
- impliquez votre auditoire (*you, Oxford students, members of the Union*) ;
- utilisez des arguments et des anecdotes ;
- utilisez des superlatifs ;
- recourez à la rhétorique (pensez à *I Have a Dream* de M.L. King).

Proposition de corrigé

Fellow Students, I stand before you, in all humility, in all modesty, but with a great sense of commitment. I do not intend to tell you how wonderful I am, for that is not how I view the role of President. On the contrary, to prove you how good a President I can be, I intend to tell you how important it is for this Student Union to be correctly represented, so that the wonderful people that you are can enjoy the best possible conditions to successfully pursue your studies here in Oxford.
The Student Union represents the students in all the different meetings concerning university life. The President must be someone who is selfless, accessible, open-minded and a good communicator. It is important for all of you to feel that the person who represents your interests is really interested in defending you. That person is me!

NOTIONS CLÉS

LE SUPERLATIF DE SUPÉRIORITÉ

- *Il correspond à « le plus... » et se forme de la façon suivante :*
– *adjectif* ***court*** : **the** + **adjective** + **-est** (ex.: the simplest) ;
– *adjectif* ***long*** : **the most** + **adjective** (ex.: the most comfortable).

LANGAGE ET POUVOIR

- Language as a social distinction: "Queen's English".
- Speech and leadership (*le discours du dirigeant*): Churchill; Bush after 9/11; the King's Speech.
- Speech and place (*le symbolisme des lieux des discours*): Lincoln + Gettysburg Address; M.L. King + Lincoln Memorial.

LA RÉSISTANCE AU POUVOIR

- Abuse of power: witch hunts, Maccarthyism, organised crime.
- Forms of protest and revolt: suffragettes, Civil Rights Movement, Occupy Wall Street.
- Pacific resistance: Gandhi, M.L King.
- Protest songs and protest marches, demonstrations.
- Other forms of resistance: Buy Nothing Day, anti-globalisation movement, Michael Moore, Occupy Wall Street...

LEXIQUE

- the command of language: *la maîtrise de la langue*
- the crowd: *la foule*
- eloquence: *l'éloquence*
- the language: *la langue*
- the listeners: *les auditeurs*
- the power of speech: *la puissance du discours*
- the public: *le public*
- rhetoric: *la rhétorique*
- a speaker: *un interlocuteur*
- a speech: *un discours*
- articulate: *distinct, net*
- eloquent: *éloquent*
- powerful: *puissant*
- rhetorical: *rhétorique*
- to address to: *s'adresser à*
- to convince: *convaincre*
- to lead: *diriger*
- to persuade: *persuader*
- to speak: *parler*
- to talk to somebody: *parler à quelqu'un*
- to transmit: *véhiculer*

Poor Doors: the Segregation of London's Inner-city Flat Dwellers

Multimillion pound housing developments in London are segregating less well-off tenants from wealthy homebuyers by forcing them to use separate entrances.

A *Guardian* investigation has discovered a growing trend in the capital's upmarket apartment blocks – which are required to include affordable homes in order to win planning permission – for the poorer residents to be forced to use alternative access, a phenomenon being dubbed "poor doors". Even bicycle storage spaces, rubbish disposal facilities and postal deliveries are being separated.

Tracey Kellett, a buying agent who trawls the capital looking for homes for wealthy clients, said a number of developments have separate entrances "so the two social strata don't have to meet". In one: "The affordable [housing] has vile coloured plastic panels on the outside rather than blingy glass."

At one building bordering the City financial district, the *Guardian* discovered wealthy owners accessed their homes via a hotel-style lobby area, while social housing tenants enter through a side door in an adjacent alley alongside trade entrances. As the London housing market has boomed the expectations of some of the capital's wealthiest homebuyers have grown and many properties now have communal areas akin to those in some of the world's best hotels.

Green party London assembly member Darren Johnson said: "This trend shows contempt for ordinary people, and is about developers selling luxury flats to rich investors who don't want to mix with local people." He added: "The mayor and councils have been turning a blind eye to this for too long, they should simply refuse applications that have separate facilities or that refuse any affordable housing on this basis."

Developers said separate doors let housing associations keep costs down as they avoided premium service charges paid by private residents. Peter Allen, sales and marketing director for *Londonewcastle* which is behind the Queens Park Place development in north London said housing associations were sometimes unable to pay for all of the facilities covered by service charges. "The simplest way from a design perspective is to have things separate."

The brochure for the upmarket apartments of One Commercial Street, on the edge of the City, boasts of a "bespoke entrance lobby ... With the ambience of a stylish hotel reception area, it creates a stylish yet secure transition space between your home and the City streets." In common with many of London's new concrete and glass residential blocks there's a concierge, on hand 24/7 to service the every need of residents paying a minimum of £500,000 – which only buys a studio flat – to live in this booming part of the city.

But the lobby is out of bounds to some of those who live in the building. What the brochure doesn't mention is a second door, with a considerably less glamorous lobby, tucked away in an alley to the side of the building, alongside the trade entrance for *Prêt a Manger*. This is the entrance for One Commercial Street's affordable housing tenants.

In north-west London the developers behind Queen's Park Place are more upfront about how its 28 affordable and 116 market-rate homes will co-exist – its marketing website says the external appearance will be uniform across all properties – or "tenure blind". But inside the building the two types of resident will be treated very differently: "Affordable tenants will not have use of the main private residential entrance, private courtyard gardens or basement car and cycle parking. Services including postal delivery and refuse storage are also divided."

However, the stark difference between the entrances and, in some cases, their positioning, rankles with some of those who live there. Through the main door of One Commercial Street the lights shine brightly in the hotel-style lobby. There is luxury marble tiling and plush sofas, and a sign on the door alerts residents to the fact that the concierge is available. Round the back, the entrance to the affordable homes is a cream corridor, decorated only with grey mail boxes and a poster warning tenants that they are on CCTV and will be prosecuted if they cause any damage.

Brooke Terrelonga lives here with her nine-month-old son – they moved into a social rented flat four months ago and she was surprised to find that she wasn't allowed to use the front entrance. Her mother, who doesn't want to be named, said she felt unhappy about her daughter returning home at night to the poorly-lit alleyway. She motioned towards two lights on the wall, either side of the door, which were the only lighting in sight. She said: "It's like the cream is at the front and they've sent the rubbish to the back."

Another tenant, Judy Brown, had also expected to be able to get to her flat through the main entrance. "I call it the posh door. I feel a little bit insulted. It's segregation." Brown said that the lifts kept breaking down and she often had to take the stairs to her ninth-floor flat. "When both the lifts weren't working they did say that if you were pregnant, had a health problem or a baby in a buggy you could use the main entrance," she said. Otherwise, the tenants said, they were "locked out" of the main lobby.

Adapted from Hilary Osborne –
Published on July 25th, 2014 in *The Guardian*, London.

KEY POINT

Controversial solutions to tackle the housing issue in London

London's house prices are rising by more than 20% annually. The city also needs 63,000 new homes each year, but only a third of these are being built and more than half of all new homes in London are now purchased by foreign buyers. For low and middle income Londoners, home ownership is increasingly out of reach, rents consume an ever increasing percentage of their income, and homelessness is rising.

A number of controversial solutions have been put forward to tackle the housing issue such as moving old people to smaller flats. Enabling people to rent better properties for longer could also be a solution and London's mayor Boris Johnson launched a scheme aimed at improving rental standards in May 2014. Besides, as more than 80,000 homes in London currently stand empty, councils could charge home owners 50% more council tax if they left properties empty.

Cachez ces pauvres...

Dans certains complexes immobiliers de Londres se développe, via des entrées distinctes, une véritable ségrégation entre locataires à revenus modestes et riches propriétaires.

Notre enquête révèle l'essor d'un phénomène nouveau dans les immeubles résidentiels haut de gamme de la capitale : les promoteurs, contraints par les règlements d'urbanisme d'y inclure des logements dits « *affordable* » [bon marché], obligent les résidents les moins favorisés à emprunter des accès séparés, déjà surnommés les « *poor doors* » [portes pour pauvres]. À chaque catégorie de population son local à vélos, son local à poubelles et son hall de boîtes aux lettres.

Tracey Kellet, une chasseuse d'appartements qui sillonne Londres pour de riches clients, confirme que plusieurs complexes sont aujourd'hui dotés d'entrées différenciées « afin que les deux strates sociales n'aient pas à se croiser » : « Au lieu de verre étincelant, la façade de la partie "bon marché" est garnie de panneaux en plastique de couleur douteuse. »

Dans un immeuble sis aux abords du quartier financier de la City, nous avons découvert que les riches propriétaires entraient par un vaste hall digne de la réception d'un hôtel, tandis que l'entrée des locataires de logements sociaux se faisait par la ruelle où passent les livraisons. Avec la flambée du marché immobilier à Londres, les attentes des plus riches acquéreurs de la capitale sont montées d'un cran, et nombre de résidences se dotent aujourd'hui de parties communes dignes des plus luxueux hôtels de la planète.

« Cette tendance est une marque de mépris pour les gens ordinaires, dénonce Darren Johnson, membre de l'Assemblée de Londres pour le Parti vert. Les promoteurs proposent des appartements de luxe à de riches investisseurs qui refusent toute mixité. La mairie de Londres et les mairies de quartier ferment les yeux sur ce phénomène depuis trop longtemps : on devrait tout simplement refuser les permis de construire aux résidences qui prévoient une ségrégation dans les infrastructures ou qui refusent d'y intégrer des logements "bon marché". »

Du côté des promoteurs, on assure que c'est là un moyen de permettre aux bailleurs sociaux de maintenir leurs charges à des niveaux raisonnables en ne leur imposant pas les services premium offerts aux résidents du parc privé. Pour Peter Allen, directeur des ventes chez *Londonewcastle* (constructeur de la résidence Queens Park Place, dans le nord de Londres), ces bailleurs n'ont parfois pas les moyens de payer l'ensemble des services proposés : « Pour les architectes, la solution la plus simple est donc de proposer des offres différenciées. »

La brochure des appartements haut de gamme du complexe One Commercial Street, en lisière de la City, vante « un hall d'entrée dédié qui, dans le style élégant d'une réception d'hôtel, vous offre un sas à la fois chic et sécurisé entre votre appartement et les rues de la City ». Comme pour nombre de ces nouvelles résidences tout de verre et de béton, à One Commercial Street un concierge est présent vingt-quatre heures sur vingt-quatre et sept jours sur sept pour répondre à tous les desiderata des résidents, qui auront déboursé au minimum 500 000 livres [630 000 euros environ] pour un simple studio afin d'avoir le privilège de vivre dans ce quartier qui monte.

Reste que ce hall avec concierge n'est pas accessible à tous. Ce que la brochure ne précise pas, c'est l'existence d'une autre entrée, au hall nettement moins chic, située dans une ruelle adjacente à côté de l'accès livraisons du fast-food *Prêt à manger*. Cette entrée, c'est celle des locataires des logements sociaux du complexe One Commercial Street.

Dans le nord-ouest de Londres, les promoteurs du Queens Park Place sont plus transparents quant au mode de coexistence choisi pour les 28 logements bon marché et les 116 appartements vendus au prix du marché : sur leur site, il est assuré que l'immeuble sera « *tenure blind* » [égalitaire] en apparence, autrement dit qu'il aura le même aspect extérieur quel que soit le type de logement. À l'intérieur, en revanche, les deux catégories de résidents recevront un traitement nettement différencié : « Les occupants des logements bon marché n'auront pas accès à l'entrée principale côté résidence privée, à sa cour paysagée, ni au parking ou au local à vélos du sous-sol. De même, les services, dont la remise du courrier et la gestion des déchets, ne seront pas partagés. »

Un traitement façon « deux poids, deux mesures » qui agace plus d'un habitant de ces complexes. À l'entrée principale du One Commercial Street, une lumière vive illumine le hall. Sur un sol en marbre luxueux sont disposés de profonds canapés, et un panneau sur la porte signale aux résidents que le concierge est à leur disposition. À l'arrière, l'entrée « bon marché » se résume à un couloir couleur crème, seulement paré de boîtes aux lettres grises et d'une affichette rappelant que l'immeuble est sous vidéosurveillance et que toute dégradation est passible de poursuites.

Brooke Terrelonga vit ici avec son fils de neuf mois : quand ils sont arrivés dans ce logement social, il y a quatre mois, elle s'est étonnée de ne pas pouvoir emprunter l'entrée principale. Sa mère, qui préfère garder l'anonymat, nous dit s'inquiéter à l'idée que le soir sa fille doive passer par la ruelle mal éclairée – elle désigne les deux lampadaires, un de chaque côté de la porte, qui sont le seul éclairage. « On garde l'élite en façade et on cache les rebuts à l'arrière », bougonne-t-elle.

Judy Brown, locataire elle aussi, s'attendait également à pouvoir rejoindre son appartement par l'entrée en façade. « Je l'appelle "la porte des snobs". Franchement, je me sens un peu insultée. C'est de la ségrégation. » Les ascenseurs sont sans cesse en panne, l'obligeant à monter à pied jusqu'au neuvième étage, où elle vit. « Quand nos deux ascenseurs ont été hors service, on nous a bien dit que les femmes enceintes, les personnes malades et les parents d'enfants en bas âge pouvaient utiliser l'entrée principale », précise Judy Brown. Mais, le reste du temps, ces locataires sont, selon leurs propres termes, « tenus à l'écart » du grand hall.

D'après Hilary Osborne – Publié le 25 juillet 2014 dans *The Guardian* (extraits), Londres. Extrait de *Courrier International*.

VOCABULARY TO REMEMBER!

- **a growing trend**: *une tendance à la hausse, un phénomène en plein essor*
- **upmarket**: *haut de gamme*
- **to be required to**: *être contraint à*
- **affordable**: *bon marché*
- **rather than**: *plutôt que, au lieu de*
- **as the London housing market has boomed**: *avec la flambée du marché immobilier à Londres*
- **expectations**: *attentes*
- **contempt**: *le mépris*
- **to boast**: *vanter*
- **otherwise**: *le reste du temps, sinon*

Scottish Independence: Old Kingdom, New Settlement

For the whole British political class, this is the morning after the night before. Washington may heave a sigh of relief, and European leaders from Madrid to Brussels rejoice that secessionist urges across the continent have now been held in check. But no such complacency is appropriate here. Despite the decisive scale of the No victory, this extraordinary and historic referendum, which prompted political participation on a level never seen before, has landed all parties and all leaders in *terra incognita*.

Alex Salmond, despite nearly doubling his party's support over the two-year campaign, has stepped down as Scottish First Minister and leader of the SNP, accepting that his life's work has now ended. David Cameron, bounced into making extravagant constitutional promises on the hoof to attempt to salvage the No campaign at the 11th hour, is now required to make good on those pledges to an impossibly tight timetable.

And if Mr Cameron carries through on his promise to balance increased powers for the Scottish Parliament with more votes for English MPs at Westminster on specifically English issues, the Labour leader could face the dizzying prospect of winning the next general election yet then being unable to pass key measures as a result of being deprived of the votes of Scottish Labour MPs.

Nor is this disorientation, the sense of having been pitched into a brave and baffling new world, confined to professional politicians. It will take all of us a while to get our bearings. In the process, some of our most settled habits will have to change.

In the first place, London will have to get used to the fact that it is not the centre of the world and the only place that really counts. Yesterday morning, the Cornish and Welsh nationalists wasted no time in demanding a Cornish assembly and more powers for Wales, respectively.

The metropolitan instinct is to flick such irritating voices away like so many midges. But it is that sort of arrogance and sense of entitlement that led directly to the panic and desperation of the past month – the sudden realisation that the Scots were in earnest, and might actually get what they wanted and break away.

Metropolitan conceit has paved the way for the rapid and apparently irreversible centralisation of power that we have witnessed in the three and a half decades since Margaret Thatcher came to power. The UK is now one of the most centralised states in the rich world, with more of its public spending coming from central government than practically any other OECD country. Its local government is weaker than any comparable country, including France.

The concomitant of the increasingly metropolitan focus of politics was a steady drop in the turnout at elections, a steep decline in the membership of parties, a gnawing and corrosive apathy and a pervading sense that politicians are all the same, all to some extent corrupt and equally remote from the concerns of the people. This slow, steady process of estrangement of the public from politics is extremely dangerous. But it is an ailment which can be cured – as this referendum campaign has demonstrated.

It has been an amazing example of democracy in action, with hundreds of thousands of normally apolitical people caught up in the debate and finally queuing in staggering numbers to make their mark. As Leanne Wood, the head of Plaid Cymru, put it on Thursday night: "This debate has been about where power lies." It's time for the rest of the country to say very clearly that it lies with the people. If we say that with sufficient vigour, and invest the same sort of passion that the Scots have shown, it will be the first step towards making our democracy fit for the future.

The Independent – September 20th, 2014

KEY POINT

The referendum on Scottish Independence took place in Scotland on 18 September 2014. The "No" side won with 55% voting against independence and 45% voting in favour. The turnout of 84.6% was the highest recorded for an election or a referendum in the UK. After voters rejected independence, Alex Salmond said he would step down as Scottish First Minister and that he would also resign as leader of the Scottish National Party which he had led for a total of twenty years. Nicola Sturgeon replaced Alex Salmond and became Scotland's first female First Minister in November 2014. The SNP which was founded in 1934 is now the third largest party in the UK. Following the results of the referendum, the UK Prime Minister David Cameron said the three main unionist parties at Westminster would follow through with their pledge of more powers for the Scottish Parliament. The Prime Minister also acknowledged that the people of England, Wales and Northern Ireland must have a bigger say over their affairs.

UN ARTICLE DU *MONDE* À CONSULTER :

- **Ecosse, Irlande du Nord : du Brexit au Royaume désuni** p. 62
(Philippe Bernard, *Le Monde* daté du 13.03.2017)

Rien ne sera plus comme avant

La classe politique britannique s'est réveillée le lendemain du vote dans un monde nouveau. Washington a poussé un soupir de soulagement et, de Madrid à Bruxelles, les chefs d'État européens se sont félicités que les velléités séparatistes qui s'étaient exprimées dans le reste du continent aient été freinées. Mais l'autosatisfaction est loin d'être de mise. Malgré la nette victoire du « non », ce référendum historique et hors du commun, qui a affiché un taux de participation record, a également parachuté tous les responsables politiques en *terra incognita*.

Bien qu'il ait fait passer le nombre d'adhérents à son parti du simple au double ou presque pendant les deux années qu'a duré la campagne, Alex Salmond a donné sa démission des postes de chef du gouvernement écossais et de dirigeant du parti national écossais (SNP), reconnaissant ainsi que l'œuvre de sa vie était maintenant terminée. David Cameron, poussé à improviser des promesses constitutionnelles extravagantes à la dernière minute pour sauver la campagne en faveur du « non », va maintenant devoir agir dans des délais si serrés que cela semble impossible.

Si M. Cameron tient sa promesse d'accroître les pouvoirs du Parlement écossais et de réserver l'exclusivité du vote aux députés anglais sur les questions qui ne concernent que l'Angleterre, le leader du parti travailliste [Ed Milliband] risque d'affronter une possibilité vertigineuse : se retrouver vainqueur des prochaines élections législatives et ne pas pouvoir faire adopter des mesures importantes parce qu'il sera privé des voix des députés travaillistes écossais.

Les professionnels de la politique ne sont pas les seuls à éprouver cette désorientation, ce sentiment d'avoir atterri dans un monde aussi nouveau que déconcertant. Il va tous nous falloir un moment pour prendre nos marques. Nous allons devoir changer quelques coutumes fortement ancrées.

Tout d'abord, Londres va devoir s'habituer à ne plus être le centre du monde ni le seul endroit qui compte. Les nationalistes cornouaillais et gallois n'ont pas perdu de temps : dès dimanche matin, les premiers ont exigé une assemblée et les seconds davantage de pouvoirs.

Le réflexe londonien est de traiter ces voix indépendantistes comme des moucherons agaçants que l'on chasse d'une chiquenaude. Mais c'est justement ce genre d'arrogance et de sentiment de supériorité qui ont engendré la panique et les solutions désespérées proposées le mois dernier, dues à la soudaine prise de conscience que les Écossais ne plaisantaient pas, qu'ils risquaient fort d'obtenir ce qu'ils voulaient et de faire sécession.

Le mépris londonien a favorisé la centralisation rapide et en apparence irréversible du pouvoir à laquelle nous avons assisté ces trois dernières décennies, depuis la prise de fonctions de Margaret Thatcher. Le Royaume-Uni est aujourd'hui l'un des États les plus centralisés du « monde riche » : les dépenses du gouvernement central sont plus élevées que dans tous les autres pays de l'OCDE ou presque. Et ses institutions locales sont plus faibles que dans n'importe quel autre pays comparable, y compris la France.

Cette concentration de plus en plus importante du pouvoir dans la capitale est allée de pair avec une diminution constante du taux de participation aux élections, une baisse importante du nombre d'adhérents à un parti politique, une apathie insidieuse et destructrice, et le sentiment généralisé que les politiciens sont tous les mêmes, qu'ils sont tous plus ou moins corrompus et éloignés des préoccupations des gens. Ce lent processus d'aliénation entre le peuple et la politique est extrêmement dangereux. Mais c'est une maladie qui peut se soigner, comme l'a montré la campagne pour le référendum.

Elle a été un exemple fantastique de démocratie en action. Des centaines de milliers de personnes normalement apolitiques ont été entraînées dans le débat et ont fini par faire la queue en nombre stupéfiant pour faire entendre leur voix. Comme l'a dit Leanne Wood, la chef du Plaid Cymru [parti nationaliste gallois], jeudi dernier : « Ce débat portait en fait sur la question de savoir qui détient le pouvoir. »

Il est temps pour le reste du pays de dire très clairement que le pouvoir est détenu par le peuple. Si nous le disons avec assez de force et avec autant de passion que les Écossais, ce sera un premier pas pour adapter notre démocratie à l'avenir.

Publié le 20 septembre 2014 dans *The Independent* (extraits), Londres. Extrait de *Courrier International*

VOCABULARY TO REMEMBER!

- **to step down**: *démissionner*
- **increased powers**: *des pouvoirs accrus*
- **the Labour party**: *le parti travailliste*
- **MPs = Members of Parliament**: *députés*
- **deprived of**: *privé de*
- **Cornish**: *cornouaillais (Cornwall: Cornouailles)*
- **Welsh**: *gallois (Wales : Pays de Galles)*
- **to waste no time**: *ne pas perdre de temps*
- **to demand**: *exiger*
- **to break away**: *faire sécession*
- **to pave the way for**: *favoriser, ouvrir la voie à*
- **to witness**: *assister, être le témoin de*
- **public spending**: *les dépenses publiques*
- **weak**: *faible*
- **a steady drop**: *une diminution constante*
- **turnout**: *le taux de participation*
- **a steep decline**: *une baisse importante*
- **remote from concerns of the people**: *éloigné des préoccupations des gens*
- **an ailment**: *une maladie*

Edith Wharton's *The Age of Innocence* (1920)

Madame Olenska put her hand on his arm, and he noticed that the hand was ungloved, and remembered how he had kept his eyes fixed on it the evening that he had sat with her in the little Twenty-third Street drawing-room. All the beauty that had forsaken her face seemed to have taken refuge in the long pale fingers and faintly dimpled knuckles on his sleeve, and he said to himself: "If it were only to see her hand again I should have to follow her –."

It was only at an entertainment ostensibly offered to a "foreign visitor" that Mrs van der Luyden could suffer the diminution of being placed on her host's left. The fact of Mme Olenska's "foreignness" could hardly have been more adroitly emphasized than by this farewell tribute: and Mrs van der Luyden accepted her displacement with an affability which left no doubt as to her approval. There were certain things, that had to be done, and if done at all, done handsomely and thoroughly; and one of these, in the old New York code, was the tribal rally around a kinswoman about to be eliminated from the tribe. There was nothing on earth that the Wellands and Mingotts would not have done to proclaim their unalterable affection for the Countess Olenska now that her passage to Europe was engaged; and Archer, at the head of his table, sat marvelling at the silent untiring activity with which her popularity had been retrieved, grievances against her silenced, her past countenanced, and her present irradiated by the family approval. Mrs van der Luyden shone on her with the dim benevolence which was her nearest approach to cordiality, and Mr van der Luyden, from his seat at May's right, cast down the table glances plainly intended to justify all the carnations he had sent from Skuytercliff.

Archer, who seemed to be assisting at the scene in a state of odd imponderability, as if he floated somewhere between chandelier and ceiling, wondered at nothing so much as his own share in the proceedings. As his glance travelled from one placid well-fed face to another he saw all the harmless-looking people engaged upon May's canvas-backs as a band of dumb conspirators, and himself and the pale woman on his right as the centre of their conspiracy. And then it came over him, in a vast flash made up of many broken gleams, that to all of them he and Madame Olenska were lovers, lovers in the extreme sense peculiar to "foreign" vocabularies. He guessed himself to have been, for months, the centre of countless silently observing eyes and patiently listening ears, he understood that, by means as yet unknown to him, the separation between himself and the partner of his guilt had been achieved, and that now the whole tribe had rallied about his wife on the tacit assumption that nobody knew anything, or had ever imagined anything, and that the occasion of the entertainment was simply May Archer's natural desire to take an affectionate leave of her friend and cousin.

DICTIONARY

- **ungloved**: without gloves
- **to forsake (forsook/forsaken)**: to leave for ever
- **to emphasise**: to stress, underline
- **farewell**: good bye
- **tribute**: something done to show respect or admiration for someone
- **approval**: favourable opinion
- **handsomely**: generously
- **thoroughly**: completely
- **a rally**: a meeting
- **a kinswoman**: a relative
- **to retrieve**: to regain
- **grievances**: complaints
- **dim**: indistinct
- **benevolence**: goodness
- **to cast glances**: to give quick short looks
- **carnations**: flowers (*œillets*)
- **odd**: unusual
- **dumb**: silent
- **to dread**: to fear
- **ill-bred**: rude

MOTS CLÉS en lien avec la thématique

NOUNS

- censorship: *la censure*
- freedom of speech: *la liberté d'expression*
- the establishment: *l'establishment, l'élite dominante*
- dictatorship: *la dictature*
- democracy: *la démocratie*
- a law: *une loi*
- a politician: *un homme politique*
- an opponent: *un adversaire*
- a supporter, an advocate: *un partisan*
- diplomacy: *la diplomatie*
- a diplomat: *un diplomate*
- a counterpart: *un homologue*

Ex.: The Prime Minister met his Italian **counterpart** yesterday in Rome.

- a spokesperson: *un porte-parole*
- a poll : *un scrutin (ou un sondage)*
- a landslide victory: *une victoire écrasante*

Ex.: He won **a landslide victory** in the presidential **poll**.

- the political landscape: *le paysage politique*
- talks: *des discussions, des pour-parlers*
- a debate: *un débat*
- a hot potato issue: *un sujet brûlant, une question controversée*

Ex.: The abortion **issue** is a political **hot potato** in the US.

ADJECTIVES

- powerful: *puissant*
- powerless: *impuissant*
- widespread: *répandu*

VERBS

- to rule: *régner, gouverner*
- to swear in (**swore/sworn**): *faire prêter serment à*

Ex.: Barack Obama was **sworn in** for a second term as US President in January 2012.

- to overthrow (**overthrew/overthrown**): *renverser (un régime, un gouvernement)*

Ex.: There was an attempt **to overthrow** the government.

- to drive out: *chasser*
- to step down, to resign: *démissionner*

Ex.: The President refused **to step down/to resign**.

It was the old New York way of taking life without "effusion of blood": the way of people who dreaded scandal more than disease, who placed decency above courage, and who considered that nothing was more ill-bred than "scenes", except the behaviour of those who gave rise to them.
As these thoughts succeeded each other in his mind Archer felt like a prisoner in the centre of an armed camp. He looked about the table, and guessed at the inexorableness of his captors from the tone in which, over the asparagus from Florida, they were dealing with Beaufort and his wife. "It's to show me", he thought, "what would happen to ME – " and a deathly sense of the superiority of implication and analogy over direct action, and of silence over rash words, closed in on him like the doors of the family vault.

Edith Wharton, *The Age of Innocence* (1920)

FOCUS ON...

Challenging old codes

The Age of Innocence, a film adaptation by Martin Scorsese (1993)

From *The House of Mirth* (1905) to *The Custom of the Country* (1913) to *The Age of Innocence*, Edith Wharton's subject is the changing scene of New York City, the foibles of its fashionable elites and the ambitions of the "new people" who she felt threatened its traditional culture.
The Age of Innocence is an accurate portrayal of how the 19th century East Coast American Upper Class lived and it questions the morals of 1870s New York society. The novel is about a gentleman who is engaged to be married, but falls in love with another woman who is separated from her husband and about to divorce. Wharton published the book in 1920, some 40-odd years after the time in which the story is set, but she was 58 years old and very familiar with the subject matter as she had been born and raised in the environment she describes. Even in the first quarter of the 20th century divorce was considered something of a taboo, so the book caused quite a stir.
The Age of Innocence won the Pulitzer Prize in 1921, making Wharton the first woman to ever win the prize.

"It was the old New York way of taking life without "effusion of blood": the way of people who dreaded scandal more than disease, who placed decency above courage, and who considered that nothing was more ill-bred than "scenes", except the behaviour of those who gave rise to them."

S'EXPRIMER

EXPRESSING OBLIGATION: HAVE TO

• "If it were only to see her hand again I should **have to** follow her."
"There were certain things that **had to** be done."
"**Have to**" is used to explain that something is **necessary**.
Ex.: I **have to** go and see her this afternoon.
• **"Must"** is also used to express that something is **necessary**. We do not use "to" after "must".
Ex.: I **must** finish my homework tonight.
• There is a difference between "must" and "have to" in some contexts. We use "**have to**" to describe **official rules**; we also use "**have to**" when a rule is made by someone else.
Ex.: English pupils **have to** wear a uniform.
• In everyday speech, we use "**have got to**" instead of "have to".
• "**Mustn't**" and "**don't have to**" have different meanings.
"**Mustn't**" describes an action which is **forbidden**.
Ex.: You **mustn't** drive on the right in England.
"**Don't have to**" describes an action which is **not necessary**.
Ex.: You **don't have to** wait for me.
• **There is no past form of "must"**. We use "**had to**".
Ex.: When I was at school I **had to** wear a uniform but my cousin **didn't have to** wear one.

USING THE PAST PERFECT

• "He noticed that the hand was ungloved, and remembered how he **had kept** his eyes fixed on it the evening that he **had sat** with her in the little Twenty-third Street drawing-room."
The **past perfect** is formed with **had + past participle**.
The past perfect is used when we need to make clear that **one event in the past happened before another event in the past**.
Ex.: When I arrived at my friend's house, she **had** already **left**.
Ex.: I thought I **had seen** the film before, but I hadn't.

Questions de compréhension

A. Choose the right answer.

1. The scene takes place ......

a. in New York.

b. in Europe.

2. Archer is ......

a. single

b. married.

3. The guests are ......

a. in the drawing room.

b. in the dining room.

4. May is ......

a. Archer's wife.

b. Archer's cousin.

5. Countess Olenska is ......

a. May's cousin.

b. Archer's cousin.

6. Countess Olenska ......

a. has just arrived in America.

b. is about to leave America.

B. Answer the questions using your own words.

1. Who is "the kinswoman about to be eliminated from the tribe"?

2. Who is the "foreign visitor"?

3. What form does "the tribal rally" take in this text?

4. What does Archer understand during the dinner?

5. Why are the guests described as conspirators?

6. "[...] now the whole tribe had rallied about his wife on the tacit assumption that nobody knew anything, or had ever imagined anything, and that the occasion of the entertainment was simply May Archer's natural desire to take an affectionate leave of her friend and cousin." What does this sentence show about the people around Archer?

7. What does Archer feel like at the end of the text?

BOÎTE À OUTILS : LE PASSIF

• "The fact of Mme Olenska's "foreignness" could hardly **have been** more adroitly **emphasized** than **by** this farewell tribute."
"There were certain things that had **to be done**."
"Archer [...] sat marvelling at the silent untiring activity with which her **popularity had been retrieved**, grievances against her **silenced**, her past **countenanced**, and her present **irradiated by** the family approval."

*Vous noterez l'utilisation du **passif** dans les phrases ci-dessus.*
*Pour rappel, le passif se forme ainsi : « **to be** » **au temps voulu + participe passé**.*
Dans la phrase 1 (« have been emphasized *»), «* to be *» est au* present perfect.
Dans la phrase 2 (« had to be done *»), «* to be *» est à l'infinitif.*
Dans la phrase 3, « had been retrieved *», «* to be *» est au plus-que-parfait.*

• ***Le passif est plus employé en anglais qu'en français** ; en français, on utilisera « on » ou des verbes réfléchis alors qu'en anglais on utilisera le passif.*
Ex.: The match **was postponed**. *(**On** a reporté le match.)*
Ex.: This word can **be written** in two ways. *(Ce mot peut **s'écrire** de deux façons.)*

• *La préposition «* **by** *» sert à introduire **le complément d'agent** (mais celui-ci est omis lorsqu'il ne présente pas d'intérêt particulier).*
Ex.: That picture **was painted by** Francis Bacon. *Ici, la préposition «* by *» est indispensable.*

• *Lorsque la phrase active a deux compléments d'objet, c'est généralement **le complément d'objet indirect qui devient le sujet de la voix passive**.*
Ex.: They gave **me** a book. *(forme active)*/**I was given** a book. *(forme passive)*

Exercices de grammaire

A. Rewrite each sentence with a passive verb.

1. People speak English all over the world.

2. They have elected a new president.

3. They are rebuilding the damaged building.

4. Someone offered him a new job.

5. They are questioning her.

6. They have stolen my bag.

7. They don't serve drinks after 11pm.

8. They will announce the results of the competition tomorrow.

9. Somebody will meet you at the train station.

10. The clubs have postponed the match.

11. Students write most of this magazine.

12. Burglars stole my laptop.

B. Translate into English the following sentences using the passive.

1. *Il était content de ne pas être sélectionné.*

2. *Je déteste qu'on m'observe.*

3. *On te demande au téléphone.*

C. Choose the correct word underlined in each sentence.

1. The children were <u>took/taken/taking</u> to the circus.

2. I was <u>sending/send/sent</u> here by my parents.

3. She has been <u>offer/offering/offered</u> a new job in New Zealand.

4. She had her windows <u>breaking/broke/broken</u> by burglars.

Sujet inédit, séries technologiques, LV1

EXPRESSION ÉCRITE : Using your own experience, explain how young people gradually gain independence from their parents. Illustrate with examples.

Analyse du sujet

Il s'agit d'exprimer votre point de vue sur la prise d'indépendance progressive des jeunes gens par rapport à leurs parents dans un essai argumentatif. Comment ce processus d'émancipation s'organise-t-il aujourd'hui ? Vous devez illustrer votre réponse avec des exemples.

Repères essentiels

– Préparez vos idées en suivant la progression de l'âge et le développement de l'indépendance.
– Rédigez votre réponse en évitant d'exprimer les idées pour lesquelles vous ne maîtrisez pas l'anglais.
– Contrôlez la qualité de votre anglais.

Proposition de corrigé

I think that to explain how people gradually gain independence from their parents, we have to consider the period of time when children have become teenagers and when they come of age to become adults. First of all, I would say that it depends on how old children are. Of course when they are young children or young teenagers, it seems quite difficult for them to go against their parents' will which is the necessary phase to become independent. As a consequence they have to impose on them a certain number of things and values children do not necessarily agree with (on account of their age and their thirst to do as they have decided). During their childhood and their youth they usually follow their parents' will even if sometimes they are quite reluctant, but that's how it all starts. Later when they grow older and after, when they come of age, they often try to talk things over with their parents to convince them they are right and should be allowed to do as they want when their decisions do not meet their parents' approval. Most parents always want the best for their children and often think that what they want or say is good for them and tend to refuse their children the right to decide on their own. This can still be true when children have become adults. I think that there comes a time when children should make their own decisions and should go against their parents' will because one has to stand on one's own two feet sooner or later and has to be given the possibility to make his own choices, even if it is sometimes difficult.

Parents can't always dictate to their children what they have to do. Parents had better give their children advice and tell them what they should think or shouldn't do but they must let them make the final decision. By gradually giving the possibility to their children to choose, to decide, parents help them to become mature, self-confident and give them the opportunity to build their own personality and consequently to become independent and adult.

Sujet 13, Sujet inédit, séries ES, S, L, LV2

EXPRESSION ÉCRITE : Are parental values the only values that can influence people's lives? Justify your answer.

Analyse du sujet

Il s'agit d'exprimer dans un essai argumentatif votre point de vue sur le rôle que jouent les valeurs parentales dans nos vies. Ces valeurs parentales sont-elles les seules qui nous guident dans nos choix de vie ?

Proposition de corrigé

Parental values are extremely important in people's lives but I believe that they are not the only values which have an influence on our lives. Everybody agrees to say that childhood is a determining period for our future. This is when our parents teach us all the basics of proper behaviour. Our parents are our role models as kids and we learn from them. The way our parents bring us up, the way they behave with other people and the way they behave with us as well as the values they teach us will have a strong influence on our lives and on the way we behave and think once we are adults. If, for instance, they tell us how important it is to be tolerant and open-minded, these values will probably stay with us for the rest of our lives. However, even though I believe parental values are the most influential values in our lives, I think that other values can be very influential too. School is also a major place where people learn how to feel, think and act. We meet friends who have been raised differently and we meet teachers who may teach us different values. We may also be influenced by religious values. If we believe in God, our faith will have an impact on the decisions we make and on how we behave. Besides, we may be influenced by the experiences we have. As we get older, we go through different experiences, we start to think for ourselves and we may question the parental values we have been taught. When we travel, for example, we find out about different cultures, different ways of thinking and different values, it gives us a new perspective on life and we may change what we believe in. In conclusion, I would say that even though parental values have a great influence on our lives, other values can be influential too.

NOTIONS CLÉS

LES DIFFÉRENTS ÂGES

- a baby: *un bébé*
- a child/a kid: *un enfant*
- chidren/kids: *des enfants*
- childhood: *l'enfance*
- a teenager: *un adolescent*
- adolescence: *l'adolescence*
- an adult: *un adulte*
- a grown-up: *un adulte* *(terme utilisé par ou pour les enfants, signifie littéralement « qui a grandi », « un grand »)*
- adulthood: *l'âge adulte*
- the elderly: *les personnes âgées*

LES LIENS FAMILIAUX

- a family: *une famille*
- parents: *des parents*
- parenthood: *la parentalité*
- a mother: *une mère*
- a father: *un père*
- a brother: *un frère*
- a sister: *une sœur*

LE RÔLE DES PARENTS

- role models/parental values/education
- to teach/to bring children up/to educate/to raise

LA NOTION D'INFLUENCE

- influence/impact/control/guidance
- to influence/to affect/to determine/to guide

LA NOTION D'EXPÉRIENCE

- experience/discovery/encounter/knowledge
- to experience/to learn/to discover

LA NOTION D'INDÉPENDANCE

- to be independent/self-supporting/self-sustaining
- to stand on one's own two feet/to think for oneself/to make one's own decisions

LA NOTION D'AUTORITÉ ET DE RESPONSABILITÉ

- authority/respect/obedience
- to obey/to comply with/to follow the rules/to behave
- to reject the rules/to disobey/disobedience/noncompliance/to rebel against
- good/bad behaviour

Colin Gordon : « *La ségrégation raciale contribue au déclin des villes américaines* »

Après les émeutes de Ferguson (Missouri) en août 2014, l'historien Colin Gordon revient sur l'histoire des discriminations à Saint-Louis.

Le 9 août, un jeune Noir a été tué dans des conditions controversées par un policier blanc à Ferguson, une banlieue de Saint-Louis (Missouri). Cette mort a déclenché aussitôt un mouvement ponctué de violences dénonçant des pratiques policières discriminatoires. Il a contraint le gouverneur démocrate de cet État du Midwest à ordonner brièvement le déploiement de la Garde nationale. La police municipale de Ferguson ne compte que trois Afro-Américains, alors qu'ils sont devenus majoritaires (67 %) dans cette ville au cours des dernières années.
Historien, spécialiste de politiques publiques et contributeur régulier à la revue américaine *Dissent*, l'Américain Colin Gordon (université d'Iowa) a consacré un ouvrage, en 2008, à l'articulation entre la ségrégation et le déclin de la ville de Saint-Louis, qui fut, au début du XXe siècle, la quatrième des États-Unis en termes de population (« *Cartographie d'un déclin. Saint-Louis et le destin de la ville américaine* », université de Pennsylvanie).

En 1904, Saint-Louis accueille les Jeux olympiques et l'Exposition universelle. Pourquoi n'est-elle plus aujourd'hui que la cinquante-troisième ville des États-Unis ?

Au début du XXe siècle, Saint-Louis est une ville déjà ancienne, dont l'économie et l'industrie reposent essentiellement sur le fleuve Mississippi. Elle amorce son déclin avant la première guerre mondiale, c'est-à-dire avant la plupart des villes américaines. Le commerce lié au fleuve est remplacé par celui du chemin de fer et elle commence à être marginalisée par les villes de Chicago et de Détroit.

La ségrégation est-elle alors en place ?

À l'époque, la population noire est concentrée principalement dans un quartier du nord de la ville et dans de très rares poches du comté. Elle ne représente qu'environ 5 % de la population totale. Elle est liée à la grande migration de la seconde moitié du XIXe siècle, c'est-à-dire au déplacement de la population noire en dehors du Sud, vers le centre des villes du Nord, après la fin de l'esclavage et de la guerre civile. Les Noirs sont attirés par le boom de l'industrie et l'espoir de trouver du travail.

Comment se structure la ségrégation ?

En 1917, une émeute raciale a lieu dans l'est de Saint-Louis en raison des discriminations à l'emploi et au logement, des violences policières… Ce soulèvement effraie de nombreux Blancs qui vivent là. C'est à ce moment-là, alors que la première guerre mondiale touche à sa fin, qu'est mise en place une politique restrictive d'accès à la propriété qui vise à empêcher les Noirs de vivre dans de larges parties de la ville. Un zonage racial est adopté au niveau municipal. Il est annulé par la Cour suprême mais les sociétés immobilières interviennent avec des contrats spécifiques qui aboutissent au même résultat : l'immobilisation de la population noire dans le nord de la ville. Ces contrats produisent leurs effets jusqu'à une décision de la Cour suprême, en 1947 : elle statue au sujet d'un contentieux qui a pour théâtre Saint-Louis.

Une nouvelle fois, la Cour suprême limite cette politique de séparation ?

Oui, mais le mal est fait. La plus grande migration d'Afro-Américains vers Saint-Louis intervient en effet pendant la Seconde Guerre mondiale, alors que ces pratiques sont toujours en place. Ces nouvelles populations se concentrent donc dans les mêmes quartiers. Ce qui se passe ensuite, c'est que les Blancs qui vivent à proximité partent vers la banlieue. Ils choisissent des endroits où ils pourront acheter de grands terrains et bâtir de grandes maisons, ce qui reste financièrement hors de portée des Noirs. Dans ces banlieues, on prend d'ailleurs soin de ne pas autoriser les immeubles collectifs, ce qui revient à différencier les populations par les revenus. On aboutit à une métropole très ségréguée, avec des banlieues aisées blanches et un centre-ville noir et pauvre.
C'est d'ailleurs à cette époque que Saint-Louis commence à s'effondrer. Sa population a alors atteint près de 900 000 habitants (300 000 aujourd'hui), le maximum de son histoire, mais une partie de ces habitants commencent à fuir parce que les services se dégradent. Dans les années 1950 et 1960, la population blanche quitte la ville. Dans les années 1970, c'est la population noire qui bouge en direction de villes de banlieue comme Ferguson, pour y trouver de meilleures conditions de vie. Ce qui accélère un déplacement des Blancs qui résident alors à Ferguson : ils partent vers d'autres banlieues.

Le mouvement pour les droits civiques, à partir des années 1960, a-t-il eu des effets à Saint-Louis ?

Ce mouvement n'ignore pas Saint-Louis, mais il est plutôt tourné vers les villes du Sud et vise les restrictions de vote et d'expression politique. Ce n'est que plus tard que la lutte s'étend à la question du logement.
En 1968, la Cour suprême rend une décision qui restreint la ségrégation par le logement mais elle n'a pas un grand effet sur le terrain : ce qui est en jeu, à ce moment-là, ce ne sont pas les lois ou les réglementations, mais le départ de la population blanche d'une banlieue vers une autre et son remplacement par une population noire moins aisée. Ce mouvement accentue la disparité entre les banlieues, qui ont des majorités écrasantes – soit blanche, soit noire.

Des politiques ont pourtant été engagées pour revitaliser la ville de Saint-Louis. Quels résultats ont-elles eu ?

Il y a eu beaucoup d'efforts destinés à bâtir un nouveau centre-ville et

POURQUOI CET ARTICLE ?

Cet entretien avec l'historien Colin Gordon fait évidemment écho à l'article du *Washington Post* reproduit en page 44, consacré aux événements survenus dans le Missouri suite à la mort du jeune afro-américain Michael Brown, tué par un policier blanc au cours de l'été 2014. Cet éclairage complémentaire permet de mettre en perspective la question de la discrimination raciale aux États-Unis, et plus particulièrement à Saint-Louis, en la replaçant dans son contexte historique local.

de nouveaux équipements – stade de base-ball, centre de conventions, logements... – mais aucun n'a eu un effet significatif sur le déclin de la ville. Les responsables locaux ont longtemps espéré que la population repartirait à la hausse au cours de la dernière décennie, entre 2000 à 2010, mais cela n'a pas été le cas.

Face à ce déclin et à ces mouvements de population, quelle a été la position de l'État du Missouri ?

L'État du Missouri n'accorde pas trop d'attention à ses villes, qu'il s'agisse de Saint-Louis ou de Kansas City. L'organisation de la politique à l'échelle de l'État fait que les villes y sont sous-représentées et qu'elles n'ont pas le poids politique que devrait leur conférer leur population. Il faut aussi tenir compte d'une composante raciste, car ces villes sont considérées comme noires. Au niveau de l'État, ce sont plutôt les nouvelles banlieues qui sont privilégiées.

Saint-Louis est-elle unique dans la fabrique de son déclin ?

La persistance de ce déclin sur des décennies en fait un cas à part, mais il existe d'autres villes comparables à Saint-Louis aux États-Unis. Certaines vieilles villes industrielles comme Détroit, Cleveland, Cincinnati ou Buffalo ont perdu jusqu'à la moitié de leur population sur deux générations. La ségrégation raciale contribue également à ce déclin : elles ont eu des stratégies immobilières qui ont renforcé la ségrégation, même si le cas de Saint-Louis est unique de ce point de vue.

Vous êtes spécialiste de politiques publiques, quelles décisions pourraient permettre de lutter contre ces évolutions ?

La première, c'est d'avoir un acteur politique, à l'échelle de la métropole, qui ait la vision d'un développement économique faisant sens à l'échelle de toute la région. C'est une idée qui fait son chemin, notamment pour des questions d'efficacité, parce que tout le monde voit bien qu'il n'y a aucun gagnant dans le système actuel.
Une fois qu'on dispose d'une gouvernance au niveau de la métropole, on peut promouvoir plus de mixité dans les modes de logement, ce qui permet d'obtenir une fiscalité plus équilibrée et donc d'éviter les dérives d'aujourd'hui – des écoles très pauvres dans des quartiers défavorisés, ce qui entretient la pauvreté. Mais cela reste un très long chemin.

Propos recueillis par Gilles Paris, *Le Monde* daté du 30.08.2014

Sadiq Khan, du HLM à la mairie de Londres

Travailliste, fils de chauffeur de bus pakistanais, il est le premier maire musulman d'une capitale occidentale.

Je serai le meilleur maire pour Londres. » Rencontré quelques jours avant son élection à la tête de la capitale britannique, vendredi 6 mai, Sadiq Khan, 45 ans, semble à première vue conforter le portrait qu'en livrent ses adversaires : sûr de lui jusqu'à l'arrogance. *« Il ne perd jamais »*, dit de lui l'un de ses conseillers, en rappelant que l'élu travailliste a appris la boxe dans son enfance. Pourtant, quand cet homme trapu aux cheveux grisonnants et aux yeux de félin prend la parole sous la pluie au milieu d'une soixantaine d'habitants de Bexley, en grande banlieue de Londres, pour défendre un espace vert menacé par des promoteurs, son empathie, son charisme et son éloquence paraissent relever de l'évidence.
« Fils d'immigré pakistanais et à l'aise, c'est un oxymore pour vous ? », tacle-t-il un peu plus tard, au cours d'un entretien dans un café italien. *« Mon parcours symbolise le fait que Londres est une ville formidable. J'aime cette cité qui m'a donné toutes mes chances »*, résume alors celui qui a été élu à la tête de la capitale britannique en rassemblant 57 % des suffrages sur son nom. Qu'il le veuille ou non, l'accession de ce fils de famille modeste et de foi musulmane au sommet d'une des villes les plus cosmopolites du monde (8,7 millions d'habitants, dont 1 million de musulmans) est regardée comme un événement. Toutes proportions gardées, Sadiq Khan serait à Londres ce que Barack Obama a été aux Etats-Unis. Loin de la masquer, il a porté sa différence en bannière pendant toute la campagne.
De fait, s'il y a deux choses qu'aucun Londonien ne peut ignorer à propos de Sadiq Khan, c'est qu'il est le fils d'un chauffeur de bus pakistanais et qu'il est musulman. Ces deux détails biographiques, pas nécessairement engageants pour tous les électeurs, il les a mis en avant comme ses principaux atouts.
Le fils de chauffeur de bus ? Sadiq Khan posait sur ses dépliants glissés dans toutes les boîtes aux lettres devant un magnifique « double-decker » rutilant, symbole du bus 44 qu'a conduit son père pendant des années. Ancien ministre travailliste des transports, il promet de geler le prix des transports en commun, dont il attribue le coût prohibitif – le plus élevé d'Europe – à la gestion de son prédécesseur, le conservateur Boris Johnson.

« Garçon élevé en HLM »

Le musulman britannique ? Croyant, pratiquant, il est le mieux placé, assure-t-il, pour *« combattre l'extrémisme »* en incitant la grande masse modérée de ses coreligionnaires à *« dénoncer à haute voix l'extrémisme »*. Les musulmans britanniques *« doivent faire davantage pour extirper ce cancer »*, a-t-il déclaré en novembre 2015, après les attentats de Paris. Lui, qui se présente comme *« le maire de tous les Londoniens »*, a critiqué le multiculturalisme en vigueur au Royaume-Uni : *« Nous avons protégé le droit des gens à vivre selon leurs traditions culturelles aux dépens du vivre-ensemble. Trop de musulmans britanniques grandissent sans vraiment connaître personne d'une origine différente. »*

POURQUOI CET ARTICLE ?

Cet article retrace le parcours exceptionnel de Sadiq Khan, élu le 6 mai 2016 à la mairie de Londres, la plus grande et la plus cosmopolite capitale d'Europe. Indéniablement, c'est la « success story » de Sadiq Khan et le fait qu'il soit le premier musulman à prendre les rênes d'une capitale occidentale qui ressortent de cette élection. Il est d'ailleurs intéressant de noter que, lors de la campagne, Sadiq Khan a mis en avant son identité religieuse ainsi que son origine sociale modeste, les transformant en atouts. Comme membre du parti travailliste, son engagement pro-européen l'oppose à son prédécesseur conservateur, Boris Johnson ; depuis le Brexit, Sadiq Khan ne cesse d'ailleurs de répéter que Londres restera une « ville ouverte ». Il a fait du logement sa priorité, mais réussira-t-il à tenir sa promesse de construction de 50 000 logements sociaux par an ?

Son troisième atout est d'être un *« garçon élevé en HLM »*, ce qui lui permet de se présenter en champion face à la toute première obsession des Londoniens : la folie des prix de l'immobilier, due notamment à une pénurie de mises en chantier. *« Londres est la plus grande ville du monde mais elle perd des points à cause de l'impossibilité d'y vivre, sauf à consacrer la moitié de ses revenus à son loyer ou à ses remboursements d'emprunt*, explique-t-il. *Ce ne sont plus seulement les chauffeurs de bus ou les professeurs qui ne peuvent plus suivre, ce sont désormais les médecins, les cadres et les banquiers ! »*

Son parcours de réussite, c'est celui de Londres, n'a-t-il cessé de répéter en substance pendant toute la campagne, transformant le conte de fées de sa propre ascension sociale en bande-annonce de ses ambitions pour une ville-monde dont le dynamisme attire la planète entière. *« La promesse de Londres a toujours été : "Quelles que soient tes origines, si tu travailles dur, tu trouveras une main pour t'aider et tu pourras tout réussir." C'est ce qui m'est arrivé*, résume-t-il. *Mais aujourd'hui, trop de Londoniens, en particulier des jeunes, ne peuvent plus aller jusqu'au bout de leur talent. Les prix des logements et de la vie sont hors de leur portée et plus personne ne les aide. Maire de Londres, je veux être cette main secourable pour les Londoniens de toutes origines. »*

Et d'égrener les étapes de sa *success story*. Premier de la fratrie à naître à Londres, il a été élevé dans un HLM surpeuplé du quartier populaire de Tooting avec ses six frères et sa sœur, par des parents durs à la tâche – un père ne refusant jamais les heures supplémentaires, sauf le dimanche pour emmener ses enfants au musée, et une mère qui cousait des robes pour 25 pence la pièce tout en préparant les repas. Il raconte son expérience du racisme ordinaire, qui l'a conduit parfois à exercer ses talents de boxeur, ses professeurs de l'école publique qui l'ont poussé vers les études supérieures, sa carrière d'avocat spécialisé dans les droits de l'homme, comme son épouse Saadiya... Puis la plongée en politique : conseiller municipal à 24 ans, député de Tooting à 34 ans, ministre à 37 ans. *« Le premier musulman à accéder au conseil privé de la reine »*, a-t-on dit de lui quand le premier ministre travailliste, Gordon Brown, lui a confié le portefeuille des transports, en 2009. Avant la première séance en présence d'Elizabeth II, Buckingham l'a appelé pour lui demander sur quel genre de Bible il comptait prêter serment. Il a demandé un Coran. Il n'y en avait pas. Il a apporté son propre exemplaire.

« Identités multiples »

A force de prétendre transformer ses origines et sa religion en atouts dans la campagne municipale, il a reçu la monnaie de sa pièce. Amplement. Le premier ministre David Cameron l'a accusé d'avoir *« servi de couverture à des extrémistes »*. Les journaux conservateurs ont sorti des photos où il figure en mauvaise compagnie : aux côtés de Suliman Gani, un imam radical de sa circonscription, ou dans une réunion d'un collectif *« contre la terreur politique »* soutenu par Al-Qaida. Dans le *Mail on Sunday*, son adversaire conservateur Zac Goldsmith a été jusqu'à associer son nom aux attentats terroristes de 2005, n'hésitant pas à le comparer aux *« dégoûtants personnages »* de l'islam radical. L'intéressé répond que dans un meeting, *« on ne sait pas toujours qui va parler après vous »* et qu'en tant qu'avocat spécialisé dans les dossiers de droits de l'homme, il a évidemment défendu de *« dégoûtants personnages »*.

La foi musulmane, *« c'est une partie de qui je suis, explique-t-il. Mais, comme tout le monde, j'ai des identités multiples : je suis un Londonien, un Britannique, un Asiatique d'origine pakistanaise, un supporteur de Liverpool, un père, un mari, un travailliste et un musulman »*. Pratiquant – il ne boit pas d'alcool et jeûne pour le ramadan – mais tolérant, en bons termes avec les autres cultes, il a été visé par une fatwa lorsqu'il a pris fait et cause pour le mariage gay. Pour la journaliste Yasmin Alibhai-Brown, l'élection de Sadiq Khan démolit le discours anti-occidental des extrémistes et apparaît comme *« le pire cauchemar pour les terroristes »*. *« Si un musulman peut être élu par des millions de citoyens de toutes origines pour diriger l'une des plus grandes villes du monde*, écrit-elle dans le *Guardian*, *comment pourraient-ils continuer de faire croire que les musulmans n'ont pas d'avenir en Europe ou que les Occidentaux les haïssent ? »*

Politiquement, Sadiq Khan s'affiche en modéré, pragmatique et proeuropéen. Alors que le Labour cumule revers politiques et défaites électorales, il est crédité de trois victoires personnelles : il a permis à Ed Miliband, dont il était le bras droit, d'être élu en 2010 à la tête du Labour contre son propre frère David. L'ex-leader l'a remercié en le nommant ministre chargé de Londres dans son cabinet fantôme, tremplin vers la candidature à la mairie. Sadiq Khan a ensuite brillamment conduit la campagne des législatives du Labour de 2015 à Londres, où, en terrain sociologiquement favorable, il a aidé le parti à conquérir 45 des 73 sièges de député de la mégapole. Dernière en date des manifestations de son habileté politique : l'an passé, contre toute attente, il a battu Tessa Jowell, la candidate de l'establishment blairiste, favorite dans la course à l'investiture pour l'élection municipale de Londres. Pour obtenir les faveurs de la gauche du parti, il a rappelé son opposition de toujours à la guerre en Irak. Il a mis aussi en valeur le parrainage qu'il a accordé à Jeremy Corbyn pour lui permettre de se présenter à la primaire du Labour, où ce dernier a été élu à la surprise générale en septembre 2015. Mais une fois choisi pour candidat pour la mairie de Londres, Sadiq Khan s'est rapidement démarqué du nouveau patron du parti, lui reprochant de renforcer l'image « anti-juive » du Labour par ses rencontres avec le Hamas et le Hezbollah. Il a aussi qualifié d'*« erreur »* son refus de chanter le God Save the Queen lors de cérémonies. D'ailleurs, M. Corbyn n'est apparu sur aucun document de campagne du candidat travailliste et pratiquement jamais sur le terrain avec lui.

Souplesse politique

Le fils de chauffeur de bus a séduit une partie de la très cosmopolite City en promettant d'être *« le maire le plus pro-business que Londres ait jamais connu »*. Une forfanterie, de la part de celui qui va succéder à l'ultralibéral Boris Johnson. Sadiq Khan veut *« aider les entreprises à prospérer »* et exclut toute augmentation de la fiscalité les visant. Face aux prix astronomiques de l'immobilier, l'ancien *« gamin élevé en logement social »* ne promet ni contrôle des loyers (hors des compétences du maire) ni réquisitions, mais un programme de construction de logements locatifs abordables et une chasse aux propriétaires voyous. Sa souplesse politique l'a conduit à abandonner son soutien à l'extension de l'aéroport d'Heathrow – une position insoutenable pour les Londoniens – pour vanter celle de Gatwick, bien plus éloigné de la capitale.

Son engagement européen est en revanche une constante. *« Comment voudriez-vous que le maire d'une ville où plus de 500 000 emplois sont directement liés à l'UE puisse souhaiter la sortie de l'Union ? »*, lance Sadiq Khan. Et d'entonner un hymne à la diversité culturelle et culinaire qu'apportent à Londres les 550 000 citoyens européens, *« ces amis »* qui y ont élu domicile et dont il n'oublie évidemment pas qu'ils font partie du corps électoral lors des municipales.

Le nouveau combat du boxeur travailliste ne fait que commencer. Boris Johnson, auquel il succède, aspire à remplacer David Cameron à Downing Street. Premier maire musulman d'une capitale européenne, Sadiq Khan va prendre des coups. Mais lui qui *« ne perd jamais »* sait depuis l'enfance comment les rendre. Avec une véhémence un peu trop appuyée, il prétend n'avoir aucune ambition de devenir premier ministre. Mais il n'ignore rien du fantastique tremplin politique sur lequel il est désormais juché.

Philippe Bernard (Londres, correspondant)
Le Monde daté du 09.05.2016

Le Royaume-Uni n'est plus le pays des libertés

En janvier 1215, exaspérés par les impôts confiscatoires et la justice arbitraire imposés par le roi Jean d'Angleterre, les barons anglais se révoltent. Le 15 juin de la même année, le bras de fer se conclut par la signature d'un texte historique : la *Magna Carta*. L'une de ses clauses, peu mise en avant à l'époque, entérine les prémices d'une société de droit : elle interdit « *d'emprisonner, de déposséder de ses droits ou de ses biens, de mettre hors la loi ou d'exiler* » tout « *homme libre* » (les serfs étaient exclus) sans un jugement impartial, qui doit reposer sur les lois du moment et nécessite d'apporter des preuves. Avec la *Magna Carta*, le Royaume-Uni inaugure une tradition de défense des libertés civiles, renforcée par *l'Habeas Corpus* (1679), qui influença le reste du monde pendant des siècles. La Constitution américaine s'en est inspirée. La charte s'applique aujourd'hui encore à travers une large partie du Commonwealth, de l'Australie à l'Inde.

Cette tradition est menacée, comme l'a illustré l'arrestation dimanche 18 août de David Miranda. Le compagnon de Glenn Greenwald, le journaliste du *Guardian* qui a révélé l'existence de Prism, ce cyberespionnage de grande ampleur mené par les États-Unis et le Royaume-Uni, a été interrogé pendant neuf heures à l'aéroport d'Heathrow sur la base d'une loi antiterroriste datant de 2000. M. Miranda, qui transportait des documents secrets venant du « lanceur d'alerte » Edward Snowden, n'est pourtant pas soupçonné de terrorisme.

Les révélations du *Guardian* ont accentué l'impression que le gouvernement britannique est devenu autoritaire. Menacé de poursuites judiciaires, le quotidien britannique a accepté de détruire les disques durs qui contenaient les informations de M. Snowden. En cette ère numérique mondialisée, le geste est surtout symbolique : d'autres copies existent à travers le monde. Mais le *Guardian* a jugé plus prudent de partager ses informations avec le *New York Times*, la Constitution américaine protégeant mieux la liberté d'expression que la loi britannique.

Pour les défenseurs des libertés civiles, ces événements récents confirment ce qu'ils dénoncent depuis des années : le pays de la *Magna Carta* ne mérite plus sa réputation. « *Frère siamois des États-Unis, le Royaume-Uni semble en train de rapidement se diriger vers une situation où la "sécurité nationale" prend le pas sur tout le reste* », accuse Philippe Sands, professeur de droit international à University College London.

Le Royaume-Uni, dont l'efficacité des services secrets est réputée, n'a jamais été un enfant de chœur. Pendant le conflit en Irlande du Nord, notamment, il avait imposé des lois dures concernant la garde à vue. Néanmoins, le pays se targuait de sa tolérance, depuis la tradition du *Speaker's corner* à Hyde Park jusqu'au droit accordé aux islamistes radicaux de s'exprimer librement dans les années 1990.

Coups de boutoir contre les libertés

Tout a basculé après les attentats du 11 septembre 2001. Sous la houlette de Tony Blair, une série de lois antiterroristes a été votée. La garde à vue pour les suspects de terrorisme a été progressivement étendue à vingt-huit jours, au lieu de quatre jours dans le droit commun. Dans un périmètre défini à l'avance, la police a obtenu le droit d'arrêter et de fouiller dans la rue qui elle voulait, sans justifier de la moindre suspicion. « *L'incitation au terrorisme* » est devenue un délit, mais sa définition est tellement vaste qu'elle risque de réduire la liberté d'expression. Enfin, le pire excès est venu du « Guantanamo britannique » : une douzaine d'étrangers, suspectés de terrorisme, mais contre lesquels ne pesait aucune inculpation, ont été mis en prison pendant trois ans sans procès. La justice a ensuite ordonné leur libération, mais ces hommes sont restés en résidence sous surveillance jusqu'en 2009.

Les coups de boutoir contre les libertés dépassent cependant le terrorisme. Le Royaume-Uni est le pays qui a installé le plus de caméras de surveillance au monde. La base d'ADN détenue par la police est l'une des plus grandes de la planète. Enfin, l'affaire Snowden l'a révélé : les services secrets britanniques réalisent une surveillance de grande ampleur du trafic Internet. Jusqu'à présent, les tentatives des gouvernements successifs d'empiéter sur les libertés ont été régulièrement bloquées par la justice. Le « Guantanamo britannique » a été fermé, la garde à vue des suspects de terrorisme a été rabaissée à quatorze jours, les droits de fouille de la police ont été encadrés... Presque à chaque fois, ces victoires se sont fondées sur la Convention européenne des droits de l'homme, que le Royaume-Uni a signée en 1951 et qu'il a incorporée dans sa loi en 1998. Mais le gouvernement de David Cameron envisage très sérieusement de sortir de la Convention. Pour lui, ce texte est désormais utilisé par des criminels qui détournent les droits de l'homme pour se défendre. Le cas Abou Qatada, un prédicateur islamiste soupçonné de terrorisme, dont l'expulsion vers la Jordanie a pris onze ans, est venu symboliser ce malaise.

Une sortie du Royaume-Uni de la Convention serait inquiétante. « *Le gouvernement a systématiquement tenté d'attaquer les libertés civiles, mais cela a été limité, grâce à la Convention*, explique Robert Wintemute, professeur de droit à King's College London. *Sans elle, on ne pourra plus résister.* » Le 800e anniversaire de la *Magna Carta*, dans deux ans, pourrait être une triste célébration.

Eric Albert, *Le Monde* daté du 28.08.2013

POURQUOI CET ARTICLE ?

Les attentats terroristes du 11 septembre 2001 ont servi de prétexte à de nombreux pays – les États-Unis et le Royaume-Uni en tête – pour restreindre les lois protégeant les libertés civiles et individuelles, au nom d'un impératif sécuritaire. Comme le montre cet article, cette évolution s'inscrit pourtant à contre-courant de la tradition britannique, le Royaume-Uni ayant toujours été considéré, depuis la *Magna Carta* de 1215, comme un pays fondamentalement attaché au respect et à la défense des libertés civiles. Le 15 juin de cette année, on célèbrera le 800e anniversaire de la *Magna Carta* – et comme le souligne l'auteur de l'article, il pourrait bien s'agir d'une triste célébration au regard de la dérive autoritaire qui caractérise aujourd'hui le Royaume-Uni.

Donald Trump, la volte-face permanente

Cent jours après son arrivée à la Maison Blanche, le président des Etats-Unis multiplie déclarations et actes en contradiction avec ses promesses de campagne. Ces réalignements sur des positions plus traditionnelles se vérifient surtout en politique étrangère.

Trois mois après son arrivée à la Maison Blanche, une phase plus difficile s'est ouverte aux Etats-Unis pour le nouveau président Donald Trump. Des élections partielles organisées en avril pour remplacer deux élus républicains – Mike Pompeo, nommé directeur de la CIA, et Tom Price, devenu secrétaire à la santé – ont souligné une nette hausse de la mobilisation des démocrates. Enhardis, ces derniers comptent même défier en mai le Grand

Old Party dans un de ses bastions, le Montana, qui doit élire un successeur au représentant Ryan Zinke, secrétaire à l'intérieur depuis le 1er mars.
Le Parti républicain a pu conserver le siège de M. Pompeo au Kansas et n'a pas perdu toutes ses chances de faire de même en Géorgie pour celui abandonné par M. Price, à l'occasion d'un second tour disputé en juin : un jeune inconnu, Jon Ossoff, a failli s'emparer dès le premier tour (48,1 % des voix) de cette circonscription que les républicains dirigent depuis 1978, en menant campagne sur l'impopularité de M. Trump. Voilà les républicains prévenus. Les premiers mois de la présidence ont été marqués, il est vrai, par une série d'échecs : sur les décrets anti-immigration du président, bloqués par la justice ; ou bien sur la réforme de la santé promise par les républicains depuis des années. Ces ratés, et de nombreux revirements, ont placé Donald Trump sur la défensive.
C'est en politique étrangère que les réalignements du président sur des positions américaines plus traditionnelles ont été les plus significatifs. Dernier en date, l'attachement exprimé à l'égard d'une *« Europe forte »* par Donald Trump, à l'occasion de la visite à Washington du président du conseil des ministres italien, Paolo Gentiloni, le 20 avril. *« C'est important pour les Etats-Unis. Nous voulons cela. Nous l'aiderons à être forte, et cela bénéficiera à tout le monde »*, a assuré le président américain. Le candidat Trump s'était, au contraire, réjoui de la décision des électeurs britanniques de quitter l'Union européenne en juin 2016. En janvier, dans un entretien accordé au *Times* et à la *Bild Zeitung*, il assurait encore que *« d'autres pays »* allaient en partir, pour s'en féliciter.
Une semaine plus tôt, le 12 avril, le président a parachevé devant le secrétaire général de l'OTAN, Jens Stoltenberg, un autre revirement. Pendant la campagne, il s'était souvent montré très critique vis-à-vis de l'Alliance atlantique, la jugeant même *« obsolète »*. Au lendemain de son feu vert à l'adhésion du Monténégro, M. Trump, qui se rendra au quartier général de l'OTAN en Belgique à la fin du mois de mai, a loué au contraire une organisation qui est un *« rempart pour la paix internationale et la sécurité »*. Pour justifier son changement de ton, le président des Etats-Unis a répété une affirmation controversée selon laquelle l'OTAN se serait tournée vers le contre-terrorisme sous sa pression. *« Je me suis longtemps plaint à ce sujet, et ils ont changé. Maintenant, ils luttent contre le terrorisme. J'avais dit qu'elle était obsolète. Elle ne l'est plus »*, a assuré M. Trump.
Le même jour, l'administration américaine remisait une autre accusation récurrente du candidat : celle selon laquelle la Chine manipulerait sa devise pour faciliter ses exportations. Dix jours plus tôt, M. Trump avait pourtant accordé le titre de *« champions du monde »* en la matière aux responsables chinois. Auparavant, la menace d'imposition d'une taxe d'importation aux produits chinois avait également disparu des éléments de langage de l'administration américaine. Au lendemain d'une visite du président Xi Jinping au club de luxe de son homologue en Floride, les 6 et 7 avril à Mar-a-Lago, la « Winter White House » fréquentée assidûment par M. Trump depuis son arrivée à la Maison Blanche, ce dernier avait également renoncé à déplorer la passivité supposée de Pékin sur la question nord-coréenne, un dossier rendu brûlant par la multiplication par Pyongyang de tests de missiles balistiques.

L'ambassade des Etats-Unis reste à Tel-Aviv

Parmi les promesses de campagne du candidat républicain figurait aussi en bonne place l'engagement de transférer de Tel-Aviv à Jérusalem l'ambassade américaine en Israël. La nouvelle administration a rapidement pris ses distances par rapport à une mesure unilatérale peu propice à la relance souhaitée d'une initiative diplomatique visant à explorer les possibilités d'un accord de paix israélo-palestinien. La Maison Blanche a également renoué avec la position critique des administrations précédentes vis-à-vis de la colonisation israélienne des territoires occupés palestiniens.
Ces changements drastiques ont trouvé leur traduction la plus spectaculaire avec la décision de Donald Trump d'ordonner le tir de 59 missiles de croisière Tomahawk contre une base militaire syrienne, dans la nuit du 6 au 7 avril, deux jours après une attaque à l'arme chimique imputée au régime de Bachar Al-Assad contre un village tenu par la rébellion, dans le nord-ouest du pays. Quelques jours plus tôt, l'administration américaine avait pourtant indiqué se résigner au maintien au pouvoir du président syrien. Cet autre revirement a eu pour conséquence de refroidir considérablement la relation déjà complexe avec la Russie. Donald Trump n'a pas renoncé à trouver un terrain d'entente avec son homologue Vladimir Poutine, dont il ne cessait de louer les qualités d'homme d'Etat pendant sa campagne, mais il a posé ses conditions. L'ambassadrice américaine aux Nations unies, Nikki Haley, a réaffirmé l'intransigeance des Etats-Unis sur le dossier ukrainien : il n'est plus question pour le moment d'une levée des sanctions adoptées par Washington au lendemain de l'annexion de la Crimée, et les deux hommes pourraient ne pas se rencontrer avant le sommet du G20 à Hambourg, en Allemagne, début juillet. Contrairement à ses prédécesseurs, M. Trump n'a effectué aucun voyage à l'étranger jusqu'à présent.
A son arrivée à la Maison Blanche, M. Trump a été classé parmi les disciples du président Andrew Jackson (1829-1837). Selon le géopoliticien Walter Russell Mead, M. Trump exprime en effet un nationalisme tournant le dos à un ordre mondial « hamiltonien » et « wilsonien » – du nom du premier secrétaire au Trésor des Etats-Unis, Alexander Hamilton (1789-1795), et du 28e président, Woodrow Wilson (1913-1921) –, d'après lequel le pays est fondé à défendre, sur toute la planète, une pax americana au nom de valeurs morales et d'une foi dans les bénéfices d'une ouverture au monde. M. Trump n'a pas forcément rompu avec cette inclination « jacksonienne », l'intervention en Syrie ayant été justifiée au nom des intérêts américains. Mais une autre grille de lecture peut être tirée de ses derniers choix : celle de se démarquer autant que possible des positions de son prédécesseur, Barack Obama. La présence dans son entourage de trois généraux influents, James Mattis, secrétaire à la défense, John Kelly, secrétaire à la sécurité intérieure, et H. R. McMaster, promu conseiller à la sécurité nationale après le départ précipité du premier titulaire, un autre général, Michael Flynn, le 13 février, tranche avec les relations notoirement complexes entretenues par le précédent commandant en chef avec les responsables de l'armée américaine.
Devant les cadets de West Point, en mai 2014, Barack Obama avait conceptualisé sa défiance vis-à-vis du recours aux militaires en estimant que *« ce n'est pas parce qu'on a le meilleur marteau qu'on doit voir chaque problème comme un clou »*. Donald Trump, comme il l'a montré en Syrie, semble estimer que l'armée est un outil comme un autre pour modifier à son profit les rapports de forces dans les relations internationales.

L'accord sur le nucléaire iranien toujours pas remis en cause

M. Trump n'a pas varié, par ailleurs, sur deux points souvent évoqués pendant la campagne. S'il n'a pas pour l'instant remis en cause, comme il s'y était engagé, l'accord conclu par la Chine, les Etats-Unis, la France, le Royaume-Uni, la Russie et l'Allemagne (P5 + 1) avec la République islamique d'Iran sur le programme nucléaire controversé de Téhéran, il n'a cessé, depuis son arrivée à la Maison Blanche, de souligner l'influence néfaste de l'Iran au Proche-Orient. Il a ainsi ravivé une relation américano-saoudienne sortie éprouvée des deux mandats de son prédécesseur.
De même, Donald Trump a continué d'exprimer son soutien aux régimes de la région considérés comme forts. Il a reçu, le 3 avril à la Maison Blanche, le président égyptien, Abdel Fattah Al-Sissi, alors que M. Obama, tout en se résignant à poursuivre sa coopération militaire avec Le Caire, s'était refusé à rencontrer dans son bureau un militaire arrivé au pouvoir par un coup d'Etat. La question des droits de l'homme, en dépit de la férocité de la répression qui vise toutes les formes d'opposition, n'a pas été mentionnée publiquement au cours de la rencontre.
M. Trump n'a pas tardé non plus à féliciter, le 17 avril, son homologue turc, Recep Tayyip Erdogan, au lendemain de sa victoire sur le fil lors du référendum visant à accroître les pouvoirs présidentiels. Le département d'Etat a fait preuve pour sa part de beaucoup plus de nuances, notamment à propos de la sincérité du vote.
Ce président peu disert sur les questions internationales a souvent frappé ses interlocuteurs étrangers par sa désinvolture et une préparation toute relative aux entretiens dont l'ordre du jour, de sources diplomatiques

convergentes, est souvent laissé à l'appréciation du visiteur. Au point d'alimenter une véritable chronique de petites gaffes, parfois difficilement vérifiables, comme cette promesse faite à l'un de ses visiteurs de le revoir au cours d'un prochain sommet international – auquel le pays dont il a la responsabilité n'est statutairement pas partie prenante.

En politique intérieure, M. Trump ne se montre pas plus attiré par *« le souci du détail »*, selon Karlyn Bowman, qui suit les tendances de l'opinion à l'American Enterprise Institute, un think tank conservateur, préférant tracer à grands traits une vision conforme à sa promesse électorale de *« rendre l'Amérique grande à nouveau »*. Cette inappétence pour les dossiers a été vérifiée lors de la tentative infructueuse de réforme du système d'assurance-maladie introduit par Barack Obama. M. Trump n'y a consacré que trois semaines, avant de décider de passer rapidement à la réforme fiscale, puis d'évoquer une nouvelle tentative de règlement du premier dossier. Les difficultés ont été amplifiées par le retard pris par le président dans les nominations des quelque quatre mille postes à pourvoir à chaque alternance, dont une bonne partie doit être confirmée par le Sénat.

Les changements de pied du président ont été rythmés par la montée en puissance d'un groupe de conseillers de la Maison Blanche considérés comme modérés. Il s'agit des anciens de la banque d'affaires Goldman : Gary Cohn, conseiller économique du président, et Dina Powell, passée par l'administration de George W. Bush et devenue adjointe du conseiller à la sécurité nationale. Ces modérés s'appuient sur les membres les plus influents de la famille du président, son gendre Jared Kushner et sa fille Ivanka, qui disposent tous les deux d'un bureau à la Maison Blanche.

La presse américaine ne cesse d'opposer ce cercle aux idéologues présents pendant et après la campagne aux côtés de M. Trump. Il s'agit de Stephen Bannon, le conseiller stratégique du président, ancien responsable du site d'information ultranationaliste Breitbart News, de Stephen Miller, son conseiller politique, et de Sebastian Gorka, son conseiller adjoint, passé lui aussi par Breitbart News.

La Cour suprême bascule dans le camp conservateur

Henry Olsen, de l'Ethics and Public Policy Institute, un think tank conservateur, juge *« surévalué »* le rôle prêté à M. Bannon. *« Ses déclarations incendiaires, notamment celles visant les médias* [qualifiés de parti d'opposition], *ont contribué à en faire un repoussoir idéal pour la presse libérale* [au sens anglo-saxon], *mais Trump n'a pas de mentor »*, estime-t-il. *« Le sentiment qui s'installe à Washington de sa normalisation me semble très prématuré. Trump est libre de toute forme d'attaches, idéologiques ou partisanes, c'est ce qui lui permet de changer très rapidement »* sur un sujet. *« Avec Trump, une décision ne mène pas nécessairement à une autre »*, met-il en garde.

Malmené par les contre-pouvoirs américains, notamment la justice fédérale, qui a bloqué à deux reprises ses décrets anti-immigration, crédité du pire taux d'approbation pour son action de l'histoire moderne des Etats-Unis, Donald Trump a pourtant rempli sa part du contrat passé avec les électeurs républicains en parvenant à faire accéder à la Cour suprême le juge Neil Gorsuch, qui a refait basculer la plus haute instance juridique américaine dans le camp conservateur. Il a par ailleurs multiplié les mesures contre l'avortement, qu'il s'agisse de la suppression annoncée d'aides internationales bénéficiant à des organisations non gouvernementales qui n'y sont pas opposées, ou bien de l'arrêt du financement fédéral des centres du Planning familial aux Etats-Unis, même pour des soins sans lien avec l'avortement (qui ne peut être financé par ailleurs par des fonds fédéraux).

Le président reste encore indéchiffrable

D'autres membres de son administration envoient des signaux favorables aux conservateurs, qu'il s'agisse des militaires Mattis et McMaster sur les questions de sécurité, ou de la secrétaire à l'éducation Betsy DeVos, qui défend ardemment le principe, prisé par les républicains, de la liberté de choix de l'établissement scolaire. *« A ce titre, on peut même dire que l'administration Trump est plus conservatrice que celle d'un président républicain traditionnel »*, assure Henry Olsen.

Il en va autrement avec les électeurs que le nouveau président se flatte d'avoir ramenés vers les bureaux de vote en novembre 2016 grâce à un discours ethno-nationaliste et protectionniste. Ces électeurs décrocheurs, concentrés dans la *Rust Belt*, l'ancien bastion industriel du nord-est des Etats-Unis, seraient pourtant les premiers touchés par les restrictions budgétaires prônées par la nouvelle administration, même si le Congrès aura le dernier mot. Ils ont de même été déconcertés par le contenu de la réforme de santé défendu par la direction du Parti républicain, avec le soutien de la Maison Blanche.

Le jusqu'au-boutisme des idéologues républicains du Freedom Caucus, à la Chambre des représentants, favorables à l'élimination de toute présence fédérale dans le domaine de la santé, a contribué à l'abandon de la réforme au sein de la Chambre basse. Mais une partie des sénateurs républicains avaient déjà fait savoir qu'ils ne voteraient pas le texte en l'état parce qu'il priverait de couverture sociale des millions d'Américains, dont une partie des anciens cols-bleus démocrates qui se sont tournés vers M. Trump lors de l'élection présidentielle.

« Ces électeurs ont exprimé un besoin de protection auquel il a répondu par ses prises de position sur l'immigration et contre le libre-échange. Ils ne sont pas opposés par ailleurs à ce qui tient à cœur à l'électeur républicain traditionnel : la réforme fiscale, la dérégulation, le conservatisme social. Ce n'est pas antagoniste. Mais pour espérer conserver ces électeurs, il faut répondre un minimum à leurs demandes. La proposition de réforme de santé a reflété l'incompréhension de la direction républicaine de ce qu'est la coalition qui a fait gagner Trump », ajoute M. Olsen.

« Il y a trois grandes questions sur lesquelles Trump peut être jugé dans les mois à venir », estime Karlyn Bowman. *« On a vu sur la santé que les gens ont été déstabilisés par le contenu du projet. Il y a ensuite la conviction qu'une réforme fiscale, plutôt vue favorablement, va créer des emplois. »* *« Enfin, il y a tout ce qui a trait à l'environnement et au réchauffement climatique. C'est un sujet qui n'était pas jusqu'à présent une priorité parce que les Américains estimaient qu'il était consensuel depuis les années 1970. Donner l'impression de remettre en cause ce consensus pourrait être coûteux »*, assure-t-elle. C'est pourtant justement sur ce point que la nouvelle administration multiplie les prises de position idéologiques, de type climatosceptique, sous couvert de la priorité donnée à l'industrie et aux créations d'emplois dans le domaine des énergies fossiles.

Après cent jours passés à la Maison Blanche, Donald Trump reste encore indéchiffrable. *« Nous sommes face à un président clairement débordé par la complexité des dossiers et par la lourdeur de l'appareil dont il a la charge, mais qui reste concentré sur sa propre réussite. Je doute fort qu'il puisse forger des alliances avec les démocrates, la polarisation extrême qui prévaut rend cela sans doute impossible, mais il ne faut pas exclure de nouvelles mutations de Trump »*, conclut Henry Olsen.

Gilles Paris, *Le Monde* daté du 02.05.2017

POURQUOI CET ARTICLE ?

C'est un bilan des 100 premiers jours de la présidence de Donald Trump qui nous est présenté dans cet article et en ressortent des positions en matière de politique étrangère en opposition à ses déclarations de campagne. L'Europe, la Syrie, la Chine, l'Otan : la liste des revirements du président est longue. L'article souligne également le manque de préparation des entretiens diplomatiques, l'acharnement du président Trump à défaire l'héritage d'Obama et conclut sur son imprévisibilité. Donald Trump pratique en effet une « diplomatie transactionnelle » afin d'obtenir les meilleurs accords possibles et cela fait dire à Ivo Daalder, ancien ambassadeur américain à l'OTAN, que « le risque d'un accident et d'une escalade imprévue vers la guerre est désormais au niveau le plus élevé depuis des décennies ».

Ecosse, Irlande du Nord : du Brexit au Royaume désuni

Dévaluation de la livre sterling, affaiblissement du statut international, incertitudes économiques… La litanie des conséquences avérées ou prévisibles du Brexit intègre généralement l'inconnue écossaise. Furieux d'être forcés par Londres de quitter l'Union européenne alors qu'ils ont voté à 62 % pour y rester, les Ecossais pourraient redemander le divorce avec Londres. Le SNP, Parti national écossais au pouvoir à Edimbourg, brûle d'impatience, rêvant d'un second référendum sur l'indépendance et d'une revanche après l'échec de celui de 2014.

Bien que les conditions économiques ne soient guère favorables, sa chef de file, la charismatique Nicola Sturgeon, ne résistera sans doute pas à la pression. On lui prête l'intention de réclamer ce nouveau vote au moment où Theresa May déclenchera la procédure de divorce avec l'UE, d'ici à la fin mars. L'intransigeance de la première ministre britannique, qui laisse entendre qu'elle n'autorisera pas un nouveau vote sur l'indépendance écossaise, agit comme huile sur le feu. *« Nous quittons l'UE comme un unique Royaume-Uni et prospérerons hors de l'UE comme un unique Royaume-Uni »*, a-t-elle martelé vendredi 3 mars. Le Royaume-Uni, qui justifie sa sortie de l'UE par le besoin de recouvrer sa pleine souveraineté, semble pourtant mal placé pour priver les Ecossais de ce droit.

Mais, pour le Royaume, le premier ébranlement consécutif au Brexit pourrait venir de cette lointaine Irlande du Nord dont les Anglais se soucient comme d'une guigne depuis que les bombes s'y sont tues. Autant la question écossaise est débattue dans les médias nationaux, largement grâce au talent de Mme Sturgeon devenue la principale opposante au Brexit dans un paysage déserté par le Labour, autant le spleen nord-irlandais d'après-Brexit est superbement ignoré. Or les 1,2 million d'électeurs de la province britannique ont penché dans le même sens que les Ecossais : 55,8 % ont voté pour rester dans l'Union européenne.

A ceux qui ne s'en étaient pas aperçus, l'élection régionale, jeudi 2 mars, a administré une sérieuse piqûre de rappel. Stormont, l'Assemblée de Belfast, dominée jusqu'à présent par le Parti unioniste démocrate (DUP, probritannique) de la première ministre Arlene Foster, s'est brusquement teinté de vert, la couleur des nationalistes du Sinn Fein, ex-branche politique de l'Armée républicaine irlandaise (IRA), partisan d'une rupture avec Londres et de la réunification de l'île. Alors que 40 000 voix et dix sièges séparaient les deux formations dans l'assemblée sortante, élue il y a dix mois, l'écart s'est réduit à 1 168 voix et un siège. Tous partis confondus, les unionistes détiennent 40 sièges, tandis que les nationalistes les talonnent avec 39 élus. Dans une assemblée de 90 sièges, les unionistes n'ont plus la majorité. C'est une première dans cette province dessinée par Londres en 1920 afin de préserver une majorité protestante. En outre, alors que le DUP avait appelé à voter pour le Brexit, une majorité des députés régionaux, élus début mars, sont partisans du maintien dans l'UE.

A première vue, le Brexit n'était pour rien dans la crise politique qui a abouti aux élections régionales. Martin McGuinness, 66 ans, figure du Sinn Fein, qui cogérait l'exécutif régional avec Mme Foster, a démissionné en janvier pour dénoncer la responsabilité de cette dernière dans le scandale « *cash for ash* ». Ce dispositif de subvention des énergies renouvelables était si généreux que les hangars vides chauffés au bois ont proliféré. Michelle O'Neill, 40 ans, une militante issue d'une famille de combattants nationalistes mais entrée en politique après la fin des *« troubles »*, a remplacé M. McGuinness, gravement malade.

POURQUOI CET ARTICLE ?

Après les résultats du référendum sur le Brexit, l'indépendance de l'Écosse a largement été évoquée dans les médias. Depuis, fragilisés par les résultats des récentes élections législatives, les nationalistes écossais ont repoussé à l'automne 2018, à l'issue des négociations sur le Brexit, la décision sur l'organisation d'un nouveau référendum d'indépendance. Mais si le cas écossais est mentionné dans l'article, c'est sur l'Irlande du Nord que ce dernier attire notre attention. Cette province britannique a en effet elle aussi voté à un peu plus de 55 % pour le maintien dans l'Union européenne et c'est le paysage politique qui en a été bouleversé. Le processus de réconciliation et la paix sociale pourraient être compromis et la réunification de l'île de nouveau envisagée. Et l'article de conclure que c'est le spectre d'un Royaume désuni qui plane désormais au-dessus du pays.

Une réconciliation en danger

Sous sa houlette, le Sinn Fein a mené campagne contre la *« corruption »* de l'exécutif. Mais il s'est aussi posé en garant du maintien dans l'UE, réclamant un statut spécial maintenant l'Irlande du Nord dans l'Union après le Brexit. Les nationalistes ont aussi capitalisé sur la crainte d'une déstabilisation du processus de paix répandue non seulement dans leurs rangs, mais aussi chez les unionistes. Le divorce avec l'UE risque de rétablir la frontière disparue entre les deux Irlandes et de compromettre la prospérité économique et la paix sociale. Il met aussi en danger un processus de réconciliation dont les institutions européennes sont garantes. *« Les électeurs ont montré qu'ils ne veulent pas du Brexit »*, a appuyé Gerry Adams, président du Sinn Fein et ancien commandant de l'IRA. Alors que l'accord de paix de 1998 prévoit un partage du pouvoir entre les deux premières forces électorales, Mme O'Neill refuse de siéger dans un gouvernement dirigé par Mme Foster. D'où la difficulté des négociations ouvertes le 6 mars.

Le bouleversement du paysage politique nord-irlandais consécutif au Brexit est plus profond encore. Rompant avec le vote « communautaire », une partie des électeurs protestants, inquiets, ont lâché le DUP, pro-Brexit, tandis que la mobilisation des nationalistes a fait gagner des points au Sinn Fein. Ce dernier, longtemps très antieuropéen, a bien perçu le parti qu'il peut tirer du Brexit pour faire avancer son combat central en faveur de la réunification de l'île. L'accord de 1998 stipule, en effet, que Londres doit organiser un référendum sur ce point si une majorité dans ce sens apparaît.

La tempête du Brexit rend cette perspective de moins en moins fumeuse. En outre, un référendum en Irlande légitimerait une consultation identique en Ecosse. Une *« ceinture euroceltique »* pourrait-elle se constituer *« autour de l'Angleterre nationaliste »* ? s'interroge dans le *Times* Adam Boulton, célébrité du journalisme. Là n'est pas le moindre paradoxe du Brexit : réaction largement nationaliste, il pourrait précipiter la désunion du Royaume.

Philippe Bernard, *Le Monde* daté du 13.03.2017

ESPACES ET ÉCHANGES

The Taming of a Vast Wilderness

Australia has a daring plan: to convert its tropical North into a huge "food bowl". The area being considered spans 3 million square kilometers. The plan offers many benefits, but the environmental risk has not yet been properly measured and may be huge.
Developing the North is a major aim of the Liberal party governing Australia. They want to double the country's agricultural output by mid-century. In a policy paper last June, they said: "No longer will northern Australia be seen as the last frontier: it is in fact, the next frontier." [...]
At first glance, north Australia is promising. It gets 1 quadrillion litres of rain a year. Most falls in just four months, so the idea is to build dams to store these wet season rains, and irrigate the land during the eight bone-dry months.
There is clearly potential, says Peter Stone of the CSIRO in Brisbane. Aquifers alone could sustain 60,000 hectares of crops, according to a 2009 report. Then there are the rivers. Dams on just two, the Flinders and Gilbert, could support 50,000 hectares of crops. [...]
Stone says 1.7 million hectares could conceivably be irrigated. But he says the government will probably miss its target. "I'd be surprised if we could double Australia's agricultural output."
A key problem is that most of the rain evaporates fast, so only 20 per cent or so enters rivers. "If you took all of that, then there would be zero stream flow," Stone says. Perhaps only 1 per cent would be available for irrigation.
The variable climate makes things even riskier. Yearly rainfall can be half or twice the average.
Then there are the downsides. Northern Australia contains 25 per cent of the world's tropical savannahs – the only significant area in a wealthy, stable country. Each wet season, rivers overflow and flood the savannah, and life blooms. The region is home to 40 per cent of Australia's reptiles and 75 per cent of its freshwater fish, says The Wilderness Society.
This environment will suffer if it is farmed. Yet the government wants to relax environmental regulations – to cut the "green tape". Prime Minister Tony Abbott has said Australia needs to throw away "green extremism". The trouble is, the "wasted" rain is all used somewhere, such as supporting fisheries. For example, damming the Gilbert river would cut the water flow to nearby wetlands by 10 per cent.
We don't know how these pros and cons will add up, says Michael Douglas of Charles Darwin University in Darwin, Australia. "We couldn't tell you exactly how much you can take out before you start to degrade fisheries or reduce the number of turtles that Aboriginal people harvest." One thing's for sure: Australia won't get something for nothing.

Invading the North?

Everyone acknowledges, at least in principle, that the development of northern Australia must benefit Indigenous Australians. They already own 30 per cent of the land and claim land rights over 80 per cent. They are concentrated in the North, where they make up 16 per cent

DICTIONARY

- **daring**: brave
- **to span**: to cover
- **huge**: enormous
- **aim**: objective
- **output**: production
- **a dam**: a wall built across a river to keep back water
- **to store**: to stock
- **bone-dry**: perfectly dry
- **crops**: harvest of fruit, vegetables
- **target**: objective
- **the downsides**: the disadvantages
- **wealthy**: rich
- **to overflow (overflew/overflown)**: to flood
- **to bloom**: to flourish
- **green tape**: bureaucratic rules concerning the environment ("Red tape" means bureaucratic rules.)
- **to throw away**: to dispose of
- **the pros and cons**: the advantages and disadvantages
- **to harvest**: to collect
- **to acknowledge**: to recognize
- **to own**: to possess
- **unlikely**: not probable
- **to rely on**: to depend on
- **gung-ho**: zealous
- **to flop**: to fail
- **seedlings**: plants
- **spare**: extra, available, not being used
- **a no-brainer**: an easy task

MOTS CLÉS en lien avec la thématique

NOUNS

- earth: *la terre*
- an inhabitant : *un habitant*
- global warming: *le réchauffement climatique*
- climate change: *le changement climatique*
- drought: *la sécheresse*
- flooding/a flood: *une inondation*

Ex.: **Climate change** causes **droughts** in some areas and **floods** in others.

- rising seas: *l'élévation du niveau de la mer*

Ex.: **Rising seas** could displace tens of millions of people.

- hurricanes: *les ouragans*
- shortage: *la pénurie*
- scarcity: *la rareté*

Ex.: Water **scarcity** already affects every continent.

- greenhouse gases: *les gaz à effet de serre*

Ex.: Human activities are increasing the concentration of **greenhouse gases**.

- growth: *la croissance*

Ex.: In the last 50 years there has been a rapid **growth** of human population.

- starvation: *la famine*
- poverty line: *le seuil de pauvreté*
- slum dwellers: *habitants de bidonville*

Ex.: The number of **slum dwellers** has continued to grow due to fast urbanization.

- developing countries: *les pays en développement*
- developed countries: *les pays développés*
- inequality: *l'inégalité*
- a disease: *une maladie*
- basic needs: *les besoins élémentaires*
- living standards: *les niveaux de vie*
- wealth: *la richesse*
- life expectancy: *l'espérance de vie*

VERBS

- to lack: *manquer de*

Ex.: Over one billion people worldwide **lack** access to water.

- to consume: *consommer*
- to waste: *gaspiller*
- to increase: *augmenter*

of the population, despite being only 2 per cent of the country's total.

Indigenous Australians have been enormously disadvantaged since the arrival of Europeans. Their life expectancy is 12 years shorter, and they are incarcerated 12 times as often as other Australians. They only got the right to vote in 1962.

For the government, redressing the balance means "creating opportunities through education and economic development." The trouble is, Indigenous Australians may not benefit from those opportunities, says Natalie Stoeckl of James Cook University in Townsville. Her research suggests they have less to gain from development than non-Indigenous people, and more to lose. They have few connections to the economy, so are unlikely to get jobs. Moreover, some Indigenous people rely on harvesting wild plants and animals, and irrigating crops threatens that.

Nevertheless, some Indigenous groups have expressed support for developing the North so long as their interests are prioritised. Stoeckl says this is essential. "New 'developments' need to forge strong financial links with existing residents, Indigenous and non-Indigenous," she says. "Otherwise, the 'development' will be similar to what the Europeans did when conquering the new world."

Lost in the Fogg

Fogg dam is an object lesson in how not to develop northern Australia. It was a gung-ho attempt to create a food bowl, one that unequivocally failed. The dam was built in 1956 to support rice farms. But the project flopped for all the reasons that are now recognised as problems in developing the region. Native wildlife [. . .] ate the seedlings, crocodiles were a risk to workers, and the little rice that did grow was far away from markets. [. . .] Instead of a big farm, the region is now a wildlife park [...].

> "Indigenous Australians have been enormously disadvantaged since the arrival of Europeans. Their life expectancy is 12 years shorter, and they are incarcerated 12 times as often as other Australians. They only got the right to vote in 1962."

Not visionary but useful

The Burdekin dam supports the largest irrigated area in northern Australia: 80,000 hectares, mostly growing sugar canes. The water comes from a combination of surface water and groundwater. Some of the water from the dam is used to top up the groundwater, preserving it for the long term.

Further developing the Burdekin is an obvious thing to do, but probably not as attractive to politicians who want to present their ideas as "visionary", says ecologist Damien Burrows [...]. "The Burdekin is underutilised," he says. "It has spare water and there's spare soil downstream." Even The Wilderness Society agrees. They say further developing existing, proven farmlands, rather than moving to risky greenfield sites, is a no-brainer. ■

Adapted from Michael Slezak – *New Scientist*, July 10th, 2014

FOCUS ON...

The driest continent on earth

Australia is the sixth largest country in the world and is about 14 times bigger than France. Desert or semi-arid land commonly known as the Outback makes up by far the largest portion of land.

Australia is a major agricultural producer and exporter. The greatest problems faced by the farms of Australia are droughts and water scarcity as Australia is the driest continent on earth.

Aborigines are Australia's indigenous people and they make up about 2% of Australia's total population. As a result of forced assimilation, by the late 1880s most Aborigines had joined white rural and urban communities. Aboriginal people became economically marginalized and were exposed to new diseases. The consequence was massive depopulation. In the 1970s, Aborigines spoke out for equal rights, and specifically for land rights for property that had been forcibly taken by British settlers. The 1990s witnessed further rights milestones, including government legislation that returned a great degree of autonomy, and increased wages and welfare benefits to aboriginal people.

UN ARTICLE DU *MONDE* À CONSULTER :

- **Australie – La repentance par l'emploi** p. 82-83
(Yves Mamou, *Le Monde* daté du 16.07.2010)

S'EXPRIMER

USING "DESPITE" TO EXPRESS CONTRAST

- "They are concentrated in the North, where they make up 16 per cent of the population, **despite being** only 2 per cent of the country's total."

Despite is used to introduce a contrasting clause. It is always followed by a noun phrase, or the verbal form of the noun (-ing). It cannot be followed by a main verb.

Ex.: **Despite** her illness, Mary went to school.

Ex.: **Despite** being ill, Mary went to school.

- **In spite of** can also be used. **In spite of** is always followed by a noun phrase, or the verbal form of the noun (-ing). It cannot be followed by a main verb.

CONNECTING IDEAS IN A SENTENCE AND BETWEEN SENTENCES

- **Adding information**

"**Moreover,** some Indigenous people rely on harvesting wild plants and animals."

Phrases that can be used to add information:

– **moreover/as well as this/furthermore/in addition** (= ***de plus***)

– **besides /also** (= ***par ailleurs***)

These phrases connect sentences and are often used at the beginning of a sentence.

- **Expressing a condition**

"**Otherwise**, the development will be similar to what the Europeans did when conquering the new world." (**otherwise** = ***sinon***)

"[...] some Indigenous groups have expressed support for developing the north **so long as** their interests are prioritized."

(**so long as** = ***tant que***)

On condition that, provided that could be used here instead of **so long as**.

- **Expressing contrast**

"**Nevertheless**, some Indigenous groups have expressed support for developing the North." (**nevertheless** = ***néanmoins***)

However could also be used here instead of **nevertheless**.

Questions de compréhension

Choose the correct answer.

1. Australia's plan is to transform the tropical North ......
a. into farmland/ **b.** into a wildlife park.
2. The environmental risk ......
a. will be limited/ **b.** hasn't been assessed.
3. The Liberal Party aims to ...... **a.** double agricultural production in Australia/ **b.** double agricultural production in north Australia.
4. The wet season in north Australia lasts ......
a. eight months/ **b.** four months.
5. North Australia gets ...... **a.** about the same quantity of rain every year/ **b.** a variable quantity of rain every year.
6. The overflowing of rivers is ......
a. a threat to Australia's reptiles/ **b.** vital for animal life.
7. The government wants ...... **a.** more flexible ecological legislation/ **b.** to reinforce ecological legislation.
8. A dam on the Gilbert river ...... **a.** would benefit the fisheries/ **b.** could have a negative impact on the fisheries.
9. Indigenous Autralians ...... **a.** do not have the same rights as other Australians/ **b.** die younger than other Australians.
10. Developing the North ......
a. will undoubtedly benefit Indigenous Australians/
b. may not be beneficial to Indigenous Australians.
11. The Fogg dam was ...... **a.** a failure/ **b.** a success.
12. The initial objective of the Fogg dam was ......
a. to create a wildlife park/ **b.** to have more farmland.
13. Politicians ...... **a.** are keen to develop the Burdekin dam/ **b.** are not really keen to develop the Burdekin dam.

BOÎTE À OUTILS : LES PROPOSITIONS CONDITIONNELLES

• "I'**d be** surprised **if** we **could** double Australia's agricultural output."
"**If** you **took** all of that, then there **would be** zero stream flow."
Ces phrases sont des conditionnelles de type 2 :
if + *prétérit* + *conditionnel présent* (would/wouldn't).
Ce type de proposition conditionnelle renvoie à une ***condition imaginaire****. On l'utilise pour parler de choses qui pourraient arriver dans le futur, ou de choses qu'on imagine.*
Would *est très souvent contracté dans le langage parlé.*
Ex.: **If** I **had** a plane, **I'd fly** to school.
Ex.: **If** they **sold** their house, they **would be** very happy.
• *Les conditionnelles de type 1 :* **if + *présent simple* + *futur*.**
On utilise les conditionnelles de type 1 pour parler d'une ***situation réelle****. Elles décrivent ce que quelqu'un pense qu'il arrivera dans une situation réelle ; on croit que les choses dont on parle arriveront.*
Ex.: **If** we **run,** we **won't be** late.
Ex.: **If** you **pay** cash, you **will get** a five per cent discount.
• *Les conditionnelles de type 3 :*
if + *plus-que-parfait* + *conditionnel passé* (would have/ wouldn't have).
Ce type de proposition conditionnelle renvoie à une ***condition impossible****. On l'utilise pour parler de choses du passé, et il est impossible de changer ce qui est arrivé dans le passé.*
Ex.: **If I had run**, I **wouldn't have been** late.
Ex.: **If** I **had known** you were waiting, I **would have come** sooner.
• *On peut donner des conseils en utilisant les conditionnelles de type 2 et en les commençant par* **if I were you**.
Ex.: **If** I **were** you, I'**d spend** more time on your written work.
Ex.: **If** I **were** you, I **wouldn't eat** so many cakes!

Exercices de grammaire

A. Choose the correct word or phrase underlined in each sentence.

1. If I'd known/ would know it was your birthday, I would send you/ would have sent you flowers.
2. If we take/ will take a taxi, we'll arrive/ we arrived sooner.
3. If I had/ would have a lot of money, I'd give/ I gave some to all my family.
4. If Sam drove/ had driven more carefully, he wouldn't have had/ didn't have a fine.
5. If I had noticed it/ would notice it, I'd have corrected/ would correct it.
6. If I studied/ will study harder, I would get/ get better marks.

B. Complete the sentence for each situation.

1. I didn't go to bed early, so I didn't wake up at 6 am.
If I .... early, I .... at 6 am.
2. I didn't turn right at the station, and I lost my way.
If I ...., I .... way.
3. I didn't buy more bread, so I didn't have enough for dinner.
If I ...., I .... enough for dinner.
4. I didn't realize you were tired when I asked you to go for a walk.
If I ...., I .... for a walk.

Sujet national, septembre 2013, séries technologiques

Document B

You Can't Pick Up Raindrops

Bob and I are Peace Corps volunteers in small, not quite a village, Puñal, twenty-five miles south of Santiago de los Caballeros in the Cibao Valley of the northern Dominican Republic.

We live on the second floor of the pale lime-green, wooden *casa curial* or parish house, next to the small wooden church. There is no electricity, running water or sewer. Rent is cheap; twenty-five dollars combined, out of ninety-five we each get monthly. You can buy a lot of rice and beans and Presidente beer with the rest.

The rest of the time, we work on projects: water supplies with water-well hand pumps, grade school and adult English classes, vegetable gardens, and hog production. We introduce new varieties of cigar wrapper tobacco. The local men learn windmill and pump repair. Periodically, the US Information Service loans us a movie projector and generator to show educational and cultural films on the outside wall of the church. What big, festive crowds we have! We do anything to keep busy and to better the lives of the Puñaleros. We enjoy life here; so quiet at night, so dark, sky full of dazzling stars. Late into the night, we often read by kerosene lamp light. An unknown admirer of the Peace Corps recently contributed 225 literary-quality books shipped in big cardboard boxes. We go through them, one by one, choosing according to our interests.

Often, after dark, we are out along the poorly paved road running north to Santiago. Here we gather with the older guys at the small *tiendas*, to spend some of our money on tiny cans of sweetened condensed milk, candies or small bottles of red Spanish wine. Along the road, we squat, knees pulled up to our chests, arms resting on our knees, Dominican style, sipping wine and watching the rickety cars and trucks trundle past.

It does not sound very exciting, does it? Actually, it is, perhaps, one of the most rewarding periods of our lives, a chance to withdraw from the rush of modern civilization, and to understand how others live.

John Charles Miller, *You Can't Pick Up Raindrops*, 2012.

EXPRESSION ÉCRITE : You are in charge of recruiting volunteers for a charitable organization abroad. You meet a group of potential candidates to explain the job profile (necessary qualities, experience, practical abilities . . .) to them.

Analyse du sujet

Vous incarnez un recruteur à la recherche de volontaires prêts à rejoindre un organisme caritatif œuvrant à l'étranger. Vous recevez un groupe de candidats potentiels. Il s'agit de leur présenter le plus clairement possible la nature du projet et le profil du poste à pourvoir. On vous demande d'insister notamment sur les qualités et compétences attendues, ainsi que sur l'expérience requise pour pouvoir mener à bien les missions confiées. Votre discours se doit d'être percutant et stimulant !

Repères essentiels

1. Commencez par noter vos idées au brouillon ; il vous faut déterminer le cadre général de votre discours : de quel organisme s'agit-il ? Quel est son objectif ? Dans quelles zones du monde intervient-il ? Comment ? Quel est le type de poste à pourvoir, pour quelle durée… ?
2. Notez au brouillon les éléments lexicaux qui vous seront indispensables pour exprimer les qualités, les compétences, la notion d'expérience, la notion de motivation…
3. Préparez un plan cohérent avant de rédiger au propre : introduction, présentation de l'organisme et du poste, attentes et exigences par rapport au profil recherché.

Proposition de corrigé

Hi everyone! Okay so settle down. I'm the recruitment officer for the Peace Corps and I'm going to explain to you what your job will entail so that you can take time to consider your application and your suitability for the job.

First and foremost, anyone who wants to work for the Peace Corps has to be motivated and ready to work in difficult conditions. **You have to** be particularly hard working and **you should** enjoy meeting people from all walks of life.

It's not necessary to have already travelled abroad. **However**, you should have at least a little experience of camping and of hiking in the great outdoors.

We don't expect you to have any particular qualifications, but you should be adaptable. And **you really need to** be practically minded: there will be all sorts of problems, and you need to find the right solution each time! **On a personal level**, you need to be independent. If you can't cook or you don't know how to wash your clothes – this job is not for you, as no one else will do it for you.

Another important point is availability. As we will be giving you two weeks' training, **we expect you to** stick to the job for a minimum of twelve months. Two years would be even better.

NOTIONS CLÉS

POUR EXPRIMER LA NÉCESSITÉ

- you need to be
- you have to be
- you must
- you should be

POUR PARLER DE L'EXPÉRIENCE

- *Le* present perfect (**have** + ***participe passé***) *permet d'évoquer des actions situées dans un passé récent, ou qui conservent un lien de continuité avec le présent.*

Ex. : **Have** you **worked** for a charitable organization before?

POUR PARLER DE CAPACITÉ

- **can + verb**

Ex.: Can you drive a truck?

- **to be able to + verb**

Ex.: You have to be able to negotiate.

- **to be capable of + V-ing**

Ex.: Are you capable of adapting yourself to any situation?

LE LEXIQUE DES COMPÉTENCES ET QUALITÉS PROFESSIONNELLES

- qualifications, skills: *les compétences*
- to be qualified for the job : *avoir les compétences requises pour la fonction*
- a career: *une carrière*
- to apply for a job: *postuler, poser sa candidature pour un emploi*
- to be adaptable: *être capable de s'adapter*
- independent: *indépendant*
- self-reliant: *autonome*
- hard-working: *travailleur (être capable de travailler dur)*
- smart, intelligent: *intelligent*
- witty: *spirituel, plein d'esprit*
- talented: *talentueux*
- wise: *sage*
- respectful: *respectueux*
- humble/ modest: *humble, modeste*
- motivated: *motivé*
- ambitious: *ambitieux*
- comitted: *engagé, convaincu, dévoué*
- to be practically minded: *avoir l'esprit pratique*
- to be efficient: *être efficace*
- to have team spirit: *avoir l'esprit d'équipe*

David Cameron Announces Immigration Benefits Crackdown

Benefits for EU migrants in the UK will be cut off after three months, says PM, as he promises Coalition changes will "put Britain first".

David Cameron is to announce tough action on immigration that will halve the amount of time foreigners can claim benefits in the UK.

The Coalition will introduce laws to ensure that European Union migrants can only claim out-of-work benefits for three months, Mr Cameron says in an article for *The Telegraph*.

The Prime Minister also pledges to stop more than 500,000 British jobs being advertised across the EU and announces tough new curbs on colleges offering visas to "bogus" students.

The Government will make changes to the immigration system that put "Britain first" and ensure that the UK is "a country that is not a soft touch," Mr Cameron says. "We changed the rules so that no one can come to this country and expect to get out-of-work benefits immediately; they must wait at least three months," Mr Cameron adds. "And we are announcing today that we are cutting the time people can claim these benefits for. It used to be that European jobseekers could claim Job Seeker's Allowance or child benefit for a maximum of six months before their benefits would be cut off, unless they had very clear job prospects. I can tell *Telegraph* readers today that we will be reducing that cut-off point to three months, saying very clearly: you cannot expect to come to Britain and get something for nothing."

Mr Cameron's latest intervention on immigration will be seen as an attempt to woo back Conservative voters who have defected to Ukip in recent months.

Under measures announced last year, European immigrants have to wait three months before they can claim out-of-work benefits. They can then claim the benefits for a maximum of six months.

Mr Cameron's announcement came as the International Monetary Fund warned that "restrictive immigration policies" in the UK "could have a negative impact on productivity growth". In a report on Britain's finances the IMF, which last week upgraded its forecast for UK growth to 3.2 per cent this year and 2.7 per cent in 2015, said: "Relaxing immigration requirements in areas with labour shortages, such as manufacturing, could provide a boost to productivity and facilitate the rebalancing of the UK economy." There was anger last year after it emerged that under an EU scheme partly funded by British taxpayers,

DICTIONARY

- **crackdown**: restraint
- **tough**: strong
- **to halve**: to cut in half
- **to claim**: to ask for
- **to pledge**: to promise
- **curbs**: restrictions
- **bogus**: false, fake
- **jobseekers**: applicants
- **prospects**: outlook for future
- **to expect**: to hope
- **attempt**: effort
- **to woo**: to charm
- **Ukip**: the UK Independence Party
- **to warn**: to inform
- **growth**: development
- **to upgrade**: to improve
- a **forecast**: prediction
- a **shortage**: deficit, lack
- **a boost**: an improvement
- **to take on (took/taken)**: to employ
- **a scheme**: a plan
- **Downing Street**: the UK Prime Minister's official residence (no. 10)
- **to request**: to ask
- **to ban**: to forbid
- **further**: additional
- **vacancies**: job offers
- **to shut down**: to close down

MOTS CLÉS en lien avec la thématique

NOUNS

- a foreigner: *un étranger*
- a newcomer : *un nouvel arrivant*
- labour: *main-d'œuvre*
- asylum seeker: *un demandeur d'asile*

Ex.: The number of **asylum seekers** is rising sharply across the European Union.

- a refugee: *un réfugié*
- undocumented worker: *travailleur sans papiers*
- immigration laws: *les lois sur l'immigration*
- working conditions: *les conditions de travail*
- intake: *le contingent*

Ex.: Australia has cut its annual **immigration intake** in the past few years.

- a citizen: *un citoyen*
- work permit: *un permis de travail*
- Green Card: *permis de séjour (US)*
- a prospect: *une perspective*
- social ladder: *l'échelle sociale*
- upward mobility: *l'ascension sociale*
- a low-paid job: *un emploi faiblement rémunéré*

Ex.: Many **immigrants** are trapped in **low-paid jobs** and are among the working poor.

- a workshop: *un atelier*
- minimum wage: *le salaire minimum*
- wealth: *la richesse*
- a border: *une frontière*
- human traffickers: *les trafiquants d'êtres humains*

ADJECTIVES

- underpaid: *sous-payé*
- low-skilled: *peu qualifié*
- rootless: *sans racines*
- uprooted: *déraciné*

VERBS

- to welcome: *accueillir*
- to gain citizenship: *acquérir une nationalité*
- to regularize: *régulariser*
- to emigrate: *émigrer*
- to flee (fled/fled) = to run away from: *fuir*
- to escape from: *s'échapper, s'évader de*
- to seek: *chercher*

all positions advertised in UK job centres also have to be offered to workers in European member states. UK firms are given as much as £1,000 as a bonus for taking on the foreign workers.

The EURES scheme offers foreigners hundreds of pounds of funding to pay for interviews in the UK, relocation costs and even English lessons. Of the 2.4 million jobs posted on the EURES site, 1,138,847 are posts in the UK. Jobs at UK firms including Tesco and Sainsbury's are advertised on the site.

Downing Street said that in future, jobs will only be uploaded to the website if an employer specifically requests that the position is offered across the EU. "Some recruitment agencies have even been recruiting directly from elsewhere in the EU without British workers ever getting a chance to apply for jobs," Mr Cameron writes. "So we are banning overseas-only recruitment – legally requiring these agencies to advertise in English in the UK. And today we are announcing a further measure. In the past, all vacancies advertised in Jobcentre Plus were automatically advertised on an EU-wide job portal. This meant advertising over a million job vacancies across the EU. So we are going to massively restrict this, aiming to cut back the vacancies on this portal by over 500,000 jobs."

There have also been growing concerns that colleges are abusing immigration rules offering visas for money so that people can come to the UK to work by pretending that they are here to study.

"Some of the most egregious examples were those claiming to be students, enrolling at bogus colleges," Mr Cameron says. "We have taken radical action – shutting down more than 750 of these colleges. Today we are announcing a further step to make sure colleges do proper checks on students: if 10 per cent of the students they recruit are refused visas, they will lose their licence."

In his article, the Prime Minister also highlights a series of measures that have come into force in recent days, including new restrictions on abuses of European human rights laws, which immigrants have used to avoid deportation.

Peter Dominiczak – *The Telegraph*, July 29th, 2014

DEUX ARTICLES DE *COURRIER INTERNATIONAL* À CONSULTER :

- **Calais heading for crisis** p. 72-73
(John Lichfield, *The Independent*, September 4th, 2014)
- **Immigrant parents urge U.S. officials to help their children flee Central American violence** p. 74-75
(Pamela Constable, *The Washington Post*, June 12th, 2014)

FOCUS ON...

Immigration in the UK

There are about eight million foreign-born residents in the UK, corresponding to about 12% of the population. The five most common foreign countries of birth are the Republic of Ireland, India, Pakistan, Germany and the United States.

Since the 1990s immigration from Australia, Canada, New Zealand and South Africa and from some countries of the EU has shifted towards migration from India and since 2004 particularly from the new EU accession countries such as Poland and Lithuania.

The UK has now for the first time a conservative government that has an explicit policy to reduce net immigration to "the tens of thousands" by 2015. While non EU net immigration has fallen by a third since the present government came to power, EU migration has increased significantly and is now almost at a similar level to non EU migration.

The electoral success of the UK Independent Party (UKIP) led by Nigel Farage in local and European elections in May 2014 shows that immigration is not an abstract, distant policy issue for voters.

There are many similarities between UKIP and the French Front national as both parties express nationalist feelings in their opposition to the EU and the appeal of both parties rests in their anti-immigrant platform.

S'EXPRIMER

EXPRESSING CONTRAST: USING "WHEREAS"

- David Cameron wants to introduce new laws "to ensure that European Union migrants can only claim out-of-work benefits for three months", **whereas** it used to be six months.

Whereas (= ***alors que***) can be used in formal speech and writing to express **contrast**.

- **While** can also be used instead of **whereas**.

Ex.: Mary gets lots of homework **whereas/while** her brother gets very little.

OTHER WAYS OF EXPRESSING CONTRAST

- **Though** (= ***bien que***) is used to introduce a contrasting clause; it is used at the beginning of a clause.

Ex.: **Though** she was ill, she went to school.

- **Though** can also mean "**nevertheless**".

When though means "nevertheless", it cannot be used at the beginning of a clause. It is used in between commas or at the end of a clause, after a comma.

Ex.: She went to school. She was ill, **though**.

- **Although** can also be used to express contrast; it is more formal than "though", and cannot be used at the end of a clause.

Ex.: **Although** she was ill, she went to school.

EXPRESSING A CONTRAST BETWEEN PAST AND PRESENT: "USED TO"

- "It **used to be** that European jobseekers could claim Job Seeker's Allowance of child benefit for a maximum of six months."

When we want to express a **contrast between past and present**, or when we want to talk about **repeated events in the past that don't happen now,** we can use **used to + infinitive**.

Ex.: I **used to play** tennis. (I no longer play tennis.)

- We can also use **would + infinitive** to talk about repeated events in the past.

Questions de compréhension

True or False?

1. European immigrants will have to wait three months before getting unemployment benefits.

2. Non EU immigrants will have to wait three months before getting unemployment benefits.

3. European immigrants will now get unemployment benefits for a maximum of three months.

4. The International Monetary Fund supports David Cameron's immigration policy.

5. The forecast for UK growth in 2015 is better than expected.

6. Under the EURES scheme British companies are encouraged to employ foreign workers.

7. Under the EURES scheme foreign workers are encouraged to come to the UK to work.

8. Job offers will only be posted on the EURES website if they have been previously checked by Downing Street.

9. Recruitment agencies won't be able to recruit overseas workers anymore.

10. The number of jobs in the UK advertised on the EU job portal will decrease sharply.

Exercices de grammaire

A. Choose the correct word or phrase underlined in each sentence.

1. I live/I have lived here since 2012.

2. I'm afraid the train left/has left ten minutes ago.

3. Yesterday I lost/I have lost my bag.

4. I've just lost/I just lost my scarf!

5. This has been/was an exciting day and it isn't over yet!

6. I feel exhausted. We went/have been to a party last night.

B. Complete the second sentence so that it has a similar meaning to the first sentence.

1. I started working here five years ago.

I .... five years.

2. This is the first time I've been on a boat.

I .... before.

3. It's a long time since I wrote to my sister.

I .... to my sister for a long time.

4. I saw a friend of yours a few moments ago.

I .... a friend of yours.

5. Is this your first visit to the US?

Have .... before?

BOÎTE À OUTILS : PRESENT PERFECT ET PRÉTÉRIT

• "[...] an attempt to woo back Conservative voters who **have defected** to Ukip **in recent years**."

"The Prime Minister also highlights a series of measures that **have come** into force **in recent days**."

Le **present perfect** (**have/has +** ***participe passé***) *est ici utilisé car on parle d'une* ***actualité récente*** (in recent years, in recent days).

• "In a report on Britain's finances the IMF, which **last week upgraded** its forecast for UK growth to 3.2 per cent this year [...]"

Le ***prétérit*** *est ici utilisé car l'action est* ***terminée*** (last week).

• ***Quand utiliser le prétérit ?***

On utilise le prétérit lorsqu'on parle de quelque chose qui est ***complètement terminé sans lien avec le présent****. Le prétérit est donc toujours associé (soit dans la phrase même, soit dans le contexte sans que cela ne soit exprimé) à une expression qui ramène à un moment précis du passé* (yesterday, last week, two years ago, when I was 16...).

Ex.: I **lived** in England **when I was young**.

Ex.: Henry James **published** *Washington Square* **in 1880**.

• ***Quand utiliser le present perfect ?***

1. *On utilise le* **present perfect** *pour parler d'une action qui* ***a commencé dans le passé*** *et qui* ***continue jusque dans le présent****.*

Ex.: She **has lived** in London **since 2010**.

Ex.: **How long have** you **known** her?

Le **present perfect** *correspond souvent à un* ***présent en français****.*

2. *On utilise le* **present perfect** *lorsque la* ***période de temps n'est pas encore terminée****.*

Ex.: I**'ve read** 12 books **this year**.

Ex.: I**'ve never been** to New York **in my life**.

3. *On utilise le* **present perfect** *lorsque* ***l'action vient de se terminer*** *ou que* ***l'actualité est récente****.*

Ex.: She **has just gone** out (= *elle vient de*).

Ex.: The bus **has arrived** (*sous-entendu :* the bus has just arrived).

4. *On utilise le* **present perfect** *lorsque* ***l'action se répercute dans le présent*** *: c'est le* ***résultat*** *qui importe surtout.*

Ex.: I**'ve already read** a lot of books on this subject.

Ex.: **Have** you **finished** your exams **yet**?

• *Le present perfect n'existe pas en français et il peut parfois se traduire par un passé composé, parfois par un présent. Pensez en anglais et* ***réfléchissez au contexte*** *pour savoir s'il faut utiliser ou non le present perfect. Et n'oubliez pas de réviser* ***votre liste des verbes irréguliers !***

Sujet national, juin 2014, séries ES, L, S

Document B

The experience of life in the city comprises the sum total of all encounters, relationships and experiences with other people during the course of the day. Well – being arises from contacts that are satisfying, and enjoyable, that affirm persons as individuals and as members of a community. The city must provide occasions and places for such good experiences to occur. Participation in social interactions makes an essential contribution to personal well – being. Impoverishment in social contact may result in a sense of isolation, meaninglessness for individuals and in the dissolution of social bonds for the community. Once we think about cities in terms of this conception, we must consider the nature of public social life, the conditions both architectural and social, under which it flourishes, and how the public and private domains interconnect.
The relation of public and private involves the flow of interest and attention from the private to the public world – to "what is happening out there" – as well as from the public to the private world. In the public realm, multiple perspectives and viewpoints prevail that inform and correct the single one-sided perspective of the private world. The public realm makes possible the exchange of opinion and information that forms the basis of civic dialogue and development of consensus. It is in the public realm that we learn about each other, through observation and participation, and develop a public conscience that pays heed to the foibles and needs of our fellow citizens. [...]
The public realm facilitates learning about ways of being and relating! We learn how persons relate within and across generational, social class, and experiential difference, and become skilled in making inferences about the fate and biography of our fellow beings. We learn about the humanity and dignity of all persons.

Henry L. Lennard, *The Essence of the City*, 1991.

EXPRESSION ÉCRITE : Discuss the importance of relating "within and across [...] social class" (document B).

Analyse du sujet

Il s'agit d'un essai argumentatif sur l'importance d'échanger au sein et au-delà des classes sociales. Dans quelle mesure ces échanges sont-ils nécessaires et enrichissants pour l'ensemble de la collectivité ? Doit-on favoriser la multiplication de ces échanges, ou peut-on au contraire s'en dispenser et se satisfaire du repli sur soi, d'un point de vue individuel comme d'un point de vue communautaire ?

Repères essentiels

1. Préparez vos idées au brouillon : des arguments en faveur des échanges, d'autres qui s'y opposent ou qui en soulignent les limites. Vous pouvez vous inspirer en partie du texte proposé (document B) : l'auteur y développe un point de vue très favorable à la nécessité d'échanger au sein et au-delà des différentes classes sociales. Pour lui, il s'agit d'un moyen d'en apprendre davantage sur l'humanité et la dignité de chacun (*cf.* dernière phrase du texte), ces échanges constituent donc clairement à ses yeux une source d'enrichissement et de progrès. Toutefois, vous devez veillez à ne pas reprendre le texte de l'énoncé mot pour mot ! Par ailleurs, rien ne vous empêche de développer un point de vue tout à fait opposé à celui de l'auteur : l'essentiel consiste à rester nuancé dans vos propos, et à présenter le plus objectivement possible l'ensemble des arguments propres à étayer des thèses divergentes (le pour/le contre).
2. Préparez un plan cohérent et équilibré avant de rédiger au propre.
3. Contrôlez la qualité de votre production en vous relisant attentivement.

Proposition de corrigé

According to the author of document B, relating within and across social class is an essential aspect of a person's participation in public life. This essay will study to what extent interaction with other people in the same class and in other classes is important today.
To my mind, the notion of social class is out-dated: in the twenty-first century, society is made up rather of different socio-professional categories than different classes. The distinction between lower, middle and upper class is no longer valid. What distinguishes the different levels of society today is undoubtedly their level of wealth. People with a similar standard of living are more likely to mix and meet at the same social events. **For example**, wealthy celebrities will attend the same charity event or congregate at the same international event such as the Cannes film festival. The homeless interact more easily with their counterparts, and people with a limited budget will find families with the same financial constraints on the campsite they choose for their holidays.
In an ideal world, interaction across all the levels of society could perhaps be a reality, but **in today's world** it's pure utopia. People associate with people who are able to offer themselves similar experiences.
However, this in itself is a form of social mixity, **as** it means meeting people from all sorts of walks of life.
In conclusion, social mixity may be an ideal, but **in reality** people generally mix with people who enjoy a similar standard of living. It's the amount of money in your bank accounts that dictates the type of people you will meet outside work.

NOTIONS CLÉS

POUR EXPRIMER L'IMPORTANCE
- important/essential
- vital/crucial
- people need to/
it's important (for people) to/
we should

POUR EXPRIMER LA NOTION D'ÉCHANGE
- to talk to each other
- to communicate
- to mix/to mingle
- to live side by side (with)

POUR OPPOSER L'IDÉAL À LA RÉALITÉ
- in an ideal world:
dans un monde idéal
- in reality:
en réalité, dans le monde réel
- utopia: *une utopie*

LE LEXIQUE DES RELATIONS SOCIALES
- socio-professional categories:
catégories socio-professionnelles
- from all walks of life:
de tous les milieux sociaux
- social condition:
la condition sociale
- social welfare:
la protection sociale
- social mixity: *la mixité sociale*
- social housing:
logement social (HLM)
- social status: *le statut social*
- social progress: *le progrès social*
- social class: *la classe sociale*
- members: *les membres*
- a community: *une communauté*
- income: *les revenus*
- the elite: *l'élite*
- wealth distribution:
la répartition des richesses
- the poor: *les pauvres*
- poverty: *la pauvreté*
- the underprivileged:
les défavorisés
- the lower class:
les classes populaires
- the middle class:
les classes moyennes
- the upper class:
les classes supérieures
- the ruling (or dominant) class:
la classe dominante
- the working classes:
les masses laborieuses
- the socially excluded,
the underclass: *les exclus*

Calais Heading for Crisis

Migrant problem threatens to escalate, and neither France nor Britain seem able – or willing – to sort it out.

Sibatu says he is 18 years old. He looks 20 years older. After travelling "with many problems" 3,000 miles from Eritrea, he has spent the past six months in the rain of the Channel coast a few miles from his destination. On Wednesday evening he was among 200 would-be asylum seekers – mostly young East African men – who tried to storm a cross-Channel ferry in the port of Calais. "The others told me this is the only way," he told *The Independent*. "Maybe, a few of us could get on a boat. Maybe none. We didn't win this time. We will try again."

After 20 years of deadlock, the never-ending saga of the Calais migrants is threatening to explode into outright crisis. The Mayor of Calais, Natacha Bouchart, spoke this week of shutting the port unless the British Government does more to help. She says her town has been "taken hostage" by the 1,300 migrants sleeping rough in the day and trying to board trucks – and now ships – by night. Relations between the two main categories of migrants – refugees from Africa and the Middle East – are increasingly tense. Wednesday's mass trespass through the main gates of the Calais ferry port is described by French police as a "worrying change in tactics." Until now, the migrants have mostly haunted approach roads and attempted to stow away in British-bound trucks or climb on to their back axles.

The French government bowed to pressure from the United Nations and announced plans to open a day centre – strictly non-residential – where the migrants can eat, shower and receive medical help. This is a significant change of policy after 12 years of harassment and the bull-dozing of squatter camps. The new centre will be the first official refuge since British pressure forced the closure of the Red Cross residential camp at Sangatte, just south of Calais, in 2002. It will inevitably be branded a "new Sangatte" by the right-wing press and politicians in Britain.

The French government and Ms Bouchart say the problem is partly of Britain's making. She and the Interior Minister Bernard Cazeneuve want the Government to pay towards policing the port (which costs France €10m a year). They also want Britain to persuade refugees that the UK is not the *El Dorado* painted by people-smugglers.

For almost 20 years, Calais has attracted an ever-changing cast of the stricken or the enterprising from Europe, Asia, the Middle East and now Africa. The problem began in 1994-5 with Bosnian refugees. The 1,300 migrants in Calais represent a mini-United Nations of conflict and oppression. About one in five are from countries such as Syria, Afghanistan and Pakistan. The great majority – and this is a relatively new development – are from Eritrea, Somalia, Darfur and the rest of Sudan. There was a street-battle last month between the Africans and Middle Eastern group over the right to exploit the most prized sections of the slip-roads approaching the ferry port.

Why do they not simply vanish into the French black economy? This is a complex issue and one frequently mis-represented in Britain. Sibatu said: "I go to England because in Eritrea there is only violence. In England, I have Eritrean friends who will get me a job, a new life." Why not apply for political asylum in France? "I no speak French. I have no friends in France." Another Eritrean, Jemal, 21, said he had tried the official asylum route in France and got nowhere. "So now I'll try and go to England because the people there are friendly. I can get a job there."

Tens of thousands of illegal migrants enter France every year. The majority want to stay in France. Some, especially the Afghans, Syrians and Pakistanis, come to France only to reach Britain. An increasing number, especially the Eritreans, emigrate to Europe without any country in mind. They are poorly treated in Italy and France and head for the Channel coast. The Calais problem is acute, and visible, because Britain is an island and does not belong to the EU open-borders Schengen Agreement.

Ms Bouchart and Mr Cazeneuve say Britain can no longer pretend this is just a "French problem." Under agreements reached in 2009 and 2010, Britain pays for body-heat-detecting equipment and other control measures. In a meeting last week with the Home Secretary, Theresa May, Mr Cazeneuve asked Britain to cover more of the cost of security and welfare. He asked her to send officials to tell the migrants Britain was a cold, wet island where illegal jobs are hard to come by.

In return, the French minister promised to prosecute migrants caught stowing away and to send them home. In practise, the systematic expulsion of migrants to war zones is opposed by French courts on human rights grounds. The mayor's threat to close the ferry port should probably not be taken seriously either. The town's economy depends on British visitors. With a British election approaching, it is equally unlikely that Ms May will give ground (or money). Crisis or no crisis, the 20-year deadlock continues.

Adapted from John Lichfield, *The Independent*, September 4th, 2014

KEY POINT

The lure of an *El Dorado*?

Since this article from *The Independent* was published, the UK has pledged £12m (five million euros a year for three years) to help tackle the problem of illegal immigrants trying to enter Britain through Calais. A plan was announced in September 2014 by Home Secretary Theresa May and her French counterpart Bernard Cazeneuve to bolster security at the port and target organized crime gangs behind people trafficking. Britain has therefore now recognized that it has a responsibility in securing the port.

El Dorado is frequently used by the French press to describe the lure that the UK holds for the migrants. Many of the 2,000 migrants living in squats in Calais desperately hope to get to the UK because they feel that they are not welcome in France and they are aware of France's high unemployment rate. The language is also another obstacle and as the migrants come from Sudan, Ethiopia, Eritrea, Afghanistan, Pakistan and Syria, if they speak a western language, it is most likely to be English and not French. They know their prospects of finding work are poor without basic French.

Calais, la crise menace

Ni la France ni la Grande-Bretagne ne semblent pouvoir contrôler la situation des migrants, dont les problèmes ne font que s'aggraver.

Sibatu dit qu'il a dix-huit ans. Il en fait vingt de plus. Après avoir parcouru « avec beaucoup de difficultés » les trois mille kilomètres depuis 'l'Érythrée, il a passé les six derniers mois sous la pluie des côtes de la Manche, à quelques kilomètres de sa destination. [Le 3 septembre], il faisait partie des deux cents candidats à l'asile politique – pour la plupart de jeunes hommes d'Afrique de l'Est – qui ont essayé de prendre d'assaut un ferry transmanche dans le port de Calais. « Les autres m'ont dit que c'était le seul moyen. Quelques-uns d'entre nous auraient peut-être pu monter à bord, peut-être aucun. Cette fois, nous n'avons pas gagné. Nous réessaierons », explique-t-il.

Après vingt ans d'impasse, la saga sans fin des migrants de Calais menace de déboucher sur une crise de grande envergure. La semaine dernière, la maire de Calais, Natacha Bouchart, a parlé de fermer le port, à moins que les autorités britanniques n'aident à régler le problème. Elle affirme que sa ville est « prise en otage » par les mille trois cents migrants qui dorment à la dure dans la journée et essaient de monter sur des camions (et maintenant des bateaux) pendant la nuit. Les relations entre les deux principales catégories de migrants – les réfugiés d'Afrique et ceux du Moyen-Orient – sont de plus en plus tendues. Le franchissement en masse des principales barrières du port de ferries de Calais est considéré par la police française comme un changement de stratégie préoccupant. Principalement, jusqu'à présent, les migrants rôdaient autour des routes d'accès et tentaient de s'embarquer clandestinement à bord de camions vers la Grande-Bretagne ou de grimper sur leurs essieux arrière. Cédant aux pressions des Nations unies, Paris a annoncé un projet d'ouverture d'un centre d'accueil de jour, sans aucun hébergement. Les migrants pourront y manger, prendre une douche et recevoir des soins médicaux. Il s'agit là d'un changement de politique important après douze années de harcèlement et de démantèlement des camps de squatters au bulldozer. Ce sera le premier centre d'accueil officiel depuis la fermeture du camp de la Croix-Rouge à Sangatte, au sud de Calais, en 2002, à la suite des pressions britanniques. Il sera inévitablement qualifié de « nouveau Sangatte » par la presse et les politiques d'extrême droite en Grande-Bretagne. Le gouvernement Hollande et Mme Bouchart estiment que la Grande-Bretagne a une part de responsabilité importante dans ce problème. Ils veulent également que Londres aide à financer la surveillance du port (qui coûte à la France dix millions d'euros par an) mais aussi convainque les réfugiés que le Royaume-Uni n'est pas l'eldorado que leur font miroiter les passeurs.

Depuis près de vingt ans, Calais attire une population toujours changeante de déshérités, souvent entreprenants, venue d'Europe, d'Asie, du Moyen-Orient et maintenant d'Afrique. Le problème a commencé en 1994-1995, avec les réfugiés de Bosnie-Herzégovine. Aujourd'hui, les mille trois cents migrants de Calais représentent une mini-ONU, marquée par les conflits et l'oppression. Environ un migrant sur cinq est originaire de pays comme la Syrie, l'Afghanistan et le Pakistan. La grande majorité – et c'est là un fait relativement nouveau – viennent d'Érythrée, de Somalie, du Darfour et du reste du Soudan. Le mois dernier, une bataille de rue a éclaté entre les Africains et les Moyen-Orientaux sur le droit d'exploiter les tronçons les plus prisés des bretelles d'accès vers le port de ferries.

Pourquoi ne se contentent-ils pas de disparaître dans l'économie parallèle française ? Le problème est complexe et souvent mal compris en Grande-Bretagne. Sibatu ajoute : « Je vais en Angleterre, parce qu'en Érythrée la violence est partout. En Angleterre, j'ai des amis érythréens qui vont m'obtenir un emploi, je pourrai repartir du bon pied. » Pourquoi ne demande-t-il pas l'asile politique en France ? « Je ne parle pas français, je n'ai pas d'amis en France. » Un autre Érythréen, Jemal, vingt et un ans, a suivi la procédure de demande d'asile en France, et cela n'a rien donné. « Alors maintenant, je vais essayer d'aller en Angleterre. Là-bas, les gens sont accueillants, je pourrai y trouver du travail. »

Des dizaines de milliers de sans-papiers entrent en France tous les ans. La plupart d'entre eux veulent rester dans l'Hexagone. Certains migrants, notamment les Afghans, les Syriens et les Pakistanais, ne passent par la France que pour se rendre en Grande-Bretagne. Un nombre grandissant d'entre eux, en particulier les Érythréens, émigrent vers l'Europe sans avoir aucun pays en tête. Mal traités en Italie et en France, ils partent pour les côtes de la Manche. Le problème de Calais est d'autant plus grave et visible que la Grande-Bretagne est une île et n'appartient pas à l'espace Schengen.

Mme Bouchart et le ministre français de l'Intérieur Bernard Cazeneuve estiment que la Grande-Bretagne ne peut plus faire semblant de croire qu'il s'agit seulement d'un « problème français ». Au terme d'accords conclus en 2009 et en 2010, la Grande-Bretagne finance des détecteurs de chaleur corporelle et d'autres mesures de contrôle. La semaine dernière, lors d'une réunion avec Theresa May, ministre de l'Intérieur britannique, M. Cazeneuve a demandé à la Grande-Bretagne de couvrir une plus grande partie des frais liés à la sécurité et à l'hébergement. Il leur a demandé d'envoyer des fonctionnaires pour expliquer aux migrants que la Grande-Bretagne est une île froide et humide, où l'on ne trouve pas facilement d'emplois illégaux.

De son côté, le ministre français a promis de poursuivre les migrants qui tentent de s'embarquer clandestinement et de les renvoyer dans leur pays d'origine. Dans les faits, l'expulsion systématique des migrants vers des zones de guerre est invalidée par les tribunaux français au nom des droits de l'homme. Quant à la menace du maire de fermer le port de ferries, elle ne devrait pas non plus être prise au sérieux. Sans les visiteurs britanniques, l'économie de la ville ne survivrait pas. De même, en cette veille d'élections britanniques [parlementaires en 2015], il est peu probable que Mme May lâche du lest (ou de l'argent). Crise ou pas, l'impasse dure depuis vingt ans, et on n'est pas près d'en sortir. ■

D'après John Lichfield, *The Independent*, le 4 septembre 2014.
Extrait de *Courrier International*

VOCABULARY TO REMEMBER!

- **deadlock**: *impasse*
- **to threaten**: *menacer*
- **to sleep rough**: *dormir à la dure*
- **relations are increasingly tense**: *les relations sont de plus en plus tendues*
- **to bow to pressure**: *céder aux pressions*
- **people's smugglers**: *les passeurs*
- **one in five**: *un (migrant) sur cinq*
- **a complex issue**: *un problème complexe*
- **to apply for political asylum**: *faire une demande d'asile politique*
- **the problem is acute**: *le problème est grave*
- **to prosecute**: *poursuivre (en justice)*
- **courts**: *les tribunaux*
- **it is unlikely that**: *il est peu probable que*

Immigrant Parents Urge US Officials to Help their Children Flee Central American Violence

Two months ago, Lucy Cabrera's adolescent son and daughter called her from Honduras in tears. They said gangs had threatened to kidnap them, and they begged her to help them flee to the United States. She borrowed $6,000 and wired the money to a series of guides in Guatemala and Mexico. On Saturday, her kids called again – from a US detention facility in Arizona. This time, there were no tears.

"Thank God they are safe now," said Cabrera. Although she is in the country illegally, she said she has been contacted by federal authorities so that both children can eventually be released to her custody. "It's truly a miracle," she marveled.

US officials are scrambling to understand and manage the exodus of unaccompanied minors from Central America who have turned up at the southern US border over the past few months. The surge has overwhelmed detention facilities, forcing the Obama administration to take emergency measures to provide shelter, hire attorneys and locate sponsors to receive the children.

The number of such minors entering the United States has crept upward since 2011, but last fall it began to skyrocket. Since October, 47,000 have arrived; officials expect another 60,000 by the end of this year. The new surge is partly seasonal, with early summer being the easiest time to travel across the region. But it is mainly driven by two other factors. One is an epidemic of gang violence across El Salvador, Honduras and Guatemala that has put many children at risk, especially when parents are not there to protect them. The second is a perception that the government is treating young illegal immigrants with unprecedented leniency.

As a result, thousands of parents like Cabrera sense both an urgent need and a unique opportunity to be reunited with children they left behind years ago. With no legal means to import their children from abroad, many are putting their hopes in an unexpected source of salvation: the US immigration system.

Word has spread through Latino communities in the Washington area and elsewhere that if their children reach the US border alone, they will be allowed to go free. The families' hopes are partly justified because officials have sped up processing the new arrivals to relieve crowded shelters and release as many as possible to relatives or guardians. Unlike children from Mexico, who can be sent back across the border right away, the law allows minors arriving from more distant countries to be sheltered and then handed over to a sponsor while awaiting court hearings.

But the speculation that these minors simply will be set free is unfounded. All of them are subject to deportation, and none are eligible for the administration's Dream Act program, which allows some illegal youths to remain if they have lived in the United States for at least five years and can meet other requirements. The newcomers, by contrast, are ordered to appear in immigration court and have no guarantee of being allowed to stay. The temptation, of course, is that families whose children face deportation may simply hide them away, shuttling them among friends and relatives in different states. On the other hand, parents or guardians must supply immigration officials with detailed information about themselves in order to receive a child from government custody, making such evasion more difficult. Before they even reach the United States, children face extreme hazards while traveling across Mexico and trying to cross the border. Smugglers often rob, abuse and abandon them; girls are sometimes raped. But more divided families are calculating that the risk is worth it. Once the children reach the border, some parents are instructing them to surrender to once-feared US Border Patrol agents as soon as they can. One Salvadoran woman in Prince George's County left her daughter as a small child a decade ago. Last year, the budding adolescent was sent north by grandparents who feared she would be abused by gangs. In Texas, scared and abandoned by smugglers, she turned herself in to the Border Patrol; after several months in custody, she was sent to live with a mother she barely knew. "She seemed more like a sister than a mother," said the girl, now 14. The mother sat close to her on a sofa, looking pensive. Both face possible deportation, but both clearly cherish their new relationship. "I was desperately worried about her, but it was definitely worth the risk," the mother confided with a shy glance at the girl. "She is everything to me." ■

Adapted from Pamela Constable, *The Washington Post*, June 12th, 2014

KEY POINT

A "humanitarian crisis" on the US border

Undocumented immigrants from El Salvador, Guatemala and Honduras have been coming to the US in massive numbers over the course of the last year as they seek to reunite with family members and escape from gang violence back home. In previous times it was primarily adult men who tried to enter the US undetected, but this time it has been a wave of women and children surrendering themselves to patrol agents on the border and asking for asylum.

According to the US Department of Homeland Security, 52,000 unaccompanied children were apprehended in 2014. President Obama has called the issue a "humanitarian crisis". Many children are being held in crowded detention centres, including makeshift warehouses, while US officials struggle to hold deportation hearings fast enough. The shelters are intended to be short-term, but the average length of stay is 35 days. Both political parties agree that the US immigration system is in need of reform.

Ces enfants qui jouent à saute-frontière

Il y a deux mois, le fils et la fille adolescents de Lucy Cabrera l'ont appelée en larmes du Honduras. Ils lui ont expliqué que des gangs avaient menacé de les enlever et l'ont suppliée de les aider à passer aux États-Unis. Elle a donc emprunté 6 000 dollars [4 400 euros] et envoyé l'argent à des passeurs au Guatemala et au Mexique. Le samedi suivant, ses enfants l'ont rappelée d'un centre de détention en Arizona. Cette fois, ils ne pleuraient pas.

« Dieu merci, maintenant ils sont en sécurité », soupire Lucy Cabrera. Bien qu'elle vive illégalement aux États-Unis, elle explique que les autorités fédérales l'ont contactée afin qu'elle puisse assurer la garde de ses enfants une fois qu'ils auront été relâchés. « C'est un vrai miracle », estime-t-elle.

Les autorités américaines s'efforcent de comprendre et de maîtriser l'exode de mineurs non accompagnés originaires d'Amérique centrale qui se présentent depuis quelques mois à la frontière entre le Mexique et les États-Unis. Cet afflux a engorgé les centres de détention, contraignant le gouvernement à adopter des mesures d'urgence afin d'assurer un hébergement provisoire aux jeunes migrants, à engager des avocats et à trouver des parrains susceptibles d'accueillir ces enfants.

Le nombre de mineurs entrant aux États-Unis augmente régulièrement depuis 2011, mais il a explosé depuis l'automne dernier. Depuis octobre, plus de 47 000 mineurs ont été interceptés à la frontière, et les autorités en attendent 60 000 de plus d'ici à la fin de l'année. Cet afflux est en partie de nature saisonnière, le début de l'été étant la saison la plus propice pour traverser la frontière. Mais il s'explique surtout par deux autres facteurs. Le premier est l'épidémie de violence des gangs qui ravage le Salvador, le Honduras et le Guatemala et met en danger de nombreux enfants, notamment ceux dont les parents sont absents. Le second est le sentiment que le gouvernement Obama traite les jeunes immigrants illégaux avec une bienveillance sans précédent. Du coup, des milliers de parents comme Lucy Cabrera ont l'impression que s'offre à eux une occasion unique de pouvoir récupérer des enfants qu'ils ont laissés derrière eux il y a des années. Et, en l'absence de moyen légal de faire venir leurs enfants de leur pays d'origine, ils placent leurs espoirs dans une planche de salut inattendue : le système d'immigration américain.

Le bruit s'est répandu à travers les communautés latinos des États-Unis que, si les enfants atteignaient seuls la frontière américaine, ils ne seraient pas inquiétés. Les espoirs des familles sont en partie justifiés, les autorités ayant accéléré le traitement des nouveaux arrivants afin de désengorger les centres de détention surpeuplés et d'en confier le plus grand nombre possible à des parents ou à des tuteurs. À la différence des mineurs mexicains, qui peuvent être renvoyés sur-le-champ dans leur pays, la loi prévoit que les jeunes arrivant de pays plus lointains peuvent être hébergés et remis à un parrain en attendant qu'un tribunal statue sur leur cas.

Mais imaginer que ces mineurs vont tout bonnement être laissés libres est une idée infondée. Tous sans exception sont susceptibles d'être renvoyés dans leur pays et aucun n'est en droit de bénéficier du programme *Dream Act*, qui autorise certains jeunes en situation illégale à rester sur le sol américain s'ils ont vécu les cinq dernières années aux États-Unis et répondent à certains critères. Les nouveaux arrivants, eux, doivent comparaître devant un tribunal qui décidera de leur sort, et rien ne garantit qu'ils seront autorisés à rester.

Bien entendu, pour les familles dont les enfants risquent le renvoi dans leur pays, la tentation est grande de les cacher en les confiant à des amis ou à des proches habitant dans d'autres États. Cela dit, les parents ou parrains d'un mineur doivent fournir aux services de l'immigration des informations détaillées afin de pouvoir se voir attribuer la garde d'un enfant jusque-là détenu dans un centre de rétention, ce qui rend plus difficile ce genre d'échappatoire. Avant même d'entrer aux États-Unis, les enfants courent de grands dangers lorsqu'ils traversent le Mexique ou tentent de franchir la frontière. Il arrive fréquemment que les passeurs les dépouillent, les maltraitent ou les abandonnent ; les filles sont parfois violées. Mais un nombre croissant de familles séparées estiment que le risque en vaut la chandelle. Certains parents conseillent à leurs enfants, une fois qu'ils ont atteint la frontière, de se rendre dès que possible aux agents autrefois redoutés de l'US Border Patrol [la police des frontières].

Il y a une dizaine d'années, une femme salvadorienne du Maryland a laissé au pays sa petite fille. L'année dernière, l'adolescente a été envoyée aux États-Unis par ses grands-parents, qui craignaient qu'elle ait des ennuis avec les gangs. Au Texas, apeurée et abandonnée par ses passeurs, elle s'est rendue à la Border Patrol ; après plusieurs mois de rétention, on l'a autorisée à aller vivre avec sa mère, qu'elle connaissait à peine. « J'ai plus eu l'impression de retrouver une sœur qu'une mère », explique l'adolescente aujourd'hui âgée de quatorze ans. Sa mère, assise à ses côtés, a l'air pensif. Toutes deux risquent le renvoi dans leur pays, mais sont manifestement ravies des liens qu'elles ont renoués. « J'étais morte d'inquiétude à son sujet, mais ça valait vraiment la peine, dit la mère en jetant un regard timide à sa fille. Elle est tout pour moi. » ■

D'après Pamela Constable, *The Washington Post*, le 12 juin 2014.
Extrait de *Courrier International*

VOCABULARY TO REMEMBER!

- **to beg**: *supplier*
- **although she is in the country illegally**: *bien qu'elle vive illégalement dans le pays*
- **so that**: *afin que*
- **eventually**: *une fois que, finalement*
- **to manage**: *gérer, maîtriser*
- **over the past few months**: *au cours de ces derniers mois, depuis quelques mois*
- **to overwhelm**: *submerger, engorger*
- **to provide shelter**: *offrir un abri, un hébergement provisoire*
- **to hire**: *engager*
- **attorneys**: *avocats*
- **it is driven by**: *cela s'explique par*
- **as a result**: *du coup, en conséquence*
- **to spread (spread/spread)**: *se répandre*
- **to reach**: *atteindre*
- **crowded**: *bondé, surpeuplé*
- **relatives**: *parents*
- **guardians**: *tuteurs*
- **unlike children from Mexico**: *à la différence des mineurs mexicains*
- **to meet requirements**: *répondre à des critères*
- **to supply someone with something**: *fournir quelque chose à quelqu'un*
- **to face hazards**: *courir des dangers*
- **to rape**: *violer*
- **to surrender**: *se rendre*
- **to fear**: *craindre*
- **scared**: *effrayé, apeuré*

Pairing Up With a Younger Mentor

In "Reverse Mentoring," Tech-Savvy Twentysomethings Help Older Managers

There is a growing digital divide in workplaces – between twentysomethings with social-media savvy and tech-impaired older managers. To address it, more companies are trying reverse mentoring, pairing young employees with older colleagues to work on tech skills.

The pair-ups don't always work. They are often intimidating to young mentors and awkward for older colleagues, who may be embarrassed to reveal how little they know. Rebecca Kaufman, a 24-year-old community manager with two years' experience in digital communications at MasterCard, says she was "definitely intimidated" when a young-professionals' network at the company paired her as a mentor with a 50-year-old executive, Ron Garrow.

Ms Kaufman had been using social media for almost a decade, but the prospect of helping a high-profile executive craft a social-media presence was daunting. The pair met twice in December and January in Mr Garrow's executive office. Mr Garrow readily embraced Ms Kaufman's first suggestion – to step up his visits on LinkedIn to daily from weekly and to begin sharing articles with his contacts. But he was unnerved by the idea of using Twitter. The importance of avoiding risky public statements was deeply ingrained in Mr Garrow, who worked at two big banking companies for 26 years before joining MasterCard in 2010. Executives there "went through rounds and rounds of approval" before saying anything publicly, he says. "Psychologically, the 140 characters is very intimidating to me."

Ms Kaufman encouraged him, saying Twitter "is a new ballgame. It opens up potential contact with anybody you're interested in." When she asked "So how do you want to brand yourself out there?", he wasn't sure how to answer. The father of four children ages 14 to 26, Mr Garrow says it was humbling to realize, "Here's this 24-year-old, the age of my kids, and I'm completely relying on her." Realizing that "Ron's reputation was on the line here," Ms Kaufman says, she did some digging to help identify human-resources experts and writers who are influential on social media. Mr Garrow opened a Twitter account, set up his profile and practiced using the site. Ms Kaufman helped him craft early tweets. On a visit to the University of Michigan last month, Mr Garrow wanted to tweet a photo of himself and a colleague with MBA students. He sent Ms Kaufman a cryptic email with a hastily written description of the complex event, a classroom simulation by students of a corporate briefing for investors, adding, "I want to tweet this but I'm not sure how," he says. Ms Kaufman suggested new phrasing. Mr Garrow rewrote the message and tweeted the photo within minutes.

Five months into their work together, Mr Garrow has 2,352 LinkedIn contacts, checks Twitter 8 to 10 times a day, follows 109 handles and tweets about 50 times a month. Ms Kaufman congratulated him recently when he passed 400 Twitter followers and praised his above-average score of 45 on Klout, a measure of social-media influence, says; "she said it was almost half of Obama's." Ms Kaufman is still pushing him to tweet about personal topics. His 14-year-old daughter Clare, he admits, "thinks I'm boring on Twitter." But sharing personal information online "crosses over into some uncomfortable spaces," he says. Mr Garrow started to tweet during a recent outing to New York City with his wife, Dana, but "I stopped, because I didn't want to cross that line yet."

Mr Garrow and Ms Kaufman have had to bridge generational differences. Riding in a car back to their offices after a recent conference, Ms Kaufman was working on her smartphone when Mr Garrow struck up a conversation about her career. They talked for a while, but she soon turned her eyes back to her phone. Ms Kaufman says she appreciated his interest, and didn't notice that he seemed uncomfortable. To Mr Garrow, her behavior "was a little awkward," he says. At her age, he would have been eagerly trying to make a good impression on a senior manager. "I thought, 'this feels no different than when my 14-year-old daughter gets in the car and won't talk to me because she's texting her friends, looking at Instagram, checking Facebook,'" he says. Resigned to differences in ways of working and relating to higher-ups, he says, he decided, "Oh well, I'll just get on my iPhone too." ■

Adapted from Sue Shellenbarger,
The Wall Street Journal, May 28th, 2014.

KEY POINT

Generation Y

Born in the mid-1980s and later, Generation Y are in their 20s and entering work. They have grown up in a world where they are surrounded by technology, technology that has developed at a faster rate than ever before. Subsequently, this new generation has an intuitive understanding of technology and is plugged in 24/7. Social media is part of their world and even more natural to them than talking on the phone.

A worldwide survey discovered that 90% of Generation Y check their emails, texts and social media accounts using their smartphones before they even get out of bed and that one in five will check their smartphone at least once every ten minutes. This apparent obsession with technology comes from a desire to ensure they aren't missing out on anything.

Although some may say that this is a distraction from work, it can be positive for employers. Generation Y are, by far, the most agile, responsive and informed generation thanks to their Internet use, smartphones and other gadgets. In an employer's eyes a Generation Y employee will have a natural ability to communicate as well as respond quickly to information.

Generation Y are also labeled as the Peter Pan generation because they tend to live with their parents for longer periods than previous generations.

UN ARTICLE DU *MONDE* À CONSULTER :

• **La traque ardue des « fake news »** p. 83-84
(Alexis Delcambre et Damien Leloup, *Le Monde* daté du 03.02.2017)

Réseaux sociaux : les jeunots à la rescousse des seniors

De plus en plus d'entreprises demandent aux jeunes employés d'aider leurs collègues dans l'utilisation des réseaux sociaux. Non sans difficulté.

Entre les jeunes d'une vingtaine d'années familiers des réseaux sociaux et les cadres d'un âge plus avancé, fâchés avec la technologie, la fracture numérique sur les lieux de travail est de plus en plus grande. Pour remédier à ce problème, un nombre croissant d'entreprises recourent au « tutorat inversé » en faisant travailler de jeunes employés avec des collègues plus âgés pour développer les compétences technologiques de ces derniers.

Les binômes ne fonctionnent pas toujours : ils peuvent être intimidants pour les jeunes tuteurs et embarrassants pour leurs aînés, parfois gênés de révéler leur faible niveau de connaissances. Rebecca Kaufman, une « community manager » de vingt-quatre ans qui est chargée de communication numérique chez MasterCard depuis deux ans, raconte qu'elle a été « terriblement intimidée » quand un réseau de jeunes professionnels de sa société lui a demandé d'être la tutrice d'un cadre supérieur de cinquante ans, Ron Garrow.

La jeune femme fréquentait les réseaux sociaux depuis une dizaine d'années, mais la perspective d'aider un cadre de haut niveau à se familiariser avec ces nouvelles technologies était assez effrayante. Deux rencontres, l'une en décembre et l'autre en janvier, ont eu lieu dans le bureau de M. Garrow. Le cadre a facilement accepté la première proposition de sa tutrice : augmenter la fréquence de ses visites sur le réseau LinkedIn en s'y rendant non plus chaque semaine, mais chaque jour, et commencer à partager des articles avec ses contacts. Mais il a été plus réfractaire à l'idée d'utiliser Twitter. L'importance d'éviter toute déclaration publique pouvant s'avérer dangereuse était d'autant plus ancrée en lui qu'il avait travaillé dans deux grandes compagnies bancaires pendant vingt-six ans avant de rejoindre MasterCard en 2010. Dans ce milieu, les cadres supérieurs devaient « obtenir une multitude d'autorisations » avant de pouvoir s'exprimer en public. « Psychologiquement, les cent quarante caractères étaient aussi très intimidants », précise Ron Garrow.

La jeune femme l'a encouragé à surmonter ses réticences en lui présentant Twitter comme « un univers entièrement nouveau, qui vous permet d'avoir des contacts avec tous les gens qui vous intéressent ». Quand elle lui a demandé « Comment souhaitez-vous vous positionner sur le réseau ? », il n'a pas su quoi répondre. Père de quatre enfants âgés de quatorze à vingt-six ans, Ron Garrow s'est dit avec humilité : « Elle a vingt-quatre ans, l'âge de mes enfants, et je dépends totalement d'elle. » Comprenant que la réputation de ce cadre supérieur était en jeu, Rebecca a fait quelques recherches pour l'aider à identifier des experts en ressources humaines et des auteurs influents sur les réseaux sociaux.

Ron Garrow a ouvert un compte Twitter, a créé son profil et s'est exercé à utiliser le site. Sa tutrice l'a aidé à formuler ses premiers *tweets*. Lors d'une visite à l'université du Michigan, en juin, il a voulu *twitter* une photo d'un collègue et de lui-même en compagnie d'étudiants de MBA. Il a envoyé à la jeune femme un courriel sibyllin contenant la description, rédigée à la hâte, d'une opération complexe – la simulation par des étudiants d'une séance d'information organisée par une entreprise pour des investisseurs –, en ajoutant ces mots : « Je voudrais le *twitter*, mais je ne sais pas comment. » Elle lui a proposé une autre formulation, lui-même a réécrit le message et a *twitté* la photo en quelques minutes.

À l'issue de cinq mois de collaboration, Ron Garrow totalise 2 352 contacts sur LinkedIn, vérifie son compte Twitter huit à dix fois par jour, suit les comptes de cent neuf utilisateurs et envoie une cinquantaine de *tweets* par mois. Rebecca l'a félicité quand il a dépassé les quatre cents *followers* et elle a salué le score supérieur à la moyenne de 45 qu'il a obtenu sur Klout, un site de classement des utilisateurs en fonction de leur influence sur les réseaux sociaux, en soulignant : « C'est presque la moitié de celui d'Obama. » Elle continue néanmoins de l'encourager à *twitter* sur des sujets personnels. Le cadre avoue que sa fille Clare, quatorze ans, trouve ses *tweets* ennuyeux. Mais, selon lui, le partage d'informations personnelles en ligne « nous place dans des situations inconfortables ». Récemment, lors d'une sortie à New York avec sa femme Dana, il a commencé à rédiger un *tweet*, mais s'est aussitôt interrompu, car il n'était « pas encore prêt à franchir cette ligne ».

Le binôme a eu à surmonter des différences générationnelles. Dernièrement, alors qu'ils rentraient en voiture d'une conférence, Rebecca était en train de travailler sur son Smartphone quand Ron Garrow a entamé une conversation sur la carrière de la jeune femme. Après avoir discuté pendant un moment avec lui, elle s'est penchée à nouveau sur son téléphone. Elle reconnaît avoir apprécié l'intérêt qu'il lui portait et n'a pas remarqué sa gêne. De son côté, le cadre a trouvé que le comportement de Rebecca « était un peu maladroit ». À l'âge de la jeune femme, il aurait cherché à faire bonne impression sur un cadre supérieur. « Je me suis dit qu'elle se conduisait exactement comme ma fille, quand elle monte dans la voiture et qu'elle ne me parle pas, occupée à envoyer des textos à ses copines, à regarder son compte Instagram ou à aller sur Facebook », dit-il. Résigné à rencontrer des différences dans le mode de travail et les relations avec les supérieurs, il s'est dit : « Eh bien, moi aussi, je vais consulter mon iPhone. »

D'après Sue Shellenbarger, *The Wall Street Journal*, 28 mai 2014.
Extrait de *Courrier International*

VOCABULARY TO REMEMBER!

- **workplace**: *lieu de travail*
- **to be social-media savvy**: *être familier des réseaux sociaux*
- **skills**: *compétences*
- **mentor**: *tuteur*
- **a prospect**: *une perspective*
- **a high-profile executive**: *un cadre de haut niveau*
- **to avoid**: *éviter*
- **to brand oneself**: *se positionner*
- **to rely on**: *dépendre de*
- **to set up a profile (set/set)**: *créer un profil*
- **to congratulate = to praise**: *féliciter*
- **to bridge generational differences**: *surmonter des différences générationnelles*
- **to strike up (struck/struck) a conversation**: *entamer une conversation*
- **for a while**: *pendant un moment*
- **behaviour**: *comportement*

Henry James' *Washington Square* (1880)

"If I don't marry before your death, I will not after," she said.
To her father, it must be admitted, this seemed only another epigram; and as obstinacy, in unaccomplished minds, does not usually select such a mode of expression, he was the more surprised at this wanton play of a fixed idea.
"Do you mean that for an impertinence?" he inquired; an inquiry of which, as he made it, he quite perceived the grossness.
"An impertinence? Oh, father, what terrible things you say!"
"If you don't wait for my death, you might as well marry immediately, there is nothing else to wait for."
For some time Catherine made no answer; but finally she said –
"I think Morris – little by little – might persuade you."
"I shall never let him speak to me again. I dislike him too much."
Catherine gave a long, low sigh; she tried to stifle it, for she had made up her mind that it was wrong to make a parade of her trouble, and to endeavour to act upon her father by the meretricious aid of emotion. Indeed, she even thought it wrong – in the sense of being inconsiderate – to attempt to act upon his feelings at all; her part was to effect some gentle, gradual change in his intellectual perception of poor Morris's character. But the means of effecting such a change were at present shrouded in mystery, and she felt miserably helpless and hopeless. She had exhausted all arguments, all replies. Her father might have pitied her, and in fact he did so; but he was sure he was right.
"There is one thing you can tell Mr Townsend, when you see him again," he said: "that if you marry without my consent, I don't leave you a farthing of money. That will interest him more than anything else you can tell him."
"That would be very right," Catherine answered. "I ought not in that case have a farthing of your money."
"My dear child," the Doctor observed, laughing, "your simplicity is touching. Make that remark, in that tone, and with that expression of countenance, to Mr Townsend and take a note of his answer. It won't be polite – it will express irritation; and I shall be glad of that, as it will put me in the right; unless, indeed – which is perfectly possible – you should like him the better for being rude to you."
"He will never be rude to me," said Catherine, gently.
"Tell him what I say, all the same."
She looked at her father, and her quiet eyes filled with tears.
"I think I will see him, then," she murmured, in her timid voice.
"Exactly as you choose!" And he went to the door and opened it for her to go out. The movement gave her a terrible sense of his turning her off.

DICTIONARY

- **wanton**: uncontrolled
- **to inquire**: to ask
- **grossness**: offensiveness
- **to stifle**: to prevent from happening
- **to make up one's mind**: to decide
- **to endeavour**: to try
- **meretricious**: attractive on the surface, but false
- **to shroud**: to cover and hide
- **a reply**: an answer
- **a farthing**: a former British coin
- **to linger**: to remain for a time instead of going
- **ungrateful**: not appreciative
- **pain**: suffering
- **to bear**: to endure
- **to overflow**: to flood
- **grimly**: with determination
- **sternly**: firmly
- **to evade**: to avoid
- **to sob out**: to say while crying
- **threshold**: doorstep
- **to remain**: to stay
- **faintly**: quietly
- **entertainment**: amusement

MOTS CLÉS en lien avec la thématique

NOUNS
- a quality: *une qualité*
- a shortcoming: *un défaut*
- a bond: *un lien*
- a dispute: *un conflit*
- a row: *une dispute*

Ex.: Family **rows** threaten children's wellbeing.
- a relationship: *une relation*
- friendship: *l'amitié*
- contempt: *le mépris*
- pride: *la fierté*
- hatred: *la haine*
- betrayal: *la trahison*

ADJECTIVES
- reliable: *fiable*
- self-confident: *sûr de soi*
- bossy: *autoritaire*
- shy: *timide*
- cautious: *prudent*
- outgoing: *ouvert*
- selfish: *égoïste*
- sensitive: sensible
- loving: *affectueux*
- nasty: *méchant*
- gifted: *doué*
- narrow-minded: *borné*
- unpredictable: *imprévisible*

VERBS
- to get on well with someone = to get along with: *bien s'entendre avec quelqu'un*
- to agree with someone: *être d'accord avec quelqu'un*
- to disagree with someone: *être en désaccord avec quelqu'un*
- to side with someone: *prendre parti pour quelqu'un*
- to change one's mind: *changer d'avis*
- to support = to back somebody up: *soutenir*
- to have an argument with: *se disputer*
- to hate = to loathe: *détester*
- to harass: *harceler*

Ex.: Children who are being **harassed** at school should talk to their parents about it.
- to make somebody do something: *forcer quelqu'un à faire quelque chose*
- to harm: *faire du mal*
- to neglect: *négliger*
- to cheat: *tricher*
- to deceive: *tromper*
- to despise: *mépriser*

"It will be only once, for the present," she added, lingering a moment. "Exactly as you choose," he repeated, standing there with his hand on the door. "I have told you what I think. If you see him, you will be an ungrateful, cruel child; you will have given your old father the greatest pain of his life."

This was more than the poor girl could bear; her tears overflowed, and she moved towards her grimly consistent parent with a pitiful cry. Her hands were raised in supplication, but he sternly evaded this appeal. Instead of letting her sob out her misery on his shoulder, he simply took her by the arm and directed her course across the threshold, closing the door gently but firmly behind her. After he had done so, he remained listening. For a long time there was no sound; he knew that she was standing outside. He was sorry for her, as I have said; but he was so sure he was right. At last he heard her move away, and then her footsteps creaked faintly upon the stairs.

The Doctor took several turns round his study, with his hands in his pockets, and a thin sparkle, possibly of irritation, but partly also of something like humour, in his eye. "By Jove," he said to himself, "I believe she will stick – I believe she will stick!" And this idea of Catherine "sticking" appeared to have a comical side, and to offer a prospect of entertainment. He determined, as he said to himself, to see it out.

Henry James, *Washington Square* (1880)

Henry James

FOCUS ON...

Henry James (1843-1916) was born in New York City into a wealthy family. He travelled widely when he was young, studying in New York, London and Paris. He spent most of his life in Europe, becoming a British citizen in 1915. His most famous novels include *The Wings of the Dove*, *The Portrait of a Lady*, *The Ambassadors* and *What Maisie Knew*. Many of the themes in Henry James' work were centered around the innocence of the New World (the United States) and the corruption and wisdom of the Old World (Europe). His protagonists are often young American women facing oppression or abuse.

Washington Square is a short novel published in 1880 that recounts the conflict between a daughter and her domineering father. Catherine Sloper is the plain, obedient daughter of the widowed Dr Sloper of Washington Square. When a handsome young man proposes to Catherine, her father forbids the marriage because he believes the man to be after Catherine's fortune. The main theme of the book is therefore family relationships. Unlike much of Henry James' work *Washington Square* is a thoroughly American novel – the characters are American as is the setting.

Washington Square is one of Henry James' most famous novels.

Washington Square, New York City

S'EXPRIMER

EXPRESSING ADVICE AND OPINION

• **Using "ought to"**

"I **ought not** in that case have a farthing of your money."

Ought to and **ought not to** give the speaker's **opinion** of what is a good or bad action.

As this is an opinion, it is often used for giving **advice**.

Ex.: You **ought to** talk to your teacher about it.

Ex.: I don't think you **ought to** go.

Ex.: You **ought not to** go out tonight because you have exams next week.

• **Using "should" and "shouldn't"**

Should and **shouldn't** can be used in the same way as **ought to** and **ought not to** to express **advice** and **opinion**.

Should is more frequently used than **ought to**.

Ex.: I think you **should** talk to your teacher about it.

Ex.: You **shouldn't** go out tonight because you have very important exams next week.

• **Using "had better"**

Had better has a similar meaning to **should** and **ought to**.

Had is usually contracted.

Ex.: They **had better** reduce their ridiculously high prices.

Ex.: You'**d better** talk to your teacher about it.

EXPRESSING A CONDITION: USING "UNLESS"

• **"Unless** you should like him the better for being rude to you."

Unless means **except if**.

Unless is used to say that something will only happen in certain circumstances (= *sauf si*).

Ex.: You can't travel on this train **unless** you have a reservation.

Ex.: **Unless** the infection is treated, there is a real danger that she will die.

• With **unless**, we use **present tenses** when we talk about the future.

Ex.: We'll go out for a walk tomorrow, **unless** it rains.

Questions de compréhension

True or false?

1. Catherine and her father are having a conversation about the date of her wedding.

2. The conversation takes place in the Doctor's study.

3. Catherine doesn't think her father will change his mind about Morris.

4. Catherine's father is convinced that he won't change his mind about Morris.

5. Morris's family name is Townsend.

6. The Doctor thinks that Morris wants to marry Catherine for her money.

7. Catherine doesn't want any of her father's money if she marries Morris.

8. Catherine's father forbids her to see Morris again.

9. Catherine informs her father that she will see Morris again.

10. The Doctor uses emotional blackmail to get her to change her mind about seeing Morris.

11. The Doctor doesn't feel any pity for his daughter.

Exercices de grammaire

A. Complete the second sentence so that it has a similar meaning to the first one.

1. My party is on Friday.

I .... on Friday.

2. Tomorrow's weather forecast is for rain.

It's .... tomorrow.

3. I don't plan to sell my car after all.

I .... my car after all.

4. I promise to phone you before our next meeting.

Before we...you.

5. The work won't take us longer than an hour.

We...the work in an hour.

B. Choose the correct form of the future (present simple, present continuous, be going to or will).

1. If you don't study enough, you .... (**fail**).

2. The film .... (**start**) in a minute.

3. The plane .... (**take off**) at 7 am.

4. What is your intention? .... (**you accept**) his offer?

5. You .... (**change**) your mind when you .... (**see**) he never keeps his promises.

BOÎTE À OUTILS : L'EXPRESSION DU FUTUR

• **Will** ***et*** **shall**

"It **won't be** polite – it **will express** irritation; and I **shall be** glad of that, as it **will put** me in the right."

"I **shall** never **let** him speak to me again."

On utilise ici **will** *et* **shall** *pour exprimer le* **futur***.*

– **Will** *s'utilise pour exprimer* ***une prédiction, une estimation concernant le futur****.*

Ex.: I **will** never be rich.

Ex.: I **will** be very pleased to meet her.

– **Will** *s'utilise pour indiquer la* **volonté** *de celui qui parle et exprimer* ***une promesse ou un refus****.*

Ex.: I promise that I **will** work harder next year.

Ex.: He **won't** change his plans for us.

Ex.: I**'ll** phone you back.

– **Will** *s'utilise pour exprimer un* ***fait simple, sans nuance****.*

Ex.: Mary **will** leave for England next week.

– **Shall** *s'utilise à la place de* **will** *dans un langage plus* **formel***.*

• *L'expression du* ***futur*** *avec le* ***présent progressif***

Le ***présent progressif*** *est utilisé pour parler de ce que l'on* ***a programmé de faire*** *dans un futur plus ou moins proche.*

Ex.: I**'m flying** to London tomorrow.

Ex.: We**'re spending** our holidays in Spain this summer.

• **L'expression du futur avec "be going to"**

– **Be going to** *est utilisé pour marquer une* ***intention.***

Ex.: She**'s going to** make coffee.

– **Be going to** *est également utilisé pour exprimer un* ***futur proche****.*

Ex.: It's already 10 am! I**'m going to** miss my plane!

• *L'expression du* ***futur*** *avec le* ***présent simple***

– *Le* ***présent simple*** *est utilisé avec un sens de futur pour indiquer un* ***horaire officiel****.*

Ex.: The plane **lands** at 6pm this evening.

– *Le* ***présent simple*** *est utilisé avec un sens de futur* ***après les conjonctions de temps*** (**when, as soon as, unless, before, until, if**).

Ex.: **As soon as I arrive** in London, I will phone you.

Ex.: I will phone you **when I arrive** at the station.

• *On utilise le* ***futur antérieur*** (**will have** *+ **participe passé***) *pour parler de* ***quelque chose qui sera terminé à un certain moment dans le futur****.*

Ex.: We **will have finished** our exams by this time next week.

Amérique du Nord, mai 2014, séries ES, L, S

Document A (extrait)

[...] Picasso snapped his fingers and asked Benoit for the bill. Soon the restaurateur did the maths, writing everything down on a yellow sheet of paper and approached the table. But just as he reached Picasso he put the bill in his pocket and slid a blank sheet of paper beneath the artist's nose.
"What's this?" asked Picasso.
"Well, Master, perhaps if... perhaps if you were to draw a quick picture...?"
The artist gazed at him with a thin smile.
"What, instead of paying?"
"Certainly sir, if you wouldn't mind..."
I felt tense, excited. Was this the moment I'd see the great artist at work? Picasso glanced around the table with a childish smile and started scribbling something on the paper. Everyone was looking. Benoit perched at his shoulder, his left eye twitching, excited.
"There!" said Picasso with a flourish, handing the restaurateur the sketch. "Will this do?"
"Monsieur Picasso! How wonderful!"
There was a murmur of appreciation around the table and every customer in the café wanted to see this spontaneous creation. Benoit sidled away, admiring the sketch. Then he stopped. He turned, then hesitated as his customer threw back some more wine, stroking the lady's arm. The restaurateur came back to the table, his eye twitching faster than ever.
"Sir," he murmured, awkward.
Picasso went on chatting and drinking.
"Sir" said Benoit, a little louder. "This is marvelous, but would maître mind signing it?"
Picasso put his glass down.
"Excuse me?"
"Just a signature, to prove it's you."
The artist gave a thin smile.
"I'm buying the meal," he said. "Not the whole restaurant."

Peter Flynn, *Picasso on the Beach and Other Stories*, 2013.

EXPRESSION ÉCRITE : Is a work of art necessarily a question of money? Discuss and illustrate by giving examples.

Analyse du sujet

Il s'agit d'un essai argumentatif au sujet du lien entre l'art et l'argent : on vous demande s'ils sont étroitement liés ou non, et d'illustrer votre argumentation avec des exemples.

Proposition de corrigé

Picasso's defense of artists in document A underlines the fact that only the most successful artists are able to make a living of their art, and that most artists lead a life of poverty hoping for the stroke of genius that will enable them to rise above mediocrity. In this essay, we will examine whether art is necessarily a question of money or not.

On the one hand, it seems obvious that initially art has nothing to do with money at all. Art is a form of creation. An artist follows his inspiration to produce a work of art that no doubt evokes a deep personal meaning for him. **Of course**, certain art forms require costly materials, **such as** precious metals or rare pigments, which means that there is a financial limitation to what an artist can produce without a patron. **However**, the true artist, **in my opinion**, is able to produce a work of art with even the cheapest of materials: art is in the inspiration and not in the materials used. So, money is by no means essential to art.

On the other hand, an artist's work only really attains the status of art if it obtains public recognition. **As** everything in our consumer society is assessed in financial terms, the artist's admirers will value his art by attributing a price. The restaurant owner's reaction in document A is a case in point: if Picasso's drawing is not authenticated by his signature, he considers it will be less valuable than the signed drawing, **and yet** the artistic value is identical.

In conclusion, it is public recognition that enables art to exist, and **as** our capitalist society values money above everything else, art is necessarily a question of money, **otherwise** it exists only in the eyes of the artist. ■

TROIS ARTICLES DU *MONDE* À CONSULTER

- **Damien Hirst pirate la Fondation Pinault** **p. 85-86**
(Emmanuelle Lequeux, *Le Monde* daté du 27.04.2017)
- **Les mots de Bob Dylan, l'émotion de Patti Smith** **p. 86-87**
(Anne-Françoise Hivert, *Le Monde* daté du 13.12.2016)
- **La voix de la douleur** **p.87-88**
(Thomas Sotinel, *Le Monde* daté du 11.04.1994)

NOTIONS CLÉS

ARTS, EDUCATION AND EXCHANGE

- Art and public spaces (*l'art et l'espace public*): poems on the underground, busking, street art, Belfast murals.
- Artistic exchange and learning in English-speaking countries (*l'apprentissage et les échanges artistiques dans les pays anglophones*).
- Public encounters and culture (*la culture et les espaces d'échanges*): book clubs, festivals, debating societies.
- an artist: *un artiste*
- an encounter: *une rencontre*
- a graffiti: *un graffiti*
- a means of expression: *un moyen d'expression*
- a musician: *un musician*
- a novellist: *un romancier*
- a poem: *un poème*
- a poet: *un poète*
- aesthetic: *esthétique*
- cultural: *culturel*
- expressive: *expressif*
- inspired: *inspiré*
- passionate: *passionné*
- permanent: *permanent*
- pleasing to the eye: *agréable à regarder*
- short-lived: *éphémère*
- valuable: *de valeur*
- to act: *jouer, faire de la comédie*
- to dance: *danser*
- to debate: *débattre*
- to draw: *dessiner*
- to paint: *peindre*
- to share: *partager*

COMMUNITY SPIRIT: BELONGING TO A WIDENED FAMILY OR COMMUNITY

- Cliques, fashion tribes, gangs, clothing, musical tastes (*cliques, tribus de la mode, gangs, tenue vestimentaire, goûts musicaux*).
- Virtual communities, gaming networks, social networks (*communautés virtuelles, jeux en réseaux, réseaux sociaux*).
- the appearance/ looks: *l'apparence*
- fashion: *la mode*
- fashionable: *à la mode*
- hip: *branché*
- in: *dans le vent*
- the sense of community: *l'esprit de communauté*
- to belong to: *appartenir à*

Australie – La repentance par l'emploi

Selon un rapport de la Commission des droits de l'homme australienne, huit Aborigènes sur dix n'ont pas accès au marché du travail. Des entreprises lancent des politiques d'embauche spécifiques.

Peau claire, cheveux longs et bouclés, petites lunettes d'intellectuelle… Rien ne signale l'appartenance de Wendy Dawson au clan aborigène des Wiradjuri de Nouvelle-Galles du Sud en Australie. « *Ma mère était aborigène, pas mon père* », dit-elle. Cette femme âgée de 53 ans, qui pourrait se fondre dans la population anglo-saxonne de l'Australie, revendique au contraire son appartenance à l'autre camp, celui des victimes.

En 2009, Wendy Dawson a quitté un poste bien rémunéré de directrice dans l'administration australienne des affaires indigènes pour devenir directrice de la diversité au sein de la filiale australienne du groupe Sodexo (6 000 salariés, 300 millions d'euros de chiffre d'affaires). « *J'aide cette entreprise à élaborer sa politique vis-à-vis des communautés indigènes.* » Wendy Dawson recrute des Aborigènes pour tous les métiers de cette multinationale de services, met en place des formations, noue des partenariats avec les différentes communautés…

Son action s'intègre à un vaste mouvement de discrimination positive que mène aujourd'hui le gouvernement australien en faveur des Aborigènes et de leurs homologues de Torres Strait Islander – une autre communauté indigène. Après des décennies de persécutions, un mouvement de repentance s'est amorcé qui oblige les entreprises à mettre en place des politiques d'embauche spécifiques.

L'intégration économique des Aborigènes n'a toutefois rien de simple : selon un rapport de la Commission des droits de l'homme australienne, huit indigènes sur dix n'ont pas accès au marché du travail pour cause d'analphabétisme, alcoolisme ou traumatisme psychologique grave. Dans certaines zones rurales, 70 % des enfants ne vont pas à l'école. Quant aux problèmes de santé, ils sont indignes d'une population vivant dans un pays développé.

À Karratha, une zone semi-désertique d'Australie de l'Ouest, Sodexo gère plusieurs villages (« *bases-vie* ») où résident les ingénieurs et techniciens chargés de construire une usine de liquéfaction de gaz naturel. Par contrat, le groupe de services s'est engagé à intégrer 15 % d'indigènes sur un effectif de 120 salariés. L'entreprise n'en salarie aujourd'hui que 10 %. Une carence qui devrait être comblée d'ici à la fin du contrat, mais qui s'explique par une forme d'« instabilité » structurelle des travailleurs aborigènes. Il n'est pas rare qu'après avoir travaillé plusieurs semaines d'affilée, ceux-ci disparaissent sans crier gare.

Cette apparente indifférence aux règles de la vie au travail s'explique avant tout par le primat de la famille et du clan sur toute autre forme de relation contractuelle. Quand un décès se produit dans la tribu, tous les proches concernés quittent instantanément leur travail et traversent ce pays-continent s'il le faut, pour participer aux cérémonies de deuil. Nul ne sait quand ils reviendront car ce sont les « anciens », les leaders du clan, qui détermineront la fin des funérailles. Lesquelles peuvent durer plusieurs semaines.

Une des manières de stabiliser le personnel indigène consiste à faire passer l'idée que l'entreprise peut, comme la famille, être pourvoyeuse de « *care* » (« protection, solidarité »). Ainsi, si un salarié qui a quitté son emploi sans avertissement retoque à la porte de l'entreprise six mois plus tard, « *notre attitude sera de rester ouvert et de l'accueillir. S'il faut changer les horaires de quelqu'un pour le garder, nous savons nous montrer flexibles* », dit Prakash Seenarain, un Mauricien francophone, chef du village de Gap Ridge, à Karratha.

Wendy Dawson le reconnaît, la mémoire de chacun est « *si lourde de griefs inexprimés et de traumas qu'ils peinent à croire qu'une entreprise puisse prendre en compte leur personne ou leurs problèmes* ».

À cet égard, l'attitude d'Annette Bennell, tribu des Noongar (région de Perth), femme de ménage depuis trois mois sur la base-vie de Gap Ridge, passe pour une victoire de Wendy Dawson. Quand on demande à Annette Bennell ce qui la retient dans l'entreprise, elle ne cite pas son salaire annuel brut de 70 000 euros, mais le fait qu'elle se sent là « *comme à la maison* » ; elle se dit « *connectée à la famille Sodexo* » et affirme ressentir le même « *caring* » que celui qui lie ensemble les membres du clan.

Pour stabiliser le personnel indigène, nombre d'entreprises investissent tôt sur des gens jeunes. Mikaela Mowarin, 17 ans, du clan des Ngarluma, est ainsi scolarisée quatre jours par semaine au collège de Karratha, mais le cinquième jour, elle travaille au village de Gap Ridge. Une insertion professionnelle progressive, ponctuée de réunions, d'entretiens, et qui a dû être négociée avec les membres de sa famille.

« *On investit sur Mikaela, mais on ne sait pas si nous arriverons à la fidéliser, ni si elle souhaitera faire carrière chez nous*, indique Wendy Dawson. *Elle a exprimé son intérêt à l'école, nous avons détecté un potentiel, on l'interviewe, on demande à ses parents. On lui parle aussi en tête-à-tête, on lui montre différentes possibilités.* »

Wendy Dawson compte sur le bouche-à-oreille pour susciter des vocations. Si Mikaela Mowarin est contente à Gap Ridge, elle le dira aux autres, qui postuleront peut-être. « *On passe beaucoup de temps à recréer un tissu de confiance. Un mensonge sera jugé par nos employés aborigènes, mais aussi par l'ensemble de la communauté, où le bouche-à-oreille est très puissant.* »

La seconde difficulté à fidéliser les salariés tient au salaire. Celui-ci est rarement perçu comme un bien individuel. Une femme de ménage peut bien gagner l'extraordinaire revenu de 70 000 euros brut par an à Gap Ridge – les salaires sont très élevés du fait des conditions de vie –, elle n'aura jamais le sentiment que cet argent lui appartient.

Naomi Knapp, de la tribu Noongar, travaille à la cuisine de la base-vie de Boddington attenante à la plus grande mine d'or d'Australie, exploitée par l'américain Newmont Mining Industries. Elle a trois garçons âgés de 18 à 22 ans. L'un est en formation, le deuxième travaille à la mine d'or, et le troisième cherche un emploi. Naomi Knapp aide financièrement ses enfants, mais aussi sa mère, qui a 66 ans. Des liens renforcés par les souffrances subies : à 4 ans, Naomi Knapp a été volée à sa mère et placée dans un orphelinat, comme ses frères et sœurs. Elle a ensuite été adoptée de force par une autre famille. « *L'administration avait fait signer à sa mère des papiers comme quoi elle renonçait à ses droits maternels. Mais elle ne savait pas ce qu'elle signait.* »

Les Aborigènes ont en effet été victimes d'une tentative de génocide très particulière qui a pris la forme d'un vol des enfants métis. Depuis les années 1920 jusque dans les années 1970, 45 000 à 55 000 enfants, nés d'un père blanc et d'une mère aborigène, ont été confisqués à leur famille pour être placés dans des orphelinats ou des familles adoptantes où ils ont grandi loin de toute affection, souvent en butte à des violences.

Ce kidnapping de masse reposait sur l'idée que la population aborigène, condamnée à dépérir, ne devait pas se renforcer par le jeu des mariages mixtes. Naomi Knapp, qui fut victime de ce phénomène connu sous le nom de « Génération volée », a revu sa mère à 9 ans, laquelle n'a pu récupérer sa fille qu'à l'âge de 13 ans. A-t-elle subi des mauvais traitements ? « *Je ne peux même pas en parler tellement ça me fait encore souffrir* », dit-elle. Pour tous les indigènes, l'argent n'a qu'une fonction : panser les plaies des membres du clan.

Si le travail des femmes aborigènes est facteur d'intégration, il accélère aussi la mutation des sociétés indigènes. Alors que les persécutions ont détruit le statut des hommes en tant que pourvoyeurs de nourriture et de sécurité, les femmes ont pu se maintenir par le rôle qu'elles ont gardé auprès des enfants. Aujourd'hui, le salaire qu'elles redistribuent sur le clan fait d'elles le pivot de la tribu et contribue à l'effacement des hommes. Plus l'employabilité des femmes s'accroît, et plus la structure familiale et tribale se déséquilibre.

POURQUOI CET ARTICLE ?

L'article de *New Scientist* reproduit en page 64 s'interroge sur l'opportunité d'un projet du gouvernement australien visant à « envahir » la région nord du pays – où la population Aborigène est très présente – pour y établir un vaste programme de développement agricole, en lien avec un ambitieux plan d'irrigation. L'article du *Monde* proposé ici vient nous rappeler à quel point les conditions de vie des Aborigènes demeurent injustement précaires depuis l'arrivée des colons européens sur cette île-continent.

Tout n'est pas tragique toutefois dans la vie des indigènes australiens. Matthew Dawson, fils de Wendy Dawson, dirige l'une des salles de sport de Gap Ridge depuis un an. C'est lui qui a donné à sa mère l'idée de passer dans le privé. « *Je savais qu'ils avaient besoin de quelqu'un comme ma mère* », dit-il.

Matthew Dawson entretient les meilleures relations avec les techniciens qui habitent Gap Ridge et construisent une usine de liquéfaction de gaz à quelques kilomètres. Il les accueille dans sa salle de sport et les conseille sur leur alimentation. Il exerce également une veille contre la dépression. S'il note le coup de blues d'un habitué de sa salle de sport, il en parle aux amis pour leur recommander d'entourer particulièrement cette personne.

Le problème de Matthew Dawson n'est pas le racisme, mais – peut-être – la possibilité de trouver l'âme sœur. Pas beaucoup de femmes, et encore moins de femmes jeunes, dans le camp. À l'exception d'Amanda, la barmaid. Amanda Korp, 24 ans, de la tribu des Wemba Wemba, aurait pu être mannequin, mais elle n'y a sans doute pas pensé. Voilà trois semaines, elle a quitté la banque où elle était chef d'agence pour tenir le bar à Gap Ridge.

La fonction est, en apparence, moins prestigieuse, mais le salaire est plus élevé. Amanda Korp est aborigène par sa grand-mère, son grand-père étant un immigré autrichien. Elle n'a pas besoin d'envoyer de l'argent, car tous ses frères et sœurs travaillent. Amanda Korp ne parle que l'anglais – le langage de son clan s'est perdu. Elle appelle ses frères et sœurs chaque jour, quelle que soit la distance. Aussi intégrée soit-elle, la famille demeure la part essentielle de son existence. ■

Yves Mamou , *Le Monde* daté du 16.07.2010

La traque ardue des « fake news »

La dirigeante écossaise, Nicola Sturgeon, a cherché, en marge du sommet, à dissiper les réserves sur l'indépendance.

Haro sur les « *fake news* ». Alors que l'onde de choc de l'élection de Donald Trump résonne encore, l'Europe se mobilise contre les « fausses informations », convaincue qu'elles ont joué un rôle dans la campagne présidentielle américaine et que leur ombre plane sur les prochains scrutins prévus en France et en Allemagne, sur fond de perte d'influence des médias traditionnels et de craintes quant aux actions de propagande étrangères – notamment russes. Utile, cette vaste prise de conscience doit se garder de toute simplification. Le phénomène des *« fake news »* ne date pas d'hier, sa mesure est difficile, la corrélation avec le résultat de la présidentielle américaine ne peut être strictement établie, et le concept même de « fausse information » – qui désigne un contenu délibérément inexact, présenté sous une apparence journalistique – recoupe d'autres réalités comme l'intoxication à visée politique, le canular, la « réinformation » d'extrême-droite, la recherche effrénée du clic et du profit...

Reste que le constat général est celui d'une expansion du phénomène, portée par l'industrialisation de la fabrication de *« fakes »*, la fragilisation de l'espace public par les communications mensongères, le conspirationnisme et les tenants de la post-vérité, et enfin l'essor spectaculaire des moteurs de recherche et désormais des réseaux sociaux comme moyens d'information. Les *« fake news »* se diffusent aujourd'hui beaucoup plus vite et efficacement qu'auparavant – la faute, en partie, aux plateformes qui privilégient *« l'engagement »* de leurs utilisateurs, c'est-à-dire le fait qu'ils partagent, commentent, *« aiment »* des contenus. Et qui donnent donc une prime aux contenus qui émeuvent, choquent, font réagir – photos d'animaux mignons ou mensonges éhontés. C'est ce parti pris qui est aujourd'hui mis en cause, après que de fausses informations, telles que le soutien du pape à Donald Trump, ont été plus largement lues et partagées que leurs contrepoints véridiques. Facebook et Google, notamment, sont désormais sommés d'agir pour maîtriser les comportements de leurs utilisateurs.

Au Royaume-Uni, la Chambre des communes vient d'ouvrir une enquête parlementaire sur le sujet. La France veut ouvrir des discussions avec Facebook et Google notamment. En Allemagne, les réseaux sociaux sont menacés d'une loi sanctionnant la diffusion de fausses informations. La Commission européenne réclame, elle aussi, une action plus déterminée des grandes plateformes par la voix du commissaire chargé du numérique, Andrus Ansip. Les pressions commencent aussi, c'est nouveau, à venir de l'intérieur : au sein de Twitter, de Facebook ou de Google, des voix s'élèvent pour demander à ces entreprises de faire plus – et mieux – contre les internautes qui usent et abusent de leur outil pour répandre des mensonges, de la propagande ou des idéologies haineuses. Mais ces demandes vont à l'encontre de la posture de ces plateformes qui se considèrent, par essence, neutres : *« nous ne sommes pas des médias »*, affirment-elles, s'abritant derrière le fait que ce sont des algorithmes qui « choisissent » les contenus mis en avant. Les Etats voudraient que Facebook ou Google agissent comme des régulateurs et trouvent les moyens de filtrer les contenus ; ces derniers considèrent que leur rôle est, au mieux, de fournir à des tiers des outils de régulation – comme Facebook l'a fait, depuis plusieurs années, sur des sujets comme la prévention du suicide. Sous la pression de l'opinion, elles ont toutefois engagé des actions, en partie pour des raisons d'image : label *« fact check »* sur Google News aux Etats-Unis, projet de vérification collective *« First Draft »* de Google en partenariat avec différents médias, dont Le Monde, système d'alerte aux fausses informations en test chez Facebook. L'autorégulation pour éviter la régulation : la recette est connue.

Des raisons économiques et culturelles

Efficacité ? L'impression que laissent jusqu'ici ces initiatives est plutôt celle de plateformes qui veulent montrer qu'elles ne restent pas inactives, mais hésitent à prendre le problème à bras-le-corps. Pour des raisons économiques : embaucher ou financer une armée de modérateurs et de *fact-checkers* mettrait à mal leur modèle, tout comme réduire le volume de contenus en circulation ou brider les utilisateurs. Mais aussi pour des raisons culturelles : fondées sur une idéologie libertaire, fascinées par le partage libre des connaissances, ces sociétés considèrent que tout ce qui limite la liberté d'expression dans son acception américaine est un danger. Non sans raison : comme l'expérimentent les internautes en Turquie, en Chine ou ailleurs, la frontière est mince entre le blocage validé démocratiquement par la loi et la censure politique.

S'ils doivent assumer une plus grande part de responsabilité, les réseaux sociaux et grands opérateurs du Web font aussi figure de boucs émissaires commodes. Le succès viral d'informations outrageusement fausses ne s'appuie pas seulement sur la puissance des plateformes de Facebook ou Google, mais aussi sur ce que l'on peut appeler, faute de mieux, « l'envie d'y croire ». Durant la campagne américaine, des millions d'électeurs ont partagé ces messages parce qu'ils n'accordaient aucune confiance aux médias, toujours suspects de parti pris, ni aux candidats, considérés comme corrompus. La propagande et la désinformation se nourrissent, d'abord et surtout, de cette terrible crise de confiance, face à laquelle représentants politiques et médias doivent faire preuve de la même énergie que celle qu'ils mettent à interpeller les plates-formes.

Alexis Delcambre et Damien Leloup,
Le Monde daté du 03.02.2017

POURQUOI CET ARTICLE ?

Les « fake news » (*fausses nouvelles*) – l'expression fait désormais partie du langage courant – sont devenues un sujet de débat pendant la campagne électorale américaine de 2016. Donald Trump se plaît à répéter que CNN, le *New York Times* et le *Washington Post* sont des « tissus de fake news ». Tim Berners-Lee, l'inventeur du Web, a lui déclaré que la propagation de la désinformation était, avec la perte du contrôle des données personnelles, l'une des plus grandes menaces pour Internet.

L'article fait un lien entre le développement de ces fakes news et l'essor des réseaux sociaux et montre que les États demandent maintenant aux plateformes qu'elles régulent leurs contenus, en opposition à l'idéologie de ces dernières, qui ne souhaite pas de limite à la liberté d'expression. La lutte contre les fakes news s'organise néanmoins et Facebook a par exemple créé un partenariat avec plusieurs médias français.

Damien Hirst pirate la Fondation Pinault

A Venise, le plus hollywoodien des artistes britanniques monte une délirante chasse au trésor sous-marine.

Pour une fois, rien d'exagéré à dire que c'est du jamais-vu. Le come-back de Damien Hirst à la collection Pinault de Venise peut être affublé de tous les superlatifs, ils ne seront pas de trop. Délirant, mégalomane, abyssal, babylonien, kitschissime, « *über-expensive* »... Le vieil enfant terrible de la scène des Young British Artists fait d'ores et déjà exploser le standard de la billetterie avec cette double exposition blockbuster. Elle envahit chaque recoin de la Punta della Dogana et du Palazzo Grassi, et fera, à n'en pas douter, date. Même si ce n'est pas forcément pour les bonnes raisons.

Le plus célèbre des aquariophiles britanniques y fait définitivement entrer la sculpture dans l'univers de la méga-super-production hollywoodienne. Son exposition se situe quelque part entre *Pirates des Caraïbes* et *Indiana Jones*, assaisonnée d'un soupçon de frères Farrell pour l'autodérision et d'une bonne giclée de *Da Vinci Code* pour les effets spéciaux volontairement outrés. Bref, un retour tonitruant après des années de silence.

Hirst s'était en effet fait discret (autant que peut l'être celui qui sculpta un crâne de platine serti de 8 601 diamants), depuis sa spectaculaire vente aux enchères de 2008 chez Sotheby's. Organisée par lui et son équipe en une sorte de déstockage de luxe des caves de son atelier londonien, elle lui aurait rapporté plus de 100 millions de livres. Elle a aussi, sans conditionnel cette fois, magnifié sa réputation de diablotin cynique qui, d'un seul geste, court-circuitait ses galeries et moquait le marché de l'art tout en en tirant le plus grand bénéfice. On comprend désormais que ces années de semi-retraite aient été mises à profit pour entamer son projet le plus grandiloquent, peut-être le plus fou qui se soit vu dans le genre : « Les Trésors de l'épave de l'*Incroyable* », si l'on traduit le titre de cette folie vénitienne. Jeff Koons, à côté, fait désormais figure de petit joueur.

POURQUOI CET ARTICLE ?

Dix ans de travail ont été nécessaires à Damien Hirst pour mener à bien ce projet narrant l'histoire du vaisseau antique *Unbelievable*, de son naufrage et de sa cargaison, l'impressionnante collection d'un esclave affranchi. L'artiste britannique de 51 ans, connu pour son requin plongé dans du formol ou son moulage en plâtre d'un crâne serti de 8 600 diamants, expose ainsi 200 œuvres dans les deux écrins de la Fondation Pinault à Venise.

L'article souligne bien le côté spectaculaire et démesuré de l'exposition ainsi que l'ambiguïté sur laquelle elle repose. Le spectateur est en effet censé se demander si les œuvres sont le résultat du travail de l'artiste ou si elles sont vraiment le fruit de fouilles sous-marines. D'après l'auteur de l'article, on n'y croit pas un instant, mais on sort néanmoins impressionné par la prouesse technique.

Entreprise de la démesure

Le pitch ? Il était une fois, il y a quelque deux mille ans, un immense collectionneur du nom de Cif Amotan II. Esclave affranchi, il possédait toutes les merveilles du monde, qu'il désira un jour abriter sur une île. Hélas – est-ce punition divine pour tant d'arrogance ou juste la faute à pas de chance ? –, le bateau coula. Il fallut attendre le début du XXIe siècle pour qu'un archéologue convainque Hirst d'allouer toute sa fortune sothebysienne à la sortie des eaux de l'antique magot. Voilà ce que raconte le livret offert à l'entrée, ainsi qu'un « documentaire » consacré à l'expédition sous-marine, dont de spectaculaires photos émaillent le parcours. La suite consiste en une accumulation absolument insensée de « richesses ». Un codex aztèque, des pépites d'or, le combat de la déesse indienne Kali avec l'hydre de Lerne, des sphinges et des masques de Bali, des pharaons et des pieds géants d'Apollon, un Pégase et une Amazone romaine, des monnaies impériales, des bouddhas et des casques khmers... Ces sculptures démesurées, dans tous les sens du terme, apparaissent rongées par les ans et la mer, recouvertes de coraux multicolores, de coquillages bienveillants, de rouille bien placée, restaurées parfois, en duplicata des « originaux ». On l'a compris, la vraisemblance historique n'entre pas dans le scénario. Mais, pour ce qui est de la réalisation technique, l'ensemble est bluffant : Hirst a en effet eu recours à des sculpteurs d'agate et de lapis-lazuli, à des fondeurs à la cire perdue et à des patineurs de résine, à des experts de la Mésopotamie et à des machines qu'on imagine dantesques. Il a fallu, à lui et à ses dizaines d'assistants, des tonnes et des tonnes de bronze, des trésors de patience et un esprit bien tordu pour mener à bien cette entreprise de la démesure. Puis, à Venise, cinquante personnes et deux mois et demi de montage pour redonner forme aux œuvres, tronçonnées pour rentrer par les portes trop petites.

Le problème, c'est qu'on n'y croit pas un instant, à ce péplum qui se rêve en série B conceptuelle. D'autant plus que Hirst fait beaucoup pour qu'on y croie, mais aussi pas mal pour qu'on n'y croie pas. Cif Amotan II ? On peut le lire comme l'anagramme de « *I am a fiction* », je suis une fiction. Au fil des vitrines, l'artiste, lui-même éminent collectionneur, sème des indices qui révèlent sans honte le mensonge, mêlant dans les cartels justesse historique et totale fantasmagorie. C'est alors que la visite tourne au vertige tendance Space Mountain. Quand apparaissent Mowgli et Baloo ; une épée superbement patinée, siglée de la marque de parc à thèmes SeaWorld ; un autoportrait vieilli, où l'artiste se singe en Walt Disney triomphant, Mickey à son bras...

Bustes de femmes pervers

Avant même d'anticiper les critiques, Hirst les digère et les incorpore à son système. C'est sans doute la marque la plus flagrante de son talent particulier d'*entertainer* qui se rêve métaphysique, et s'amuse à perdre dans toutes sortes d'abymes ces mille et une nuits de l'héroic fantasy. Ainsi, de cette salle du Palazzo Grassi, une des plus réussies, qui rassemble des dessins sur le thème du naufrage par des artistes de la Renaissance. Des sanguines belles à s'y tromper, frappées du sceau de prestigieuses bibliothèques ou… de marques automobiles. Elles sont toutes signées Is it Dream. Soit, on l'a compris, un quasi-anagramme de Damien Hirst. Plus pervers encore, ces bustes de femmes prétendument antiques, prétendument source d'inspiration des mannequins de l'exposition surréaliste de 1936. On découvre ici leurs avatars, frappés du label Mattel, fabricant de la poupée Barbie. On peut être aussi saisi devant quelques morceaux de bravoure, comme cette silhouette de Protée, divinité marine dotée du pouvoir de se métamorphoser sans cesse. Hirst la représente à moitié mangée par le corail, défi permanent au sculpteur démiurge autant qu'au collectionneur d'œuvres d'art : ces deux êtres rongés par un seul et même désir d'arrêter le temps.

Emmanuelle Lequeux, *Le Monde* daté du 27.04.2017

Les mots de Bob Dylan, l'émotion de Patti Smith

Absent à Stockholm de la cérémonie de remise des prix, le Nobel de littérature a fait part de son incrédulité.

Les Nobel sont une machine parfaitement huilée, qui ne laisse aucune place à l'improvisation. Les soubresauts parfois suscités par le choix d'un lauréat controversé sont vite effacés, pour permettre à la cérémonie de se dérouler dans toute sa splendeur pompeuse. Cette année aura été différente.

Bob Dylan n'est certes pas le premier lauréat du Nobel de littérature à ne pas venir à Stockholm recevoir son prix des mains du roi de Suède, Carl XVI Gustave, qui lui a déjà remis le Polar Prize en 2000. Mais il est le seul à avoir prétexté *« de précédents engagements »* pour justifier son absence. Le seul aussi à avoir tenu l'Académie suédoise en haleine pendant douze jours, ne répondant à aucun des appels de sa secrétaire perpétuelle, Sara Danius, et exaspérant l'académicien Per Wästberg, qui a fini par le juger *« impoli et arrogant »*.

Si le musicien américain n'était pas assis sur la scène du Stockholm Concert Hall, samedi 10 décembre, aux côtés des neuf autres nobélisés en queue-de-pie, devant un parterre d'invités prestigieux, il n'en était pas complètement absent. Visiblement bouleversée, sa consœur Patti Smith, chemise blanche boutonnée jusqu'au cou et blazer bleu marine, est venue interpréter *A Hard Rain's a-Gonna Fall,* écrite en 1962. La chanteuse américaine s'est interrompue au second couplet, s'excusant de sa nervosité, avant de reprendre, les yeux fermés, sous de longs applaudissements, faisant couler des larmes dans la salle.

Bob Dylan avait envoyé un texte de remerciement, lu par l'ambassadrice des Etats-Unis en Suède, Azita Raji, à la fin du banquet donné dans la salle d'honneur de la mairie de Stockholm. Il y exprime son incrédulité de se retrouver en *« si rare compagnie »* que celle de Rudyard Kipling, George Bernard Shaw, Thomas Mann, Pearl Buck, Albert Camus ou Ernest Hemingway. Si on lui avait dit qu'il recevrait un jour le Nobel, assure-t-il humblement, il aurait cru ses chances identiques à celle de *« se trouver sur la Lune »*. D'où son silence, après l'annonce. *« Ce sont mes chansons qui sont au centre vital de presque tout ce que je fais »*, dit-il. Est-ce de la littérature ? Il invoque Shakespeare, qui n'a jamais dû se poser la question lorsqu'il écrivait *Hamlet*. Bob Dylan remercie l'académie de l'avoir fait pour lui, et *« finalement, d'y donner une réponse aussi fantastique »*.

Pendant la cérémonie, l'académicien Horace Engdahl a défendu un choix *« audacieux »*, rappelant que *« dans un passé lointain, toute la poésie était chantée ou récitée, les poètes étaient des rapsodeurs,*

POURQUOI CET ARTICLE ?

C'est à la grande surprise générale que le prix Nobel de littérature de 2016 a été attribué à Bob Dylan, un choix que cet article tente d'expliquer. Le chanteur, originaire du Minnesota et engagé contre la guerre et pour le mouvement des droits civiques, est en effet un troubadour des temps modernes qui a « créé une nouvelle forme d'expression poétique au sein de la grande tradition de la chanson américaine ».

L'article revient également sur l'absence de Bob Dylan à la cérémonie et sur son mutisme. Le chanteur américain finira par envoyer l'enregistrement de son discours dans lequel il soulignera le lien entre ses chansons et la littérature et parlera de ses influences littéraires, de *Moby Dick* à *l'Odyssée*.

En 2017, l'académie suédoise est revenue à un choix plus classique en attribuant le prix à l'écrivain britannique Kazuo Ishiguro.

des bardes, des troubadours, la poésie venait de la lyre ». Bob Dylan, c'est comme si *« l'oracle de Delphes lisait à haute voix les nouvelles du soir »*, lance-t-il, avant d'enfoncer le clou, sourire en coin : *« Si les gens du monde littéraire grognent, rappelons-leur que les dieux n'écrivent pas, ils dansent et ils chantent. »*

L'académie suédoise, créée en 1786 sur le modèle de l'Académie française, aura en tout cas frappé un grand coup, dépoussiérant son image parfois un peu désuète. Lisa Irenius, chef des pages Culture du quotidien *Svenska Dagbladet*, a beau témoigner de son *« scepticisme »* à l'égard du choix du lauréat, elle reconnaît *« une volonté de surprendre, d'étonner, de montrer qu'on suit ce qui se passe dans le monde »*.

« Aucune différence de genre »

Composé de dix-huit romanciers, poètes, historiens et linguistes, cooptés à vie, le cénacle s'est largement renouvelé ces dernières années, faisant descendre la moyenne d'âge à 68 ans. Il s'est aussi féminisé, avec la présence de cinq académiciennes, dont Sara Danius, professeure de littérature, première femme à occuper le poste de secrétaire perpétuelle, et bientôt l'arrivée de l'écrivaine Sara Stridsberg, 44 ans, qui y fera son entrée le 20 décembre. Plusieurs sont des inconditionnels de Bob Dylan, assure le professeur Ola Holmgren, auteur d'un ouvrage prémonitoire, publié au printemps et intitulé *Huit raisons pour lesquelles Bob Dylan devrait être récompensé du prix Nobel*. Lui-même n'y croyait pas.

Rejetant l'hypothèse d'une expérimentation, Asa Beckman, directrice ajointe du service Culture du journal *Dagens Nyheter*, y voit *« un effort visant à élargir le concept de littérature »*, après le prix accordé en 2015 à l'écrivain biélorusse Svetlana Alexievitch, *« à la frontière du roman et du journalisme »*.

L'académicien Per Wästberg souligne que *« le testament d'Alfred Nobel ne fait aucune différence de genre »* et n'exclut pas qu'un auteur de livres pour enfants soit un jour récompensé, du moment que son œuvre est *« de haute qualité et marque son époque »*.

Hakan Bravinger, éditeur chez Norstedts, rappelle qu'en 1953, Winston Churchill a été honoré pour ses discours : *« Nous avons peut être réduit le Nobel, en pensant qu'il se limitait à la poésie et à la prose, tandis que l'académie en a peut être toujours eu une conception plus large. »*

La controverse a du bon. *« Rarement, le prix Nobel de littérature aura suscité un tel engagement »*, constate la journaliste Lisa Irenius. Elle regrette cependant que les discussions se soient vite transformées en *« un métadébat sur la personnalité de Dylan »*. La presse du royaume s'en est donné à cœur joie, fustigeant le *« manque de politesse »* du chanteur et raillant la *« gifle »* à l'académie. Les Suédois se sont finalement consolés en constatant que le musicien avait aussi boudé l'invitation de Barack Obama à la Maison Blanche, le 1er décembre.

« La réaction de Bob Dylan n'était pas attendue, mais les lauréats sont imprévisibles », résume Per Wästberg, qui rappelle que si l'artiste veut toucher l'argent qui accompagne le prix (850 000 euros), il devra se rendre à Stockholm pour y livrer son discours officiel, avant le 1er juin 2017.

Anne-Françoise Hivert, *Le Monde* daté du 13.12.2016

La voix de la douleur

Kurt Cobain, chanteur et guitariste du groupe de rock Nirvana, s'est donné la mort vendredi 8 avril 1994 dans l'État de Washington.

Le troisième et dernier album de Nirvana aurait dû s'appeler *I Hate Myself and I Wanna Die* : je me déteste et je veux mourir . Kris Novoselic, le bassiste du groupe, disait en juillet dernier au mensuel *Les Inrockuptibles* pourquoi il avait obtenu que le disque s'appelle *In Utero* : *« Je n'aimais pas ce titre et j'ai dit à Kurt : que ferons-nous si un môme de douze ans se met une balle dans la tête après avoir écouté notre disque ? »* Au bout du compte, l'enfant de douze ans, ce fut Kurt Cobain, qui a choisi de partir en laissant derrière lui une poignée de chansons, trois albums et un rock américain profondément changé, pour le meilleur et pour le pire.

Aux yeux du monde entier, l'histoire de Nirvana a commencé à l'automne 1991, lorsque MTV – la chaîne musicale américaine – s'est mise à diffuser à forte dose la vidéo d'une chanson accrocheuse et déjantée au titre incompréhensible, *Smells Like Teen Spirit*. On y voyait trois jeunes gens, un guitariste blond, Kurt Cobain, un bassiste géant, Kris Novoselic, et un batteur furieux, Dave Grohl, s'agiter – vêtus comme l'as de pique – au milieu de majorettes frénétiques. Le succès de la chanson porta celui de l'album, intitulé *Nevermind*, qui se vendit mieux, cette année-là, que celui de Michael Jackson.

D'un coup, cette irruption, contemporaine des étonnants succès de rappers ou de chanteurs de country, mit à bas les règles du show-business. Le marketing n'était plus tout à fait roi, il fallait compter avec le hasard, avec les rencontres entre les tribus et des porte-parole surgis de nulle part. Un temps, Nirvana

devint le porte-parole de la jeunesse blanche américaine, de ses frustrations, de son trouble endémique.
Cobain et Novoselic avaient formé le groupe en 1987, à Aberdeen, une ville de l'État de Washington située à 100 km de Seattle. Tous deux ont souvent raconté à quel point la vie y était ennuyeuse, coupée du monde. On n'y entendait, à la radio, que les grands succès du moment, et il fallut aux deux jeunes gens la rencontre avec les Melvins, un groupe de la région, pour découvrir le rock punk plus de dix ans après sa naissance.
En arrivant à Seattle quelque temps après, Cobain et Novoselic découvrent une scène extrêmement vivace. Là, des groupes comme Mudhoney, Alice In Chains ou les musiciens du futur Pearl Jam font leur apprentissage à l'abri des regards du show-business. Ils passent leur culture musicale extrêmement conformiste – le hard-rock, de Led Zeppelin à Def Leppard – aux filtres de leurs frustrations adolescentes, de leur mal de vivre, ou peut-être même du climat pluvieux de la région. Les tempos se ralentissent, la distorsion et le flou prennent le pas sur l'agressivité directe. Ces jeunes gens tous plus fauchés les uns que les autres achètent leurs vêtements au kilo. Un jour, l'un d'eux, musicien de Mudhoney, décrit ce style de vie comme *grunge*, un mot enfantin qui évoque la crasse et la négligence. Le terme fait fortune. Au fur et à mesure que les groupes de Seattle arrivent à une certaine maturité, ils vont frapper à la porte du label indépendant Subpop. Nirvana ne fait pas exception et enregistre l'album *Bleach*, pour la somme princière de 900 dollars, en 1989. Le disque est remarqué dans les cercles éclairés, se vend à 80 000 exemplaires. Le groupe joue à travers le monde, entre autres au Fahrenheit d'Issy-les-Moulineaux.

Fragile et approximatif

En 1990, le groupe signe avec Geffen, filiale de MCA-Matsushita. À l'automne de la même année, le batteur Dave Grohl, originaire de la côte Est, rejoint le groupe, qui enregistre *Nevermind* sous la direction du producteur Butch Vig. Le disque se vend à plus de 5 millions d'exemplaires aux États-Unis, à 730 000 en France. Mais, on l'entend bien lors de son passage au Zénith de Paris, les musiciens, et plus particulièrement Kurt Cobain, n'ont pas vraiment de goût pour le métier de rock star, contrairement à leurs collègues de Pearl Jam, par exemple. Le groupe garde une fragilité, une approximation dans le jeu, qui minent et magnifient les chansons de Kurt Cobain. Lui chante d'une voix plaintive et coléreuse pour dire qu'il ne s'aime pas, qu'il s'en veut d'être apathique, mais qu'il ne sait pas être autrement, que personne ne le lui a appris. En même temps, ils font beaucoup de bruit et aiment à fracasser leurs instruments en fin de concert.

POURQUOI CET ARTICLE ?

La disparition prématurée, en 1994, du chanteur de Nirvana a d'autant plus profondément marqué toute une génération que Kurt Cobain, presque malgré lui, était devenu la figure emblématique du mouvement grunge, ralliant des milliers de jeunes derrière lui. Trop fragile et très réfractaire au statut de rock star qui lui était « tombé dessus », Kurt Cobain a choisi de mettre fin à ses jours alors qu'une longue et riche carrière semblait lui tendre les bras – mais vingt ans plus tard, l'héritage laissé par Cobain et la vague grunge issue de Seattle continue à influencer divers styles et courants, aussi bien dans le domaine du rock alternatif que dans celui du « look » vestimentaire.

L'année 1992 est celle de l'oisiveté. Le groupe ne tourne plus, n'enregistre pas encore. Kurt Cobain se marie avec Courtney Love, musicienne de la scène alternative de Los Angeles, chanteuse du groupe Hole. La presse s'intéresse beaucoup à leur héroïnomanie. Cobain et Love affirment avoir décroché, ce qui n'empêche pas le mensuel américain *Vanity Fair* d'accuser la chanteuse de s'être injecté de l'héroïne pendant qu'elle attendait leur enfant. À l'automne naît Frances Cobain, ainsi prénommée en hommage à Frances Farmer, l'actrice hollywoodienne dont la carrière fut brisée par un internement en hôpital psychiatrique.
Au début de 1993, Nirvana entre en studio pour enregistrer le successeur de *Nevermind*. Le groupe travaille avec le producteur Steve Albini, qui finit par abandonner le projet en affirmant que Nirvana s'est rendu aux raisons de Geffen et a renoncé aux audaces sonores enregistrées avec Albini. Le groupe dément vigoureusement, et l'écoute d'*In Utero* donne du poids à ce démenti. Le disque est conçu en partie pour dérouter, pour éloigner tous ces fans d'occasion qui, en 1991, sont passés *« de la guerre du Golfe à Nevermind »*, comme le remarquait avec amertume Kris Novoselic lors du passage du groupe en France en février dernier (*Le Monde* du 13-14 février 1994). Le disque se vend très bien, malgré le boycottage de quelques grandes chaînes de magasins américains, comme Walmart, choquées par la couverture du disque, qui représente un écorché féminin. Plus désespéré, plus violent encore que son prédécesseur, *In Utero* indique clairement que la souffrance de Cobain ne s'était pas dissipée avec l'argent ou la reconnaissance.
Pourtant, il se prête de bonne grâce au jeu des interviews, s'affirme guéri de son héroïnomanie et *« plus heureux que jamais »*. Ce n'était sans doute pas encore assez, puisque le 4 mars dernier, alors que Nirvana était en tournée en Europe, Kurt Cobain est hospitalisé, dans le coma, à Rome, à la suite d'une surdose de somnifères. Il était depuis retourné à Seattle, où il habitait une petite maison. C'est là qu'il s'est donné la mort. ■

Thomas Sotinel, *Le Monde* daté du 11.04.1994

CORRIGÉS DES EXERCICES

Mandela p. 8

Compréhension

A.

1. False/ 2. True/ 3. True/ 4. False/ 5. False/ 6. False/ 7. False/ 8. True/ 9. True/ 10. False

B.

Hero, icon, leader, warrior, saint, martyr.

C.

Courage, humility, sense of humour, fortitude, magnanimity, dignity.

Grammaire

A.

1. Mary is the tallest in the class.
2. Your mobile phone is more expensive than mine.
3. Emma didn't eat as much as David.
4. Helen's hair is longer than Jane's.
5. I am the noisiest student in the school.
6. The play wasn't as good as we expected.

B.

1. Today is less cold than yesterday so I'm wearing my shorts.
2. What a terrible novel. It's one of the least interesting I've ever read.
3. This is one of the most famous paintings in the world.
4. Nobody knows more about computers than Jane does.

C.

1. This is the worst TV programme I've ever watched.
2. Our house is bigger than the one next door.
3. I think this book is much better than the other one.
4. I was disappointed as the film was less funny than I expected.
5. Yesterday was one of the hottest days of the year.
6. The Nile is the longest river in the world.
7. The first exercise was easy but this one is more difficult.
8. Today, I feel worse than I did yesterday.

Frankenstein p. 16

Compréhension

A. Compréhension générale

1. He is creating a new being/ a female being.
2. He had created a male being.
3. He fears that the two beings will have children and that they will threaten the whole human race.
4. He destroys the new creature.

B. Compréhension détaillée

1. a. False/ b. False/ c. True/ d. True/ e. False.
2. The creature is ugly. "The creature who already lived loathed his own deformity."
3. He thinks that he has created a monster, that he is malicious and barbarous. His creature embodies evil.
4. The narrator had promised to create a mate for his creature. The creature had promised to live in deserts, far away from human beings.

Grammaire

A.

1. must/ 2. can/ 3. must/ 4. may/ 5. could/ 6. might

B.

1. might/ 2. could/ 3. must/ 4. can't/ 5. must/ 6. might/ 7. can't come/ 8. can't be

---

The app that lets you spy on yourself p. 26

Compréhension

1. True/ 2. False/ 3. True/ 4. False/ 5. True/ 6. False/ 7. True/ 8. True/ 9. True/ 10. False/ 11. False/ 12. True/ 13. False/ 14. True/ 15. False

Grammaire

A.

1. whose/ 2. which/ 3. who/ 4. who/ 5. who/ 6. whom/ 7. who/ 8. whose

B.

1. The museum that we want to visit opens at 10 am.
2. The boy whose bike was stolen went to the police station.
3. The friend who met me at the station carried my bag.

Pride and Prejudice p. 34

Compréhension

A.

1. b/ 2. b/ 3. b/ 4. a/ 5. b/ 6. b/ 7. a/ 8. b/ 9. a

B.

1. She means that it is not acceptable for women to go and visit a man they do not know. She has to wait for her husband to go first.
2. Mr. and Mrs. Bennet do not seem to be sharing the same interests. Mr. Bennet uses sarcastic humour and seems to take pleasure in making fun of his wife.
3. Mrs. Bennet seems to care for nothing else but seeing her daughters married. She is portrayed as a foolish woman and Jane Austen stresses her lack of intelligence ("she was a woman of mean understanding").

Grammaire

A.

1. She's as friendly as her sister. / She's not as friendly as her sister.
2. Your solution is as good as Sam's. / Your solution is not as good as Sam's.
3. The station is as far as the airport. / The station is not as far as the airport.
4. The table is as heavy as the sofa. / The table is not as heavy as the sofa.
5. Her ring is as expensive as my car. / Her ring is not as expensive as my car.

B.

1. as/ 2. like/ 3. as/ 4. like/ 5. as/ 6. like

In Missouri, artists broadcasting pain through hip hop p. 46

Compréhension

1. a/ 2. a/ 3. b/ 4. b/ 5. b/ 6. b/ 7. a/ 8. b/ 9. a/ 10. b/ 11. b/ 12. a/ 13. a/ 14. a

Grammaire

1. a. has disappeared/ b. have been disappearing
2. a. has been staying/ b. have stayed
3. a. haven't run/ b. have been running
4. a. have been checking/ b. have already checked

The Age of Innocence p. 54

Compréhension

A.

1. a/ 2. b/ 3. b/ 4. a/ 5. a/ 6. b

B.

1. Countess Olenska.
2. Countess Olenska.
3. The tribal rally takes the form of a farewell dinner.
4. Archer understands that the people around him believe that he and Mrs Olenska are lovers.
5. Because they have succeeded in separating Archer and Mrs Olenska.
6. This sentence shows that the people around Archer are hypocritical; they conduct themselves by the rules and standards of the New York society that they reside in and they want to avoid scandal at all costs.
7. Archer feels like a prisoner.

Grammaire

A.

1. English is spoken all over the world.
2. A new president has been elected.
3. The damaged building is being rebuilt.
4. He was offered a new job.
5. She is being questioned.
6. My bag has been stolen.
7. Drinks aren't served after 11 pm.
8. The results of the competition will be announced tomorrow.
9. You will be met at the train station.
10. The match has been postponed by the clubs.
11. Most of this magazine is written by students.
12. My laptop was stolen by burglars.

B.

1. He was glad not to be selected.
2. I hate being observed.
3. You're wanted on the phone.

C.

1. taken/ 2. sent/ 3. offered/ 4. broken

The taming of a vast wilderness p. 66

Compréhension

1. a/ 2. b/ 3. a/ 4. b/ 5. b/ 6. b/ 7. a/ 8. b/ 9. b/ 10. b/ 11. a/ 12. b/ 13. b

Grammaire

A.

1. If I'd known it was your birthday, I would have sent you flowers.
2. If we take a taxi, we'll arrive sooner.
3. If I had a lot of money, I'd give some to all my family.
4. If Sam had driven more carefully, he wouldn't have had a fine.
5. If I had noticed it, I'd have corrected it.
6. If I studied harder, I would get better marks.

B.

1. If I had gone to bed early, I would have woken up at 6 am.
2. If I had turned right at the station, I wouldn't have lost my way.
3. If I had bought more bread, I would have had enough for dinner.
4. If I had realized you were tired, I wouldn't have asked you for a walk.

David Cameron p. 70

Compréhension

1. True/ 2. False/ 3. True/ 4. False/ 5. True/ 6. True/ 7. True/ 8. False/ 9. False/ 10. True

Grammaire

A.

1. I have lived/ 2. left/ 3. I lost/ 4. I've just lost/ 5. has been/ 6. went

B.

1. I have worked here for five years.
2. I haven't been on a boat before.
3. I haven't written to my sister for a long time.
4. I have just seen a friend of yours.
5. Have you been to the US before? / Have you visited the US before?

Washington Square p. 80

Compréhension

1. False/ 2. True/ 3. False/ 4. True/ 5. True/ 6. True/ 7. True/ 8. False/ 9. True/ 10. True/ 11. False

Grammaire

A.

1. I am having a party on Friday.
2. It's going to rain tomorrow.
3. I am not going to sell my car after all.
4. Before we meet again, I'll phone you.
5. We will have finished the work in an hour.

B.

1. [...] you will fail.
2. The film is starting [...] / The film starts [...]
3. The plane is taking off [...] / The plane takes off [...]
4. Are you going to accept his offer?
5. You will change your mind when you see [...]

LE GUIDE PRATIQUE

Méthodologie et conseils

L'épreuve écrite

Si vous êtes en Série L (LV1 et LV2), séries S et ES (LV1) : l'épreuve dure 3 heures. 10 minutes sont consacrées à la première lecture, environ 1 heure et 15 minutes à la partie « Compréhension écrite » et environ 1 heure et 15 minutes à la partie « Expression écrite ».

Si vous êtes en Séries S et ES (LV2), séries technologiques (LV1 et LV2) : l'épreuve dure 2 heures. 10 minutes sont consacrées à la première lecture, environ 45 minutes à la partie « Compréhension écrite » et environ 45 minutes à la partie « Expression écrite ».

L'épreuve est composée de deux parties :

– La compréhension de l'écrit (10 points) prend appui sur un, deux ou trois documents en anglais qui renvoient à des notions du programme. Certains documents peuvent comporter des éléments iconographiques.

– L'expression écrite (10 points) est évaluée à partir d'une ou plusieurs tâches. Vous devrez rédiger un ou plusieurs textes construits, en lien avec les documents servant de support à l'épreuve de compréhension écrite. Pour l'épreuve de LV1, il peut être proposé un nouveau document « tremplin » en relation thématique avec les documents-supports de la compréhension écrite. Ce document vous servira à contextualiser et à nourrir votre expression écrite.

La lecture du sujet

Pensez à identifier le thème principal, la situation et les personnages. Soulignez dans le texte les expressions qui vous aident à les repérer.

La compréhension du ou des textes

Les questions, en général, suivent l'ordre du ou des textes. Elles sont formulées en anglais. On ne vous demande pas une analyse du texte ou un avis personnel. Vous devez répondre brièvement et précisément aux questions posées.

Lorsque vous répondez à une question, assurez-vous que vous avez bien lu et compris ce que l'on vous demande.

On vous demande de vous exprimer de manière compréhensible. N'hésitez pas à utiliser un brouillon pour noter et organiser vos idées. Si l'on vous demande de justifier votre réponse à l'aide du texte, pensez qu'il s'agit souvent de relever quelques mots, parfois une phrase entière et en aucun cas plusieurs phrases. Ne retenez donc que les éléments pertinents et pensez à indiquer le ou les numéros de lignes où figure la citation.

L'expression personnelle

Là encore, le brouillon est indispensable pour organiser son travail. Lisez bien le sujet et respectez la forme que doit prendre votre production. Attention, il est possible que l'on vous demande de rédiger plusieurs textes, de formes différentes.

En ce qui concerne l'argumentation, réservée aux LV1 (niveau B2), elle peut prendre appui sur le ou les textes de compréhension écrite mais aussi sur un nouveau document traitant du même thème, qui devrait enrichir votre réflexion et vous apporter une aide lexicale sur ce sujet.

Chaque texte doit être structuré (logique, cohérent) et rédigé dans une langue correcte et de qualité (richesse du vocabulaire, des expressions ; respect des structures ; articulation des différentes parties, etc.). Pensez à utiliser des tournures idiomatiques, des mots de liaison, en tâchant de vous exprimer dans un anglais recherché.

L'épreuve orale

Compréhension de l'oral (toutes séries sauf L)

Vous serez évalués lors du deuxième trimestre par les enseignants de votre établissement. La note obtenue ne vous sera pas communiquée.

– Vous écouterez un ou plusieurs documents audio (ou vidéo) d'une durée d'1 minute 30 maximum, en lien avec les notions étudiées pendant l'année. Vous écouterez le ou les documents trois fois, avec

GESTION DU TEMPS LORS DE L'ÉPREUVE ÉCRITE

• Selon les séries, vous disposez de 2 ou 3 heures. Utilisez-les complètement et ne vous débarrassez pas du travail.
• On peut considérer qu'il est nécessaire de consacrer au moins 15 minutes à la lecture du sujet.
• Pour les LV1 des séries L, ES, S et les LV2 de la série L (durée de l'épreuve : 3 heures) : environ 1 h 15 consacrées aux questions de compréhension et 1 h 15 à l'expression écrite.
• Pour les autres séries (durée de l'épreuve : 2 heures) : environ 40 minutes consacrées aux questions de compréhension et 50 minutes à l'expression écrite.
• Le temps restant (soit 15 minutes) est utilisé à la relecture de l'ensemble du travail.
• Ces indications restent des conseils. Vous devez bien entendu adapter le temps disponible à vos besoins.

CONSEILS POUR L'ÉPREUVE ÉCRITE DE COMPRÉHENSION DE TEXTE(S)

• Lors de la lecture du sujet, ne cherchez pas à vouloir tout comprendre tout de suite. Prenez le temps de relire le texte. Pensez également à utiliser le contexte pour trouver le sens des mots inconnus.
• Lisez toutes les questions plusieurs fois. Les questions sont souvent posées dans un ordre qui va de l'explicite vers l'implicite, et parfois certaines questions fournissent un indice.
• Si une question vous pose problème, ne restez pas bloqué. Il n'est pas impossible que les réponses à venir éclairent la question sur laquelle vous butiez.
• Évitez d'écrire au fil de la plume : c'est la pire des méthodes, elle ne vous permettra pas d'arriver à une réponse correcte et structurée.

une pause d'une minute entre chaque écoute. Vous pouvez prendre des notes pendant ces écoutes.

– Vous disposerez ensuite de 10 minutes pour rédiger un compte rendu en français de ce que vous avez compris.

Expression orale (épreuve obligatoire LV1 ou LV2, toutes séries sauf L)

Vous serez évalués au cours du dernier trimestre par un des enseignants de votre établissement. La note obtenue ne vous sera pas communiquée. L'épreuve dure 20 minutes : 10 minutes consacrées à la préparation et 10 minutes à l'interrogation. Vous tirerez au sort une des notions du programme étudiées dans l'année.

L'interrogation se déroule en deux parties :

– 5 minutes de prise de parole en continu où vous présentez la notion étudiée (ce que vous avez étudié pendant l'année, votre approche personnelle, ce que vous avez aimé ou pas). Le but est d'exposer clairement et efficacement votre opinion sur ce qui a été découvert, étudié, retenu.

– 5 minutes en interaction avec le professeur.

Expression orale (épreuve obligatoire LV1 seule ou LV2, série L uniquement)

Vous serez interrogé par un examinateur extérieur à votre établissement. Vous lui présenterez la liste des notions étudiées dans l'année et les documents qui les ont illustrées. L'examinateur choisira l'une de ces notions. L'épreuve dure 30 minutes : 10 minutes consacrées à la préparation et 20 minutes à l'interrogation.

L'interrogation se déroule en deux parties :

– 10 minutes de prise de parole en continu où vous présentez la notion étudiée (ce que vous avez étudié pendant l'année, votre approche personnelle, ce que vous avez aimé ou pas). Vous pourrez vous appuyer sur les documents que vous aurez apportés.

– 10 minutes en interaction avec le professeur.

Expression orale (épreuve orale de langue de spécialité ou LVA), série L, LV1 ou LV2)

Cette épreuve remplace l'épreuve orale de LV1 ou LV2 si vous avez choisi votre LV1 ou votre LV2 en spécialité.

Vous serez interrogé par un examinateur extérieur à votre établissement. Celui-ci choisit l'une des deux notions présentées par le candidat et étudiées pendant l'année.

Vous devez avoir constitué pour chacune de ces deux notions un dossier comportant :

– deux documents étudiés en classe ;

– un document de votre choix qui illustre ou complète cette notion.

L'épreuve dure 30 minutes, dont 10 minutes consacrées à la préparation, 10 minutes de prise de parole en continu où vous présentez votre dossier et justifiez vos choix et 10 minutes en interaction avec le professeur.

Expression orale (épreuve obligatoire de littérature étrangère en langue étrangère (LELE), série L)

Cette épreuve a lieu à la suite de l'épreuve obligatoire ou de l'épreuve de spécialité de la langue choisie par le candidat pour cet enseignement (LV1 ou LV2). Il n'y a pas de temps de préparation spécifique.

Vous serez interrogé par un examinateur extérieur à votre établissement. L'examinateur choisit l'une des deux thématiques du programme de littérature étrangère en langue étrangère présentées par le candidat.

Vous devez avoir constitué pour chacune de ces deux thématiques un dossier comportant :

– deux textes extraits d'une ou de plusieurs œuvres étudiées en classe (roman, théâtre, poésie) ;

– un troisième document de votre choix qui permet d'analyser la réception de la ou des œuvres (extrait de critique, adaptation, illustration iconographique, etc.).

Immédiatement après l'épreuve obligatoire ou de spécialité, vous disposez en premier lieu de 5 minutes pour présenter le dossier portant sur la thématique choisie par l'examinateur et pour justifier votre choix de documents. Cette prise de parole en continu est suivie d'une phase d'interaction avec l'examinateur qui n'excède pas 5 minutes.

CONSEILS POUR L'ÉPREUVE ÉCRITE D'EXPRESSION PERSONNELLE

• Utilisez le ou les les texte(s) que vous aurez lus : ils peuvent vous servir de « réservoir lexical » : sans faire de paraphrase, vous avez la possibilité de réemployer des mots et des expressions tirés du texte proposé.

• La relecture est une étape absolument indispensable : il convient donc de lui consacrer tout le temps nécessaire.

• N'oubliez pas non plus que l'on vous impose un certain nombre de mots ou de lignes (une ligne fait environ 10 mots). Pensez à indiquer, à la fin de chaque texte, le nombre de mots utilisés.

CONSEILS POUR L'ÉPREUVE ORALE

• Vous devez présenter l'une des quatre notions du programme de Terminale. Il vous est conseillé de trouver une problématique reliant la notion que vous devrez présenter aux documents que vous aurez étudiés en classe avec votre professeur.

• Présentez un plan organisé en plusieurs parties (introduction, deux ou trois arguments ou idées importantes, conclusion). Pensez à relier les idées entre elles par des liens logiques.

• Vous serez surtout évalué sur votre niveau de langue. Il faut donc soigner votre expression, votre prononciation et votre accent. Reprenez-vous si vous pensez avoir fait une faute et parlez à un rythme normal.

• N'oubliez pas que l'interaction compte pour moitié de la note finale. Montrez que vous comprenez les questions. Ne laissez pas l'examinateur parler seul : vous devez prendre part à l'échange.

Crédits

Couverture

Big Ben et le palais de Westminster, Londres (Angleterre) © sborisov/iStock

Mythes et héros

p. 5 © Daniel Berehulak/Getty Images News ; © The British Library/Rue des Archives ; DR ; © iStockphoto/Thinkstock
"Madiba: South Africa's loss is the world's loss too"
p. 6 © 58shadows/iStock Editorial
Frankenstein
p. 14 © Rue des Archives/BCA
p. 15 © Lebrecht/Rue des Archives ; © The British Library/Rue des Archives

L'idée de progrès

p. 23 DR ; DR ; DR ; © Getty Images/Thinkstock
"The App That Lets You Spy on Yourself and Sell Your Own Data"
p. 24 © iStockphoto/Thinkstock
p. 27 © Ingram publishing/ Thinkstock
Pride and Prejudice
p. 32 © GeorgiosArt/iStock
p. 33 © ClaudeLux/iStock ; © BasPhoto/iStock

Lieux et formes du pouvoir

p. 43 © Goodshoot ; © chrisdorney/Essentials/iStock ; © william87/Essentials/iStock ; © Getty Images/Thinkstock
"In Missouri, artists broadcasting pain through hip hop"
p. 44 © william87/Essentials/iStock
p. 45 © william87/Essentials/iStock
The Age of Innocence
p. 52 © Rue des Archives/PVDE
p. 53 © MEPL/Rue des Archives ; © Rue des Archives/RDA

Espaces et échanges

p. 63 © Goodshoot ; © art2002/iStock ; © mattjeacock/Signature/iStock ; © Petar Chernaev/Signature/iStock
"The taming of a vast wilderness"
p. 64 © shells1/iStock
p. 65 © Goodshoot
"David Cameron announces immigration benefits crackdown"
p. 68 © EdStock/Signature/iStock
p. 69 © mattjeacock/Signature/iStock
Washington Square
p. 78 © Rue des Archives/PVDE
p. 79 © Granger NYC/Rue des Archives ; © art2002/iStock

Le guide pratique

p. 93 DR

EAN : 9782820807380

Achevé d'imprimer en France par Aubin Imprimeur, en mars 2018
Dépôt légal : décembre 2017

Réviser son bac avec Le Monde

CAHIER SPÉCIAL

Testez-vous pour le bac

ANGLAIS

60 questions

corrigées et commentées

rue des écoles

Grammaire

Indéfinis, quantifieurs

Question 1

Complete the sentences below with either *much* or *many*.

1. There are .... reasons for this.

2. The document does not give .... information about the situation.

3. At the time, people didn't show .... interest in the event.

Question 2

Complete the sentences below with either *little*, *a little*, *few* or *a few*.

1. JFK is one of the .... people I really admire.

2. I've been to England .... times!

3. I enjoy reading, but unfortunately I've got .... time at the moment.

4. If I had .... more time, I would read a Stephen King novel.

Question 3

Complete the sentences below with *some*, *any*, *no* or *none*.

1. .... of the stories about the Loch Ness monster are true – pure invention!

2. We have .... evidence to prove the veracity of these stories. They are hoaxes.

3. There are .... people who are ready to believe anything.

4. We have not got .... reason to believe these stories.

5. I would not believe such a story without .... proof.

6. A story without .... witnesses is hard to believe.

Question 4

Complete the sentences below, using *all*, *both*, *each of*, or *neither*.

1. .... the documents we studied are direct illustrations of this notion.

2. .... the documents we studied illustrates this notion from a different angle.

3. There are two North American authors. .... of them are from the States.

4. .... of these two writers seems to approve of JFK's attitude to women.

5. We have studied four documents; .... four authors are quite critical of JFK.

Adjectifs

Question 5

Which statements are correct ?

☐ **A.** *Interesting* means « intéressé » and *interested*, « intéressant ».

☐ **B.** *Interesting* means « intéressant » and *interested*, « intéressé ».

☐ **C.** *Disappointing* means « déçu » and *disappointed*, « décevant ».

☐ **D.** *Disappointing* means « décevant » and *disappointed*, « déçu ».

Comparatifs, superlatifs

Question 6

Complete the sentences below, using either *than* or *as*.

1. British pop music is less well-known internationally .... American pop music.

2. Most British artists are not as eccentric .... their American counterparts.

3. I suppose David Bowie has become just as mythical .... Michael Jackson.

4. There are more British artists working in the States .... the other way round.

Articles

Question 7

Complete the following sentences with a definite article, if necessary.

1. Everybody loves .... music.

2. But not everyone likes .... music (that) other people listen to.

3. .... children spend more and more time interacting with screens, but .... children with attentive parents are less in danger than others.

Question 8

Complete the following sentences with either *the*, *a* or *an*, if necessary.

1. Florence Nightingale was .... nurse. She helped English soldiers during the Crimean War.

2. Doctors and nurses in hospitals often work more than 10 hours .... day.

3. .... John Watson's home was supposedly at 22 Baker Street, where Sherlock Holmes also lived.

4. The building still stands today, but it's such .... ordinary house!

Prépositions

Question 9

Complete the following sentences with *at*, *by*, *in*, *on*, or *until*.

1. He lives .... number 10, ... Downing Street, ... London.

2. His parents expected her home .... 10 p.m. They waited for her .... midnight.

3. Her latest book was published .... 2016, to be precise .... July 12th, so .... a Tuesday.

Question 10

Match each expression with its opposite.

outwards •	• behind
towards •	• inwards
close to •	• under
downwards •	• away from
over •	• far from
in front of •	• upwards

Question 11

Complete the sentences below with either *since* or *for*.

1. The main character hasn't seen his parents .... three years.

2. He hasn't seen them .... last year.

3. The family lived in London .... 5 years before emigrating to the States.

Verbes à particules

Question 12

Complete each sentence with the correct preposition.

1. The passengers had been waiting

…………… the ferry from Ellis Island for ages.

2. They enjoyed listening …………… music during the voyage.

3. Most immigrants succeeded …………… getting a job quite quickly.

4. It depended …………… their ability to speak English.

Passif

Question 13

Use the following elements to describe the situation in South Africa

1. During apartheid – Black population – discriminate against

……………………………………………

……………………………………………

2. They – not allowed – vote.

……………………………………………

……………………………………………

3. Most of them – confine – in townships.

……………………………………………

……………………………………………

4. Nelson Mandela – imprison – for 27 years.

……………………………………………

……………………………………………

5. Thanks to Mandela – Blacks and coloured people – finally – give – the vote.

……………………………………………

……………………………………………

6. Mandela – elect – President – in 1994.

……………………………………………

……………………………………………

7. Today – all South Africans – consider – as equals – in theory.

……………………………………………

……………………………………………

Auxiliaires modaux

Question 14

Complete the following sentences with either *can*, *may* or *must*.

1. Education is compulsory up to the age of 16, so all children …………… go to school.

2. That's not entirely true: parents …………… homeschool their children too.

3. The law …………… change in the future so that school becomes compulsory until 18.

Question 15

Complete the following sentences with either *mustn't* or *needn't*.

1. You …………… present your passport at the border with UK: your ID card will do.

2. You …………… drive on the right in the UK.

Question 16

Which of the following statements are correct?

☐ **A.** Modal verbs do not take -s in the 3rd person singular present.

☐ **B.** Modal verbs are followed by to + verb.

☐ **C.** Modal verbs do not exist in the infinitive form.

☐ **D.** To form the negative, you just add not after the modal verb.

☐ **E.** It's possible to juxtapose two or more modal verbs.

Présent simple et présent continu

Question 17

Write sentences using the prompts. Use either the simple present or the present continuous.

1. phrase interrogative : *you/ to wear/ gloves*

....

....?

2. phrase affirmative : *she/ to eat/ too much/ often*

....

....?

3. phrase interrogative : *he/ to come/ tonight*

....

....?

4. phrase négative : *I/ to understand/ German*

....

....?

Question 18

Say if the following temporal expressions are used with the simple present, the present *be* + V-*ing* or neither of them.

☐ **A.** yesterday

☐ **B.** at the moment

☐ **C.** always

☐ **D.** sometimes

☐ **E.** now

☐ **F.** everyday

Temps du passé

Question 19

Which of the following statements are correct?

☐ **A.** The simple past is used to describe an action which started in the past and ended in the past.

☐ **B.** The present perfect is used for past events with a connection to the present.

☐ **C.** The past continuous (*was/ were* + V-*ing* is used to describe a past action which continues in the present.

☐ **D.** The past perfect is used to describe an action that happened before another action in the past.

☐ **E.** Each tense in English corresponds to a tense in French.

Question 20

Match the two halves to form correct sentences.

1. He had watched TV...
2. He was watching TV...
3. He watched TV...
4. He has watched TV...

☐ **A.** and then he went to bed.

☐ **B.** before he started cooking

☐ **C.** for so long now that his eyes are red.

☐ **D.** when the police officers rang the doorbell.

Question 21

Use the expression in bold to choose the correct tense. Then, write the sentence.

1. The Vikings – already – visit – North America – **before Christopher Columbus arrived in 1492.**

....

2 . **Between 1492 and 1503** – Columbus – complete – four round-trips between Spain and America.

....

3 .**While** – he – cross the Atlantic – for the second time – **Columbus discovered the Virgin Islands.**

....

4 . Americans – celebrate – Columbus Day – as a statutory holiday – **for more than a century now**

....

L'expression du futur

Question 22

Complete these sentences by putting the verbs in brackets into the correct form: ***will*** or ***be going to***.

1. What is your intention? .... (you/ accept) this job?

2. If you don't study enough, you .... (fail).

3. We must hurry up, otherwise we .... (miss) the train.

4. When .... (you/ move) to Canada?

L'expression du conditionnel

Question 23

Complete these sentences by putting the verb within brackets into the correct form.

1. If I .... (be) rich, I would set up a charity to help the homeless.

2. I .... (express) my indignation, if other wealthy people .... (refuse) to donate money.

Question 24

Complete these sentences by putting the verb within brackets into the correct form.

1. If they had offered her a job, she .... (be) very happy.

2. She would have written a letter home, if she .... (have) better news.

3. If her parents .... (know) of her difficulties, they .... (try) to help her.

Pronoms relatifs

Question 25

Complete the following sentences, using either ***who***, ***whom*** or ***whose***.

1. Andy Murray, ... brother also plays tennis, has been knighted by the Queen.

2. His brother, ... plays doubles with him, persuaded Andy to accept the honour.

3. In 2015, Murray married Kim Sears, with .... he has one daughter.

Question 26

Complete the following sentences, using either ***which*** or ***what***

1. There is one positive outcome of the First World War, ... is the birth of feminism.

2. .... is most frustrating, is the slowness of the evolution of sexual equality.

3. Men are still paid more than women for the same work, ... is totally unjustified.

4. We must ask ourselves .... can be done to improve the situation.

Question 27

Join these sentences using relative clauses.

1. The museum you can't miss in NYC is MOMA. It is ideally situated in Manhattan.

2. The MOMA is actually in Central Park. You can enjoy nature in the heart of the city there.

3. Visitors can see masterpieces of famous artists including Monet. He is very popular in the US.

4. It's a good idea to visit on Saturday evening. There is a free guided tour then.

Discours direct et discours indirect

Question 28

Change the following sentence to indirect speech.
He said: "She is going to marry me!"
What is the correct answer?

☐ **A.** He said that she was going to marry.
☐ **B.** He said that she is going to marry me.
☐ **C.** He said she was going to marry him.

☐ **D.** He said she was going to marry her.

Question 29

Complete each sentence with the correct tag question.

won't they? – did you? – didn't you? – was it? – wasn't it? – will they?

1. That wasn't very nice, ...

2. It was cold, ...

3. They won't bring their children ....

4. You went to London, ...

Verbes irréguliers

Question 30

Which statement below is correct ?

☐ **A.** The past form of irregular verbs is used in the present perfect.

☐ **B.** The past participle of irregular verbs is used with have, has or had.

☐ **C.** You need to know your irregular verbs when you use the simple present.

Question 31

Which of the following verbs are irregular? Give the past form and the past participle of irregular verbs.

	past form	past participle
to check		
to try		
to throw		
to understand		
to clean		
to stay		
to fall		
to wish		
to say		
to hold		
to finish		
to trust		

Lexique

Mythes et héros

→ Le thème p. 6

Question 32

Which of the following statements are correct?

☐ **A.** The American dream consisted of emigrating to the USA and believing that anyone could go from rags to riches.

☐ **B.** Nowadays the myth of the self-made man is still strong and climbing the ladder of success is possible as long as you are hard-working and stubborn.

☐ **C.** The founding fathers or "Pilgrim Fathers" showed themselves adventurous and finally grateful for their successful harvests.

☐ **D.** The Pilgrim Fathers taught their ancestors courage and self-confidence.

☐ **E.** On the second Thursday of November, the American people celebrate Thanksgiving to pay tribute to them.

Question 33

Which of the following statements are correct?

☐ **A.** The protagonist is also called the hero or main character.

☐ **B.** The antagonist is a character that helps to resolve a plot.

☐ **C.** The plot is the order of events in a narrative structure.

☐ **D.** The climax is the point of highest tension in a narrative work.

☐ **E.** An imbroglio is a simple plot such as a setup, a conflict and a resolution.

Question 34

Which myth do Romeo and Juliet represent? Choose the right answer.

☐ **A.** the myth of the road

☐ **B.** the quest for eternal youth

☐ **C.** the myth of the initiatory voyage

☐ **D.** the myth of eternal love

Question 35

Which of the following words are used to describe a nasty or evil character? Choose the right answer(s).

☐ **A.** a traitor

☐ **B.** a puritan

☐ **C.** a goodie

☐ **D.** a villain

☐ **E.** a devil

☐ **F.** a rogue

☐ **G.** a patriot

☐ **H.** a rascal

☐ **I.** an outlaw

Question 36

Which of the following attributes are given to good characters? Choose the right answer(s).

☐ **A.** selfishness

☐ **B.** slyness

☐ **C.** loyalty

☐ **D.** malevolence

☐ **E.** devotion

☐ **F.** bravery

☐ **G.** virtue

☐ **H.** kindness

L'idée de progrès

→ Le thème p. 23

Question 37

Which of the following new technologies cannot store data?

☐ **A.** a cell phone

☐ **B.** a laptop

☐ **C.** headphones

☐ **D.** a memory card

☐ **E.** a hard disk drive

☐ **F.** a tablet

Question 38

Find the odd one out in the following list of words/ expressions.

☐ **A.** a factory

☐ **B.** to be/ live on welfare

☐ **C.** an assembly line

☐ **D.** robotics

☐ **E.** to clock in/ out

☐ **F.** to operate three eight-hour shifts

Question 39

Which of the following words refer to novelty or creation?

☐ **A.** enhancement

☐ **B.** improvement

☐ **C.** innovation

☐ **D.** discovery

☐ **E.** experiment

☐ **F.** invention

Question 40

Which invention is referred to in the following sentence?

This invention was a revolution in 1997, it made the reproduction of an entire organism from a single cell possible.

☐ **A.** vaccination against smallpox

☐ **B.** magnetic resonance imaging

☐ **C.** law of gravitation

☐ **D.** invention of penicillin

☐ **E.** animal cloning

☐ **F.** space conquest

Question 41

What do you know about women's rights in the 20th century in Great Britain? Find the sentence which is not correct.

☐ **A.** In 1903 Mrs Pankhurst and the suffragettes demanded the right to vote in a radical movement called the Women's Social and Political Union (WSPU).

☐ **B.** The suffragettes put an end to their campaign at the beginning of the war in 1914.

☐ **C.** After the 1st World War in Britain, women over 30 were allowed to vote, and later on, in 1928 they were allowed to vote at the same age as men (21).

☐ **D.** In 1919 Nancy Astor became the first female lawyer and in 1929 Margaret Bondfield became the first female Chancellor of the Exchequer.

☐ **E.** In 1979 Margaret Thatcher became the first female Prime Minister, she remained in government until 1990.

Lieux et formes du pouvoir

→ Le thème p. 43

Question 42

Find the odd one out.

☐ **A.** ballot-paper

☐ **B.** polling-day

☐ **C.** trade union

☐ **D.** candidates

☐ **E.** election campaign

☐ **F.** to canvass

Question 43

Find the odd one out in the following list of verbs.

☐ **A.** to protest

☐ **B.** to march

☐ **C.** to denounce

☐ **D.** to revolt

☐ **E.** to rebel

☐ **F.** to investigate

Question 44

What are the main British political parties?

☐ **A.** the Labour party

☐ **B.** the Democratic party

☐ **C.** the Conservative party

☐ **D.** the Republican party

☐ **E.** the Liberal Democrats

Question 45

Find the odd one out in the following list.

☐ **A.** Prime Minister

☐ **B.** House of Lords

☐ **C.** Congress

☐ **D.** Parliament

☐ **E.** Constitutional Monarchy

☐ **F.** Chamber of Commons

Question 46

Fill the gap with the correct word(s).

A. tabloids / B. daily magazines / C. weekly / newspapers / D. quality press / E. broadsheet

The press may be seen as an opposition force, it allows readers to keep up to date with the news through newspapers, magazines and the internet. In the UK .... publish sensational headlines and outrageous photos that are not censored in order to raise the circulation figures.

Espaces et échanges

→ Le thème p. 63

Question 47

Find the odd one out among the following verbs.

☐ **A.** to flee

☐ **B.** to settle down

☐ **C.** to escape
☐ **D.** to run away from
☐ **E.** to sail away
☐ **F.** to emigrate
☐ **G.** to undertake a journey

Question 48

Which of the following words can be translated by "frontière"?

☐ **A.** boundary
☐ **B.** outlaw
☐ **C.** frontier
☐ **D.** border zone
☐ **E.** territory
☐ **F.** dividing line
☐ **G.** limit

Question 49

Which of the following words are related to travel?

☐ **A.** trip
☐ **B.** tour
☐ **C.** pilgrimage
☐ **D.** brotherhood
☐ **E.** wanderings
☐ **F.** journey
☐ **G.** cruise

Question 50

Among the following reasons for choosing to immigrate to the USA, find the one that doesn't apply to Mexicans.

☐ **A.** to flee from poverty
☐ **B.** to seek political asylum
☐ **C.** to escape from the economic crisis
☐ **D.** to settle down in the south
☐ **E.** to help one's family to survive by sending them money

Question 51

Which of the following countries is no longer a member of the Commonwealth?

☐ **A.** Australia
☐ **B.** New Zealand
☐ **C.** The Republic of Ireland
☐ **D.** Kenya
☐ **E.** Canada
☐ **F.** South Africa

Question 52

Which of the following statements are correct?

☐ **A.** The exploration of new territories has contributed to commercial relationships between countries or continents.

☐ **B.** In the 16th century British explorers discovered new territories and offered the natives presents such as cocoa, rum or spices.

☐ **C.** The British Empire exploited the natural resources and commodities of its colonies in order to make the most of them.

☐ **D.** In the 17th century the British Empire was the largest and the most important in the world.

☐ **E.** The exchange of commodities has allowed countries to establish strong links which led to a decolonization movement in the 20th century enabling most former colonies to regain their independence.

Question 53

Which of the following statements are correct ?

☐ **A.** English was the official language of 30 sovereign states in 2015.

☐ **B.** English is the official language of the UK.

☐ **C.** Australia doesn't have any official language.

☐ **D.** India is the third-largest English-speaking country in the world by number of speakers, after the United Kingdom.

☐ **E.** English is an official language in Ireland.

Grammaire

Question 1 : 1. many ; 2. much. ; 3. much

Much est suivi d'un singulier et *many* est suivi d'un pluriel. On utilise de préférence *much* et *many* dans les phrases négatives.

Question 2 : 1. few ; 2. a few ; 3. little ; 4. a little.

Little (« peu de ») est suivi d'un indénombrable alors que *few* (« peu de ») est suivi d'un dénombrable. Pour dire « un peu de », on utilise *a little* ; « quelques » se traduit par *a few*.

Question 3 : 1. none ; 2. no ; 3. some ; 4. any ; 5. any ; 6. any.

• *Some* est utilisé dans les phrases affirmatives pour exprimer une certaine quantité (phrase 1).
• On emploie *any* dans les phrases déclaratives à la forme négative pour compléter la négation (phrase 4), et avec des adverbes à valeur négative telles que *hardly* ou bien *without* (phrase 5). *Any* dans une phrase affirmative a le sens de « n'importe quel(le) ... » (phrase 6).
• *No* s'utilise devant un substantif dans une phrase affirmative pour exprimer une négation.

Question 4 : 1. all ; 2. each of ; 3. both ; 4. Neither ; 5. all.

• *All* désigne l'ensemble des éléments d'une même catégorie (*all the documents* + verbe au pluriel) ou bien la totalité d'un ensemble (*all my money* + verbe au singulier).
• *Both* renvoie à deux personnes ou choses prises ensemble et s'accorde avec un verbe au pluriel. La place de *both* est variable. *Both my parents are doctors. I like them both.*
• *Neither* renvoie à deux personnes ou choses prises ensemble et s'accorde avec un verbe au singulier, car il signifie « ni l'un, ni l'autre ». Contrairement au français, ce verbe est à la forme affirmative.
• *Each of* (« chacun de(s) ») se réfère à tous les éléments d'une quantité, il accompagne donc un nom au pluriel, mais sera suivi d'un verbe au singulier.

Question 5 : B ; D.

• Les adjectifs formés à partir d'un verbe au participe présent ont un sens actif, donc *disappointing* se traduit par « décevant ».
• Quant aux adjectifs formés à partir d'un verbe au participe passé, ils ont un sens passif. C'est pourquoi *disappointed* se traduit par « déçu ».

Question 6 : 1. than ; 2. as ; 3. as ; 4. than.

• On utilise *than* pour les comparaisons de supériorité (*more* + adjectif + *than* ou adjectif + *er* + *than*) ainsi que pour les comparaisons d'infériorité (*less* +adjectif + *than*).
• On utilise *as* pour les comparaisons d'égalité (*as* + adjectif + *as*) et d'égalité négative (*not as* + adjectif +*as*) ainsi que dans la structure *all the* + comparatif + *as* qui signifie « d'autant plus...que ».

Question 7 : 1. pas d'article défini ; 2. the ; 3. pas d'article défini, the.

On n'utilise pas d'article défini pour désigner une chose ou une personne prise en général (noms indénombrables et noms dénombrables au pluriel). Par contre, on emploie l'article défini lorsqu'on prend un mot dans un sens restreint (phrase 2 et deuxième proposition, phrase 3).

Question 8 : 1. a ; 2. a ; 3. pas d'article ; 4. an.

• On utilise l'article indéfini devant les noms de profession (phrase 1) sauf s'il s'agit d'une fonction unique. On l'utilise également dans des expressions du type *seventy miles an hour, twice a week et $5 a kilo* (phrase 2) ainsi qu'après l'adjectif emphatique *such* suivi d'un dénombrable au singulier (phrase 4 = une maison si/ tellement ordinaire).
• On n'utilise pas l'article défini avec le cas possessif (phrase 3).

Question 9 : 1. at, in, in ; 2. at/by, until ; 3. in, on, on.

• *At* s'utilise avec un lieu précis et l'heure (à la maison, à 10 heures du soir).
• *By* suivi d'une expression temporelle signifie « avant ».
• *In* s'emploie pour indiquer la localisation au sein d'une certaine zone géographique (dans la rue, à Londres) et pour indiquer l'année d'un événement (en 2016).
• *On* s'utilise pour une date précise (le 12 juillet) ainsi que le jour de la semaine (le vendredi).
Until s'emploie avec une unité de temps et signifie « jusqu'à » (jusqu'à minuit).

Question 10 :

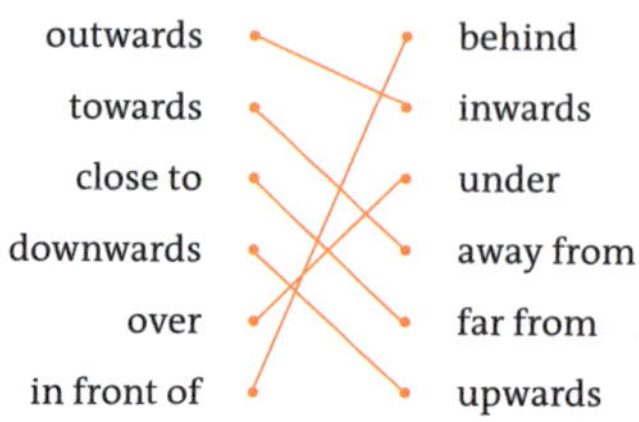

Question 11 : 1. for ; 2. since ; 3. for.

• On utilise *since* avec un point de départ (*last year*, phrase 2) et *for* avec une durée (*three years*, phrase 1). Dans ces deux phrases, le *present perfect* est utilisé et *since* et *for* se traduisent par « depuis ».

• Dans la phrase 3, le prétérit est utilisé et *for* se traduit par « pendant », car l'action est déconnectée du présent.

Question 12 : 1. for ; 2. to ; 3. in ; 4. on.

Question 13

1. During apartheid the Black population was discriminated against.
2. They were not allowed to vote.
3. Most of them were confined in townships.
4. Nelson Mandela was imprisoned for 27 years.
5. Thanks to Mandela, Blacks and coloured people were finally given the vote.
6. Mandela was elected President in 1994.
7. Today, all South Africans are considered as equals in theory.

• Lorsque l'on souhaite décrire la situation de soumission de quelqu'un, c'est à dire une situation où la personne subit l'action de quelqu'un d'autre, c'est la voix passive qui convient.

• Une phrase à la voix passive se construit de la façon suivante : sujet + *be* (conjugué au temps de la voix active) + participe passé.

Question 14 : 1. must ; 2. can ; 3. may.

• *Must* exprime une obligation (parfois morale), et *can* une capacité physique ou intellectuelle (ce qu'on sait ou ne sait pas faire).

• *May* exprime une éventualité.

Question 15 : 1. needn't ; 2. mustn't.

Needn't exprime une absence de nécessité et *mustn't* une interdiction formelle.

Question 16 : A ; C ; D.

• Les auxiliaires modaux ne se conjuguent pas comme les autres verbes : la plupart d'entre eux n'ont pas de forme prétérit, de futur, ni de conditionnel. Ils ne prennent pas de *-s* à la 3e personne du singulier, et ne possèdent pas d'infinitif.

• Les auxiliaires modaux *may* et *might* ne se contractent pas avec la négation.

• En revanche, les autres modaux peuvent se contracter à la forme négative : *can't, mustn't, couldn't, won't, needn't, shouldn't.*

Question 17 :

1. Are you wearing gloves? ; 2. She often eats too much. ; 3. Is he coming tonight? ; 4. I don't understand German.

• On utilise le présent *be* + V-*ing* :
– dans la première phrase car il s'agit d'une description ;
– dans la troisième phrase car il s'agit d'un futur proche.

• On utilise le présent simple :
– dans la deuxième phrase car elle est comporte l'adverbe de fréquence *often*. L'action se produit donc régulièrement ;
– dans la quatrième phrase car *understand* ne s'emploie pas à la forme *be* + V-*ing ;* on doit utiliser l'auxiliaire *do* suivi du verbe à l'infinitif (ou base verbale) car il s'agit d'une phrase négative.

Question 18

Simple present : C ; D ; F.

Il s'agit de *always, sometimes*, qui sont des adverbes de fréquence indéfinie (comme *never, usually, often, rarely*), et *everyday* qui indique que l'action est répétée. En effet, on emploie le présent simple pour décrire des actions habituelles et des généralités.

Present *be + V-ing* : B ; E.

• On utilise la forme *be* + V-*ing* pour focaliser sur le moment présent plus particulièrement. *At the moment* et *now* sont des expressions temporelles qui désignent ce moment présent.

• *Yesterday* signifie « hier » et s'utilise donc avec le prétérit simple.

Question 19 : A ; B ; D.

• Le prétérit *be* + V-*ing* décrit une action qui a duré dans le passé, par opposition au prétérit simple qui décrit une action brève.

• L'action évoquée au prétérit *be* + V-*ing* est souvent interrompue par une action exprimée au prétérit simple.

• Il n'y a pas d'équivalence entre les temps du français et de l'anglais. Cependant, on peut dire que le *past perfect* correspond au plus-que-parfait.

Question 20

1A. He had watched TV before he started cooking.

• La première action est antérieure à la seconde. Toutes deux se situent dans le passé.

• L'action antérieure est indiquée par le plus-que-parfait (*had* + V-*en*), l'action qui s'est produite par la suite par le prétérit simple.

2D. He was watching TV when the police officers rang the doorbell.

• La première action fut interrompue par la deuxième. Toutes deux se situent dans le passé.

• L'action interrompue est indiquée par le prétérit en V-*ing* (*was/ were* + V-*ing*), l'action qui l'a interrompue par le prétérit simple.

3A. He watched TV and then he went to bed.

Les deux actions se sont succédé au passé : on utilise le prétérit pour les deux.

4C. He has watched TV for so long now that his eyes are red.

L'action a débuté dans le passé, mais c'est son impact sur le présent (= bilan) qui nous intéresse ici : il se manifeste par l'emploi du *present perfect* (*have* + V-*en*).

Question 21

1. The Vikings had already visited North America before Christopher Columbus arrived in 1492.

• La première action est antérieure à la seconde. Toutes deux se situent dans le passé.

L'action antérieure est indiquée par le plus-que-parfait (*had* + V-*en*), l'action qui s'est produite par la suite par le prétérit simple.

2. Between 1492 and 1503 Columbus completed four round-trips between Spain and America.

L'action s'est déroulée à une autre époque : le prétérit simple s'impose.

3. While he was crossing the Atlantic for the second time, Columbus discovered the Virgin Islands.

• La première action fut interrompue par la deuxième. Toutes deux se situent dans le passé.

• L'action interrompue est indiquée par le prétérit en V-*ing* (*was/ were* + V-*ing*), l'action qui l'a interrompue par le prétérit simple.

4. Americans have celebrated Columbus Day as a statutory holiday for more than a century now.

L'action a débuté dans le passé, mais c'est son impact sur le présent (= bilan) qui nous intéresse ici : il se manifeste par l'emploi du *present perfect (have + Ven)*

Question 22 : 1. going to ; 2. will ; 3. will ; 4. going to.

• On utilise *be going to* + infinitif pour exprimer une intention. *Be going to* + infinitif indique également la conviction de celui qui parle.

• On utilise généralement *will* + base verbale dans une proposition principale accompagnée d'une proposition conditionnelle. *Will* + base verbale exprime aussi une prévision.

Question 23 : 1. were (ou was) ; 2. would, refused.

• Dans ce type de phrases conditionnelles (type 2), on utilise le conditionnel présent (*would* + V) dans la proposition principale et le prétérit dans la proposition subordonnée.

• On emploie souvent la forme subjonctive *were* du verbe *be* à toutes les personnes dans ce type de phrases conditionnelles.

Question 24 : 1. would have been ; 2. had had ; 3. had known, would have tried.

Dans ce type de phrases conditionnelles (type 3), on utilise le conditionnel passé (*would have* + V-*en*) dans la proposition principale et le plus-que-parfait (*had* + V-*en*) dans la proposition subordonnée.

Question 25 : 1. whose ; 2. who ; 3. whom.

• *Whose* est la forme possessive du pronom relatif. Il peut désigner des personnes et des choses (il se traduit par « dont » dans la phrase 1).

• On utilise *who* pour désigner des personnes. *Who* est un pronom relatif sujet.

• On utilise *whom* après des prépositions pour désigner des personnes.

Question 26 : 1. which ; 2. What ; 3. which ; 4. what.

• On utilise *which* comme pronom relatif pour désigner des choses. *(positive outcome* phrase 1), mais aussi pour reprendre l'idée exprimée dans une proposition (phrase 3). Dans la phrase 1, *which* se traduit par « qui », et dans la phrase 3, par « ce qui ».

• *What* correspond à *the thing which*. *What* se traduit par « ce qui », « ce que ».

Question 27

1. The museum you can't miss in NYC is MOMA which is ideally situated in Manhatttan.
2. The MOMA is actually in Central Park where you can enjoy nature in the heart of the city.
3. Visitors can see masterpieces of famous artists including Monet who is very popular in the US.
4. It's a good idea to visit on Saturday evening when here is a free guided tour.

• *Who* s'utilise pour des personnes et *which* pour les objets inanimés.
• *Where* et *when* peuvent s'employer comme relatifs. On utilise *when* pour le temps et *where* pour le lieu.

Question 28 : C.

• Le présent *be* + V-*ing* se transforme en prétérit *be* + V-*ing* au discours indirect : c'est le système de la concordance des temps.
• Le pronom *me* est changé en *him* car il correspond au masculin du sujet.

Question 29 : 1. was it? ; 2. wasn't it? ; 3. will they? ; 4. didn't you?

1. On reprend le verbe *be* qui est présent dans la première partie de la phrase, ainsi que le pronom sujet *it*. La *question tag* est affirmative, étant donné que la phrase à laquelle elle est accolée est négative.
2. On reprend le verbe *be* qui est présent dans la première partie de la phrase. Le pronom *it* remplace *that* qui ne peut se trouver dans une *question tag*. La *question tag* est négative, étant donné que la phrase à laquelle elle est accolée est affirmative.
3. On utilise l'auxiliaire du futur *will* qui est déjà présent dans la première partie de la phrase, ainsi que le pronom sujet *they*. La *question tag* est affirmative, étant donné que la phrase à laquelle elle est accolée est négative.
4. Il faut utiliser l'auxiliaire du prétérit *did* pour accompagner la négation.

Question 30 : B.

• Le participe passé des verbes irréguliers est précédé de l'auxiliaire *have*, *has* ou *had* selon que l'on utilise le *present perfect* simple (*have/has*) ou le *past perfect* simple (*had*).
• La forme prétérit des verbes irréguliers est utilisée uniquement au prétérit (simple past) dans les phrases affirmatives.
• Dans les autres types de phrase, on utilise l'auxiliaire *did*, suivi de la base verbale.

Question 31 : to throw ; to understand ; to fall ; to say ; to hold.

To throw, I threw, thrown ; to understand, I understood, understood ; to fall, I fell, fallen ; to say, I said, said ; to hold, I held, held.

Lexique

Question 32 : A ; B ; C.

• The founding fathers or "Pilgrim Fathers" taught their descendants courage and self-confidence.
• On the fourth Thursday of November, American people celebrate Thanksgiving to pay tribute to them.

Question 33 : A ; C ; D.

• The antagonist is the character opposed to the protagonist or main character. He acts in order to prevent the protagonist from reaching his/her goal or accomplishing his/her mission.
• An imbroglio is a **complicated** or an intricate plot with much interference.

Question 34 : D.

• *Romeo and Juliet* is a tragedy written by the playwright William Shakespeare about two young star-crossed lovers. The plot is based on the myth of eternal love, they die but reconcile their feuding families as if it was a sacrifice.
• The myth of the road is found in Jack Kerouac's famous novel *On the Road*, the myth of the initiatory voyage is found in Tolkien's *Lord of the Rings*, and the quest of eternal youth is best showed in *The Picture of Dorian Gray* written by Oscar Wilde.

Question 35 : A ; D ; E ; F ; H ; I.

• Un personnage méchant en littérature sera globalement désigné par le terme *villain*. Ses synonymes sont : *a bad guy* ou *a baddie*, *a traitor* (« un traître »), *a devil* (« un démon »), *a rogue* (« un voyou »), *a rascal* (« un coquin »), *an outlaw* (« un hors-la-loi »), mais aussi *a scoundrel* (« un scélérat »), *a criminal* (« un criminel, un délinquant »), *an evildoer* (« un personnage infâme »), *a gangster*.
• Pour un personnage gentil on utilise les termes suivants : *a goodie* ou *a good guy*, *a puritan* (« un puritain »), *a patriot* (« un patriote »), *a (good) fairy* (« une (bonne) fée »).

Question 36 : C ; E ; F ; G ; H.

• Les qualités attribuées aux personnages gentils sont la loyauté (*loyalty*), le dévouement (*devotion*), le courage (*bravery*), la vertu (*virtue*) et la gentillesse ou la bonté (*kindness*).
• *Selfishness* désigne l'égoïsme, *slyness* la ruse, et *malevolence* la malveillance.

Question 37 : C.

Un casque (*headphones*) ne peut stocker des données. *A cell phone* est un téléphone mobile, *a laptop* un ordinateur portable, *a memory card* une carte-mémoire, *a hard disk drive* un disque dur et *a tablet* une tablette électronique.

Question 38 : B.

- *To be on welfare/ to live on welfare/ to be on the dole* signifie « recevoir l'aide sociale/ être au chômage ».
- *A factory* désigne une usine, *an assembly line* une chaîne de production, *robotics* la robotique, *to clock in/ out* « pointer à l'arrivée/ au départ » et *to operate three eight-hour shifts* « faire les trois huit ».

Question 39 : C ; D ; E ; F.

- Les mots *innovation, discovery, experiment* et *invention* désignent une nouveauté ou création.
- Les mots *improvement* et *enhancement* désignent quant à eux une amélioration, s'appuyant donc sur un élément déjà existant.

Question 40 : E.

- En 1997, le clonage animal est une révolution : il rend possible la reproduction d'un organisme entier à partir d'une simple cellule. L'animal cloné est la réplique exacte de son parent, il a la même ADN.
- *Vaccination against smallpox* désigne la vaccination contre la variole, *magnetic resonance imaging (MRI)* est l'équivalent de l'imagerie par résonance magnétique (IRM), *law of gravitation* est la loi de la gravitation, *invention of penicillin* l'invention de la pénicilline et *space conquest* la conquête de l'espace.

Question 41 : D.

- La phrase inexacte est la suivante : *In 1919 Nancy Astor became the first female MP and in 1929 Margaret Bondfield became the first female cabinet minister*.
- *The Chancelor of the Exchequer* se traduit par le Chancelier de l'Échiquier, c'est-à-dire le ministre des Finances : il s'agit de la fonction la plus importante après le Premier ministre.
- *MP* signifie *Member of Parliament*, l'équivalent d'un député exerçant le pouvoir législatif, alors que *a cabinet minister* est un ministre.

Question 42 : C.

- L'intrus est *trade union* qui désigne un syndicat, alors que les autres mots se rapportent au champ lexical des élections. En Grande-Bretagne, le syndicalisme apparaît peu après la révolution industrielle, ce qui permet aux ouvriers d'obtenir dès 1824 la légalisation des *trade-unions* et le droit de grève (*the right to strike*). Le syndicalisme britannique est marqué par la pensée socialiste modérée du philanthrope Robert Owen.
- Les autres mots se rapportent au champ lexical des élections : *a ballot paper* désigne un bulletin de vote, *polling day* le jour des élections, *candidates* les candidats, *election campaign* la campagne électorale et *to canvass* faire une campagne électorale.

Question 43 : F.

- L'intrus est *to investigate* qui signifie « enquêter », alors que les autres verbes expriment un point de vue pour ou contre une idée : *to protest* « protester » ; *to march* « défiler » (dans une manifestation = *a demonstration*) ; *to denounce* « dénoncer » ; *to revolt* « se révolter » ; *to rebel* « se rebeller ».
- À chacun de ces verbes correspond(ent) un ou plusieurs noms de la même famille : *a protest* (une protestation, une manifestation), *a march* (un défilé, une marche), *a denunciation* (une dénonciation), *a revolt* (une révolte), *a rebellion* (une rébellion), *an investigation* (une enquête).

Question 44 : A ; C ; E.

Les principaux partis politiques britanniques sont le *Labour party* (Parti travailliste), le *Conservative party* (Parti conservateur) et les *Liberal Democrats* (libéraux démocrates). Theresa May est la Première ministre du gouvernement actuel depuis juillet 2016. Elle est membre du Parti conservateur.

Question 45 : C.

- Le Congrès est l'intrus car il s'agit d'une institution législative américaine. Le Congrès américain siège au Capitol à Washington DC, il comprend deux maisons : la Maison des Représentants et le Sénat. Les Représentants (435 membres élus pour deux ans) et les Sénateurs (100 membres élus pour 6 ans, un tiers renouvelé tous les deux ans) sont tous élus au suffrage universel direct. Les élections ont lieu tous les deux ans le Jour de l'Élection le premier mardi de novembre.
- Tous les autres termes font référence au système politique britannique qui est une monarchie constitutionnelle : le Premier ministre se trouve à la tête du gouvernement, la chambre des Lords et la chambre des Communes légifèrent sur le pouvoir législatif au Parlement situé au bord de la Tamise, à côté de Big Ben. Finalement, la Reine (ou le Roi) a la plus haute position à la tête de l'État.

Question 46 : A.

- La presse peut être vue comme une force d'opposition, elle permet aux lecteurs de s'informer par le biais de journaux, de magazines et d'internet. Au Royaume-Uni, la presse à sensation publie des titres choquants et des photos scandaleuses qui ne sont pas censurées afin de faire monter les chiffres de vente (tirages).

• Les magazines (*magazines*) sont habituellement des hebdomadaires (*weekly*), des mensuels (*monthly*) ou bimensuels (*bimonthly* ou *fortnightly*), et les journaux (*newspaper*) sont souvent des quotidiens (*daily*). La presse de qualité (*quality press*) s'oppose à la presse à sensation (*tabloids*) qui se partage en deux groupes : les *red tops* accusés de sensationnalisme et les *compacts* qui autrefois utilisaient un grand format (*broadsheet*).

Question 47 : B.

L'intrus est *to settle down* qui signifie « s'établir, s'installer » (pas de mouvement).

Les verbes *to flee* (« s'enfuir »), *to escape* (« (s')échapper »), *to run away from* (« partir en courant »), *to sail away* (« s'éloigner en bateau »), *to emigrate* (« émigrer ») et *to undertake a journey* (« entreprendre un voyage ») incluent un mouvement d'éloignement, alors que *to settle down* est au contraire un point d'ancrage.

Question 48 : A ; C ; D ; F ; G.

• Les autres mots signifient « hors-la-loi » (*outlaw*) et « territoire » (*territory*).

• Le terme *frontier* est un concept clé dans l'histoire des États-Unis : il était utilisé pour décrire la conquête du territoire américain au temps des pionniers (*pioneers*) dans un mouvement qui va d'est en ouest (*westwards*). Cette « frontière » était donc géographiquement instable (*unsettled*).

• *Frontier* évoque plus globalement l'esprit de conquête des Américains et dans tous les domaines, par exemple l'innovation technologique (*technological innovation*) ou encore exploration de l'espace (*space exploration*). Cette notion reste fermement ancrée (*rooted*) dans leur conscience collective (*collective consciousness*). Les pionniers ou premiers colons (*Pilgrim Fathers*) font toujours figure de héros (*hero*) et de modèle.

Question 49 : A ; B ; C ; E ; F ; G.

Les mots qui évoquent le voyage sont *a trip* (« voyage, excursion »), *a tour* (« visite guidée »), *a pilgrimage* (« pèlerinage »), *wanderings* (« pérégrinations »), *a journey* (« voyage, trajet, parcours »), *a cruise* (« croisière »). *Brotherhood* désigne la fraternité.

Question 50 : D.

• The United States of America is situated northwards of Mexico, if Mexican people want to travel south they go to Guatemala.

• Mexicans who cross the border are courageous people who often choose to leave their family in order to earn a living in the USA so that they can send back money to them in Mexico. Life in Mexico is dreadful, a lot of people live in a poverty stricken environment and their future is bleak. Therefore their reasons for emigrating to the USA is to flee from poverty, to seek political asylum, to escape from the economic crisis and to help their family to survive by sending them money. Indeed the USA represents a land hope and abundance.

Question 51 : C.

• Le Commonwealth est une association volontaire de 54 États libres et égaux qui s'est faite au fil du temps depuis 1931. La plupart sont d'anciennes colonies avec qui la monarchie britannique a établi des liens commerciaux privilégiés.

• C'est la reine Élisabeth II qui est à la tête de cette institution, mais sa position reste très symbolique : elle n'a aucun pouvoir politique ou exécutif. Le vrai pouvoir est détenu par le Secrétaire général du Commonwealth.

• Le Canada fut le premier pays à y entrer, suivi par l'Australie, la Nouvelle-Zélande, et l'Afrique du Sud (qui se retira durant l'Apartheid pour y revenir en 1994). L'Irlande en fut membre de 1931 jusqu'en 1947, date à laquelle la république d'Irlande a été instituée. C'est donc l'Irlande qui ne fait plus partie du Commonwealth aujourd'hui.

Question 52 : A ; C ; E.

• In the 16th century British explorers discovered new territories and brought back goods such as cocoa, rum or spices.

• In the 19th century the British Empire was the largest and the most important in the world.

Question 53 : C ; E.

• English was the official language of 54 sovereign states in 2015.

• The UK has no official language. The languages spoken in the UK are English, Welsh, Scottish, Cornish and Irish.

• India is the second-largest English-speaking country in the world by number of speakers, after the United States.